BOUTS of MANIA

ALI, FRAZIER, AND FOREMAN
AND AN AMERICA ON THE ROPES

RICHARD HOFFER

Aurum
Press

First published in Great Britain
2014 by Aurum Press Ltd
74—77 White Lion Street
Islington
London N1 9PF
www.aurumpress.co.uk

This paperback edition first published in 2015 by Aurum Press Ltd

First published in 2014 in the United States by Da Capo Press,
A member of the Perseus Books Group
www.dacapopress.com

A catalogue record for this book is available from the British Library.

ISBN 978 1 78131 336 7
EBOOK ISBN 978 1 78131 320 6

1 3 5 7 9 10 8 6 4 2
2015 2017 2019 2018 2016

Designed by Jack Lenzo
Typeset in 12.5 point Perpetua by the Perseus Books Group
Printed and bound by CPI Group (UK) Ltd, Croydon, CR0 4YY

*CONTENTS

1974

1975

1996

2011

2013

* PROLOGUE

The three men marched, year by year and fight by fight, across a nation's time line of deepening shame. It so happened they began their riotous roundelay in the spring of 1971, about when the Pentagon Papers were published, outlining the gross deceptions that kept the United States in the Vietnam War (the death toll reaching forty-five thousand that year), about when Lieutenant Calley was convicted in the murder of civilians there, needless slaughter now the reasonable residue of Americans' good intentions. And it so happened they completed their furious tournament—bouts of hysteria indeed—in the fall of 1975, about when the United States left Saigon, the surrender not nearly as sickening as the terrible waste, helicopters pushed off aircraft carriers to make room for refugees the least of it, that the pullout acknowledged.

Bookended by dishonor and dysfunction, these three men and their five fights provided an alternate and highly necessary reexamination of certain American qualities, whether they be courage, stamina, or just a wholesome capacity for mischief. A country lurched from one catastrophe to the next, no end in sight, and these characters, in their stubborn insistence upon personal glory, made a case for an upside, an argument for ancient values of righteousness, a reminder of achievement's availability, a claim to this country's undeniable right to fun.

Their arrival together would have been outrageous under any conditions, during any time. For that matter, any one of them might have carried the day—Muhammad Ali, fresh off a political exile, his hands still as quick as his mouth; Joe Frazier, the sharecropper's son, the heavyweight champion in Ali's absence, a virtual threshing machine; George Foreman, the huge and thunderous puncher who was promising to make both his elders, and maybe even the sport, obsolete. Each an Olympic gold medal winner, each undefeated, each in his time heavyweight champion of the world. Pick one and he might have dominated boxing, during a period when the game still mattered, galvanized this country for years with his oversized exploits. He might, in other words, have dominated the sports and celebrity culture that was then taking full bloom, all on his own.

But put them together? Three powerful and contrasting personalities (not to mention boxers), each a proxy for competing belief systems, each a highly visible (if not always willing) symbol for divided constituencies, each a complete variation of our most potent icon—and set them in pursuit of a single prize? The urgency, the sheer desperation of these men, produced a screeching period of tumult never before seen, never seen again. The nearly four years they spent in their fabulous entanglement—and even the year that preceded it—were as much commotion and excitement as this country, any one country, could bear.

And set loose upon the world? As America contracted, these three exploded the borders, crashing into each other around the globe. New York, yes, but also Zaire and Manila and Jamaica. Homicidal dictators were now players, joining an already colorful cast of characters. It was more pageantry than it was boxing, more theater than sports, almost more, really, than we could handle. Thrillas, Rumbles, Fights of the Century—all set pieces in our sports culture, all of them. Some still resonate in ways that go beyond any appreciation for the sport of boxing, that go right to our understanding of manhood. Each of these fights came to stand for some kind of effort, perseverance, defiance, amazement, or maybe foolishness, none of which could be confined to a single country.

It was an accident of history, these three men converging in a single place during a particular time, their fights giving us an irreproducible pandemonium, just when we needed it most. Their clashes over the heavyweight belt, an irrelevant trinket almost any other time, had an unlikely significance in these otherwise dispiriting years. This country could get nothing right; it was emerging from the convulsive 1960s, racial and generational aftershocks still booming across the nation. Just the year before, in 1970, after National Guardsmen had opened fire on a college campus and, for no real good reason, killed four students, only 11 percent of the country disapproved of their actions. The easy answers of sweeping legislation and reform, the promise of the 1960s, eluded the nation, and it remained so divided that it did not care to stand up even for its children.

And so as the country careened from one depressing disaster to the next—a president hounded out of office, a military occupation ending in humiliation, the richest people in the world rationing gasoline—Ali, Frazier, and Foreman gave a glimpse of better times to come. Their headlong struggles, life-and-death fights, engaged a troubled nation in ways that could never happen again. At once boxing and burlesque, at once comic and tragic, at once sport and national imperative, their fights offered a strange reassurance that ambition remained possible, that it was not so ridiculous—although not so easy, either—to fight for something better.

These three men, and their five fights, might have been athletic footnotes in any other age, but in this one they became necessary diversions, required antidotes to toxic times. They became history themselves. A country—well, a world, too—sat ringside and gaped at their effort and determination (and their nonsense, also), and wondered at these new and astounding levels of resolve. This was truly possible? Somebody could get off a stool after that? Somebody could endure this, return for more? Wait, there's a trilogy in this madness?

The psychic doldrums, even a prolonged enervation, could not withstand this wild hullabaloo. Political shame, a sense of national retreat, they were no match for shenanigans of this scale. Their frantic competition, so far beyond reckless it became nearly ruinous, bridged social divides and, while it couldn't heal a nation, did create a common ground. The nation just sat at ringside. It could scarcely believe its eyes.

1970

RAT BINS, UNWASHED PUNKS, AND WHITE OWL CIGARS

The exile had been devastating, a public relations catastrophe of course, an athletic interruption of near-tragic consequence, a financial disaster above all else. Things were at last looking up on that last score, a little; student unions were flush with cash these days and happy to pay him as much as $25,000 an appearance, way up from the $1,500 the Muslims negotiated when he first hit the campus trail. In fact, he had motored here in his pink Cadillac, about a block long, and, although he didn't know it when he accepted the gig, he was about to get an auditorium full of grief for living in a $91,000 house in a Philadelphia suburb, a backward validation of sorts. "Why do I want to live in a rat bin and have a rat bite my child?" he argued, the crowd booing this little comfort. So, no, he didn't have to live in a rat bin, at least that.

But even after all this time, three years since they stripped him of his title and since the US government began prosecution for his refusal to serve in Vietnam, or wherever they'd post him, the heavyweight champion of the world, after all, he remained Public Enemy No. 1 most places. Even what little money he could scrounge on these economic and political fringes were totally resented. It was absurd. All he'd done was convert to this little religion, more of a cult really. And change his name, Cassius Clay becoming Muhammad Ali. And dare to wonder why the hell he'd travel half the globe to fight some other minority. That was back in 1967, and even if a generational tolerance was trending his way, it was still unforgivable, to the point that the threat of a prison sentence hung over him.

Here at Muhlenberg, a small college at the edge of Pennsylvania Dutch country, Ali strained to represent his pre-exile self, when his presence ensured hilarity and high jinks. Back then, his pie-eyed bravado and his rants were a source of consternation for white America, or maybe just older America, but also, more and more, a guilty pleasure. Going from the 1960 Olympics, when he won a gold medal, and right up to his championship, when he improbably knocked out the formidable Sonny Liston in 1964, the sleek and irrepressible kid had become one of those love-him-or-hate-him personalities. Toward the end, right before he decided to really stir things up, announcing he had "no quarrel with those Vietcong," he was probably more loved than hated, even the old-timers coming around to his insistence on fun and, if not that, his astonishing abilities in the ring. Nobody had ever seen anything like him, fluid, full of improvisation, just a marvel.

About two hundred people had crowded in the office of the athletic director (AD) this February night, another twenty-five hundred massing in Memorial Hall beyond. Ali shucked and jived, just the way he used to, tossing out some rhymes, the way he used to do that, too, everybody hooting in delight. He had just turned twenty-eight, and it was impossible to imagine he'd ever recapture that athletic excitement, or even have the opportunity. But here he was, biting his lower lip, shooting the jab, promising to knock out whomever. The room was in a frenzy, the way he liked it. "The champion of the world!" he yelled out, although he was nothing of the sort, hadn't been for nearly three years, the division doing fine without him. He was wearing a gray sharkskin suit, after all, the trunks of his trade these days. Still, the students in the room obliged his whimsy and ducked and laughed.

He'd come a long way in this line of work. He was always a willing-enough speaker and had been giving campus speeches even before he became a national pariah. But he was without a hint of seriousness or importance back then, his vanity unadulterated by a sense of purpose. In 1965 a student escort met him in the student union at Randolph-Macon College and was almost appalled by the fighter's complete lack of attention to the speech at hand. All the young Cassius Clay wanted to talk about was his portable phone, some kind of gadget that occupied an entire suitcase, like a World War II walkie-talkie but with more wires and cables. The escort was not certain it was even operable.

That was a long time ago, though. Back when he had a title, some influence over the national media and money. The exile had been punishing, brutally so. The money was long gone, and nobody was in a rush to replace it. The Black Muslims, as they were simply known at the time, the Nation of Islam, to give the religion its proper name, had given him little but a new name in recompense for his sacrifice. Joe Frazier, who'd gone on to win the heavyweight title in Ali's absence, had loaned him some money. There were a few odd paydays, a computerized matchup with Rocky Marciano (which the computer said he lost, and which he immediately regretted). But he was mostly on his own, picking up scraps here and there. Champburger: that was one of the scraps, a short-lived fast-food franchise.

Another prospect of the time, himself only one year removed from glory in the 1968 Olympics, remembered Ali bounding up the steps of the 5th Street Gym in Miami. "George Foreman!" Ali screamed, Foreman hearing that familiar whoop and dropping his mitts in absolute joy. Here was Ali, onetime champion of the world, his idol, and fun was always at hand when he was around, that much Foreman knew. "Once you get to be champion," Ali said by way of introduction, "I'm gonna show you what you'll have." He bounded back down the stairs and returned from his car—a pink El Dorado—and produced a black briefcase for Foreman to ogle. Was it full of money, hundreds of thousands? "See that," Ali said. "A portable telephone." Ali talked about the phone a bit and then wondered if Foreman would be needing those shoes, those wraps.

That was a bad time, Ali desperate enough at one point that he agreed to become a sparring partner for Joe Bugner, a young fighter of few dimensions aside from his breadth. Bugner paid him $1,000, the former champion not bitter a bit, cheerful even. He tried to get $1,200 more out of Bugner for that phone. "Joe," he said, as serious as he could ever get, "it's just what you need."

Now, in 1970, he was neither as broke nor as indifferent to his audience as before. After hundreds of campus speeches, he was in fact a practiced messenger of the Nation of Islam's message, primarily black separatism. This, of course, was the single most offensive stance possible. The nation had been trying to confront its history of institutionalized racism and had, only two years before, made integration the law of the land. The Civil Rights Act of 1968 may not have been popular in every corner of the country, but overall it was recognized as progress, a way toward the future, a way out of discrimination. It was hard-won, Martin Luther King Jr. assassinated for his black leadership just the week before, and who knows how many protesters, bus riders, or just innocent bystanders firehosed and beaten, or possibly even lynched, in the violent decade previous.

Yet Ali and his Black Muslim brothers would undo all that if they could. It was beyond infuriating, this mockery of equality, this perversion of justice. It had always been something of a mystery, why Ali, or Cassius Clay, as he was born, had ever been attracted to the Nation of Islam, an irrelevant, quite small, and bizarre sect that involved fleets of spaceships in its creation myth. Certainly, Malcolm X, the primary recruiter and top lieutenant in the religion (he reported directly to Elijah Muhammad, who had somehow made the Nation of Islam the biggest black-owned business in America), was persuasive. But still: a mystery. Ali, nothing if not impressionable, could just as easily have come under the sway of civil rights leaders and could have more profitably and with less disruption pushed forth a necessary and increasingly popular and inevitable reform. Instead, he had acquired the hatred of the white establishment while, at the same time, earned the distrust of the black movement.

The only saving side effect of his conversion, at least in terms of public opinion, was the Nation of Islam's stance against the Selective Service, which happened to coincide with Ali's own. Whereas Ali might have been left on culture's curb as a religious kook, a slightly dangerous one at that, his refusal to serve in Vietnam, whether his convictions were religious or political, recast him as a bona fide member of a growing antiwar movement. There was a near-comic aspect to it, the younger Clay initially classified as unfit for service, having scored just 16 on the mental aptitude test, needing 30 to qualify. It was embarrassing, more than funny, really—"I said I was the greatest, not the smartest"—but certainly acceptable. Then, in 1966, the requirement was lowered to 15, which Ali found suspicious, but which was probably intended to make more than just him available for the incredible ramping up halfway across the world. And that's when, sitting on his porch in Miami when he heard the news, Ali, surprised and hurt, articulated a generation's objection: "I ain't got nothing against them Vietcong."

History inserted "quarrel" in the quote, but no matter. Ali had now picked a side, and whether it was grounded in religious belief, well, that didn't matter, either. He was part of a political process now, one of the "unwashed punks who picket and demonstrate," according to columnist Red Smith. Reaction was swift and unequivocal. He managed to get a few more fights in, but in April 1967, when he refused induction on religious grounds (which the government had long since swept aside), it was over for him as a boxer and maybe even as a citizen. He was quickly stripped of his title, even before the grand jury could indict him. He was without a job, even without a country, and imprisonment, pending legal maneuvers that would not end until reaching the Supreme Court, loomed over him all the while. "I will not be what you want me to be," he'd told the draft board, the semiliterate once more giving words to a percolating movement that was still searching for its vocabulary of protest. Perhaps, but he could no longer be what he wanted to be, either.

But by 1970, as the Vietnam War was pronounced unwinnable, perhaps even a moral failure as well as a strategic and political disaster, antiwar activists were no longer traitors and Muhammad Ali was no longer, as columnist Jim Murray called him in 1967, a "black Benedict Arnold." Ali's stance, when removed of religious and racial objections, now seemed almost reasonable, perhaps even correct. Only a few months before, a million people had marched on Washington in protest, millions more across the country. As the war grew unpopular, Ali's persecution was taken up by a more liberal media than was represented by Jimmy Cannon. "Muhammad Ali Deserves the Right to Defend His Title" was the cover story in *Esquire*.

In any case, America's dissident youth becoming the outspoken norm, he was at home on campuses throughout the land.

"Everybody out," Ali suddenly yelled, "except that Polish boy over there." Ali was pointing to Ron Czajkowski, the junior journalism major who'd been assigned to introduce him to the Muhlenberg crowd. The room emptied, just the two of them left, and Ali got down to business. "Give me a read on the demographic tonight," Ali said. Czajkowski told him to expect a mostly white, mostly conservative student body and, if what the local radio reporter had told him was true, a smattering of black activists from nearby Lehigh University. He'd heard they meant trouble. They might even have been Black Panthers. Ali considered the information and then opened a brown leather briefcase, which had as many as fifteen sets of note cards, each bundled up in rubber bands. Ali dug around and took one and put it in his suit pocket.

"Nervous?" Ali asked him. Of course! "Don't be. Just remember, you're walking out there with the champeen of the world. Son, you won't have a thing to worry about."

Czajkowski led him to the stage, where he was greeted with pronounced hooting and laughter. What the hell? He turned around and saw Ali was shadowboxing him from behind.

Some of Ali's speeches—it all depended on which bundle of notes he pulled out of his briefcase—were more provocative than others. He might talk about poverty, he might talk about Vietnam, or, more dangerously, he might talk about the need for the separation of races, as ordained by the Nation of Islam. Usually, he couched that topic in homespun logic, tigers keeping with tigers, and so on. Other times he put it to work in comic riffs. "There's Snow White," he'd begin, going on to offer the inescapable reality of white America. To-night's speech was along those lines: "Solutions to the Racist Problem as Taught by the Black Muslims." That was the bundle, although he never once referred to the cards he'd put in his coat pocket.

It did not go that well. Ali's black-white routine went fine, his comic representation of an all-white country getting laughs. Santa Claus is white; Miss America is white, he pointed out. Cigars are White Owl! "Even Tarzan, the king of Africa, is white," he said. But his answer to the "racist problem," a nonviolent separation of the races, was not popular, especially among the dashiki-wearing militants who'd come in from Lehigh. Why, they wondered, was this separatist living in such a grand house in a white neighborhood?

It grew heated, Ali trying to reconcile his ambitions with a di-vided country, the black kids in their dashikis having none of it. "We must go to war!" one in the crowd shouted. "You go ahead," Ali said. "I'll read about you tomorrow in the newspapers." They continued to bark at him from the wooden bleachers, Ali growing increasingly frustrated at the interruptions. "You niggers give me more trouble than the whites," he finally said.

With that, the black students, as if prompted, stood up and walked out, Ali running off the stage after them, biting his lower lip, as if ready to fight. He returned and summarized the proceed-ings for the remaining white students: "You have just witnessed those boys arguing among themselves while I have given up things for them." And he accepted the ensuing melee, everybody riled now, police taking nearly twenty minutes to escort him along the thirty-second walk back to the athletic director's office, some of the white students now wanting to fight him. Wanting to fight Ali! "Let me at him!" one of them yelled.

In the AD's office, crowded with those two hundred people again, Ali exulted in the commotion he'd just created. This had been an excellent night. He flipped his keys to Czajkowski, told him to bring the Cadillac around and leave the motor running. Ali and his little entourage—a lawyer, a neighbor along for the ride—sailed off into the night, leaving this mini-maelstrom behind, everybody pawing and hollering at him. Of course, to be fair, they hadn't seen anything yet.

CHAPTER 2

PHILCO DREAMS, PHILADELPHIA'S FINEST, AND A FLAT-FOOTED BULL

Joe Frazier had avoided the tournament, partly in deference to Muhammad Ali's claim to the championship, but mostly because of the economic realities of heavyweight boxing. His manager, Yancey (Yank) Durham, using the managerial pronoun, had said, "Screw the tournament. I don't need them, they need me. Let them fight it out and I'll fight the winner." Durham had little trouble convincing Frazier, and then the Cloverlay syndicate that was fronting the fighter, that there was much more money to be made in the tournament's aftermath than during it. Scarcely two weeks after the World Boxing Association (WBA) had stripped Ali of his title and announced an eight-man elimination, Cloverlay was telling the press that Frazier was going to fight George Chuvalo in New York's Madison Square Garden instead; let the WBA squabble over their own made-up champion.

If Frazier, and by that we mean Durham, didn't like the tournament, plenty of others did. By 1967, when Ali—or Cassius Clay, as many still insisted upon—got into a little hot water for refusing induction into the armed services, heavyweight boxing had become a kind of bum-of-the-month club. Defenses against Brian London,

Karl Mildenberger, and Cleveland Williams were highly noncompetitive, the events surviving entirely on the basis of Ali's charisma. Now, with a prison sentence looming for his steadfast refusal to buckle under to the US government, that charisma was essentially a black-market attraction, no longer available to legitimate promoters. A long-suffering contingent of challengers was poised to take advantage of his absence.

In fact, the tournament seemed a sudden breath of fresh air for everybody, just what boxing needed after three years of Ali's increasingly boisterous dominance. "Muhammad who?" asked Bob Arum, who was none other than Ali's promoter. It seemed everybody was energized by the idea. "This type of tournament could be the shot in the arm the ailing boxing business needs," wrote *Ring* magazine. "An entire new notion of competition emerges."

Not only would there be a slate of interesting matchups—six leading up to the championship—but they'd all be available free of charge to the fight fan, the whole thing backed by the ABC Network and a pile of cash said to be $300,000—"an unimaginable sum," it was reported. It might be difficult, given the pedigrees of the assorted applicants, to ensure quality control, but it shouldn't be that hard to produce some intrigue here and there among such various contenders. That is the beauty of the format, a ruthless winnowing of effort and talent, conducted within a scant six months.

It's just that none of it would involve Frazier, who'd lately been positioned as Ali's obvious, if somewhat eventual, successor. Just as the tournament was being announced, *Ring* magazine was going to press with a Frazier cover: "They're Talking Frazier Now!!!" Even the WBA had him ranked second (this was before he rejected its tournament), while taking into account some very careful grooming by the Cloverlay bunch. It was, after just fourteen fights, too soon for a proper anointment; not all of his early opposition was tainted by qualities of ability. For that matter, Frazier was not yet a complete fighter. "Scrap Iron Johnson gave him all he wanted," hollered one of the heavyweight contestants, Thad Spencer. "And Scrap Iron can't walk from here to the door without falling down." Still, in an apprenticeship that had covered just eighteen months, Frazier had knocked out thirteen of those fighters, his fast-closing style, his punishing up-front barrages, a conversation starter for sure.

Frazier could probably use a little more seasoning, anyway. The eight fighters the WBA and Sports Action, Inc., picked—none of them Sonny Liston—would not have sufficiently interested Ali to inspire so much as a couplet (Eduardo Corletti?), but most of them were at least distinguished by a respectable amount of ring experience. There were some tough guys such as Jimmy Ellis, Oscar Bonavena, and Jerry Quarry, real trial horses, not to mention former champion Floyd Patterson. These would be tests, as Durham guessed, that Frazier could afford to postpone just a bit further.

Because, face it, Frazier had arrived prematurely. Maybe even accidentally. He would never have gone to the 1964 Games in the first place if the blubbery, but surprisingly deft, Buster Mathis had not broken his hand on Frazier's skull during the Olympic run-up. If Frazier did manage to capitalize, returning from Tokyo with a gold medal, just like Ali had returned from Rome four years earlier, it was to paltry advantage. Prospects for a 200-pound heavyweight—not really a heavyweight at all—who was not even six feet tall, arms so stubby his reach was fully two feet shorter than, say, Liston's, were not high. When Frazier got back to Philadelphia, he excited no interest, attracted no support, and received little attention.

Further, Olympic success aside, his preparations had been ragged and hurried, not reassuring to potential backers at all. He'd come a long way from the South Carolina low country where, as a thirteen-year-old dropout, he worked the dirt behind a team of mules. He'd come a long way from his daddy's porch, where the two watched Sugar Ray Robinson and Rocky Marciano—and Joe Louis!—on a fifteen-inch Philco. A long way from that swinging burlap bag, filled with rags and corncobs, a brick in the middle to give it some weight, young Frazier making it swing anyway. Boxers are not expected to materialize with advanced degrees, but, even by the low standards of admission for this game, Frazier had a woefully incomplete dossier.

Even in Philadelphia, a destination he didn't achieve until the "dog" finally established a stop in Beaufort, his preparations had been uncertain. He had not been especially driven to box, those early Philco dreams aside, and had appeared in the Police Athletic League gym only out of a kind of self-loathing, his thighs rubbery, his middle spreading. That was only five years earlier, back in 1967, when Yank Durham, a full-time welder and sometime bootlegger, found him hitting a real heavy bag. Progress, at least enough of it to get him in the Olympic Trials with Mathis, was swift, if you care to remember that Frazier had been working old plantation fields just a few seasons before.

But now, back home in Philadelphia, a gold medal tucked away, Frazier was facing a sudden career deceleration, his credentials entirely discounted. No takers. And, as he'd broken and dislocated his thumb before his gold medal bout, he couldn't even return to his old job at Cross Brothers, the kosher slaughterhouse where he used to practice his combinations on sides of beef in the refrigerated lockup. He worked for a moving company, $2.50 an hour. He cleaned up at the Bright Hope Church for even less. If not for Florence, whom he married at the age of sixteen, and her job at Sears Roebuck, their family of five would be no better off than if he'd stayed in Beaufort.

Not even his first pro fight, he and Durham selling tickets for their end of the purse, satisfied much more than a weekly grocery bill. He made $125 for his debut, almost a full year after his gold medal bout. But that career, which had seemed stillborn so recently, picked up sudden steam, now everybody willing to climb aboard. It happened quite quickly. In 1965, after just four fights against some fairly forgettable opposition, Philadelphia's finest began angling for a piece of Frazier's future. A man named Bruce Baldwin, president of Horn & Hardart Baking Company, got forty friends to buy shares in an outfit that would be called Cloverlay. Altogether, buying eighty shares, they put up $20,000, guaranteeing the fighter a weekly wage of $100, plus half of his purses for the first three years of the deal. With Durham choosing carefully, Frazier began plowing through opponents, and now, in the summer of 1967, Cloverlay's investment had proved somewhat more than prescient. That original $250 share was worth $3,600, and it was increasing with every win. Speculative or not, Frazier's stock was growing in other quarters besides the open market. He was, with considerate handling, heir to a valuable franchise.

That tournament, which proceeded without Frazier's involvement but with Ali's reluctant blessing ("With me around," he admitted, "nobody gonna take these guys seriously"), concluded in April 1968, to less acclaim than the organizers might have hoped, although the TV ratings had been very good. As Teddy Brenner, matchmaker for the rival Madison Square Garden, said of the elimination tournament, "It was a complete success in that it successfully eliminated all the fighters." Frazier got a jump on it, fighting for Madison Square Garden's version of the heavyweight championship in May 1967, and had indeed beaten Chuvalo, a brutal stoppage in just four rounds. The WBA was impressed enough that it dropped Frazier from no. 2 to no. 9, just below its eight-man depth chart. Frazier was okay with it, having earned $50,000 in his desertion (compared to $23,000 purses for some of the WBA's first-round bouts).

Cloverlay shares continued to soar throughout that year—one of those shares, even diluted by repeated "stock" offerings, was now worth $7,200. Then, just two months before Jimmy Ellis, Ali's former sparring partner, emerged from the WBA tournament with the championship, Frazier met his old Olympic rival Buster Mathis for the New York State Athletic Commission's version of the title. Fighting for a purse of $175,000 (Ellis received $125,000 in his elimination fight with Jerry Quarry), Frazier floored Mathis in eleven rounds. The stock doubled.

So now there were two champions, not counting Ali, of course. Further consolidation was required, and the inevitability of a Frazier-Ellis match grew. Ellis dallied as long as he could, traveling to Sweden to defend his interim title against Patterson later in 1968, postponing other defenses here and there, finding an excuse as well to postpone Frazier, the so-called champ of five states. Frazier, despite or perhaps because of his smaller constituency, prepared far more anxiously for the eventuality, fighting four more times, including a knockout of Quarry, whom Ellis had struggled to outpoint for the WBA crown.

And all the while, Ali was stirring rumors of a comeback, even as he awaited sentencing. Said one heavyweight at the time, "In the gyms guys are whispering, Ali's coming back, Ali's coming back. That cat Ali drives everybody crazy."

Certainly, comeback or not, which still seemed highly doubtful, he was pushing Frazier to his limits. Once a title unification fight was signed—Ellis and Frazier each guaranteed $150,000 for the bout at Madison Square Garden, to be held in February 1970— Ali began to systematically haunt Frazier, as if laying the groundwork for their own fight. He'd called in to aggravate Frazier on a Philadelphia radio talk show, tried to force his way into the dressing room after the Quarry fight, and then, in September 1969, showed up at Frazier's gym, having tipped the media he'd be ready to fight.

Whether Ali had acquired any ring rust during his exile was impossible to say, but he had not lost the gift of provocation. At the PAL gym Ali challenged Frazier, for no obvious reason except for the sheer foolishness of it, to a fight at a park about a mile away. Ali led a crowd of several hundred there and bemoaned Frazier's cowardice when he didn't show. "Here I am," he said, "haven't had a fight in three years, 25 pounds overweight, and Joe Frazier won't show up. What kind of champ can he be?" The headline in the *Philadelphia Inquirer* appeared to have been dictated by Ali himself: "Ali and 10,000 Fans Disappointed, Frazier Skips Battle in Park."

This sort of mischief had long been Ali's stock in trade, difficult to take seriously. Frazier was nonetheless frustrated, wondering why he had to look like the fool when he was the guy out there facing the Quarrys, the Bonavenas, Ali parading his smirk on the lecture circuit. It was maddening, of course. It helped Frazier to know that, while he was set for a big payday with Ellis, getting ready to become the more or less undisputed champion of the world, Ali was enjoying less fortunate circumstances, never mind the bluster. In fact, at the time, Ali was earning $100 a day as Ellis's sparring partner.

Ali had offered to attend the fight at the Garden and, in a final show of grace, present his championship belt to the winner. This offer was declined, and Ali instead held court at the Arena in Philadelphia, where he was considerably less gracious, noting that the two contestants vying for his long-vacated title were "my sparring partner" and a "flat-footed bull who moves like a plow horse."

He might have had the sparring-partner characterization right. Ellis managed one and a half rounds of boxing before Frazier began landing his left hooks to his head. There were fighters Frazier had difficulty with—Bonavena gave him twenty-five hard rounds in their two fights—but Ellis was not going to be one of them. In the third round, before a record crowd for an indoor heavyweight championship fight, Frazier stung Ellis again with left hooks. "Sissy, you can't hit," Frazier hissed through his mouthpiece. "You got nothing." Frazier hit him with a left hook to the jaw, decking Ellis at the start of the fourth round, and then, Ellis up at the count of nine, sent him to the canvas at the bell. Ellis, trained by Angelo Dundee, Ali's longtime cornerman, would not be allowed out for the fifth. Ellis never did remember that second knockdown. "You mean I was knocked down twice?" he asked later.

Finally, after three years, there was once more a single heavyweight champion. Frazier was without the charms of Ali, perhaps, but he did not feel counterfeit, or otherwise inauthentic, in this new office. Ali was running up and down the aisles at the Arena, shadowboxing and promising a comeback, delighting the crowd. "This town is too small for both of us," he said. In fact, it was big enough for Frazier. It suited him fine.

CHAPTER 3

HOROSCOPES, THE FIFTH WARD, AND A LITTLE MEAN GUY

Sonny Liston, embittered and sullen in the twilight of his career, was an imperfect role model. Even in his heyday, his prospects bright, he would by any measure have been a flawed mentor. He'd been a thief, a leg breaker, a two-time loser concerning time served, Mob flunky, all-around menace when it came to St. Louis criminal enforcement, all while he was climbing up the division's rankings. He was not considered to have cleaned up his act in any appreciable way once he became heavyweight champion of the world in 1962, having demolished Floyd Patterson. In fact, wrote *Sports Illustrated* at the time, in the year that separated the equally noncompetitive rematch (another first-round knockout), Liston had "become insufferable . . . giving back all the abuse he ever had to take."

By 1970 he'd become just a little bit more insufferable, and understandably so. He'd been beaten by Muhammad Ali twice, the first time quitting on his stool, the sight of his surrender once more inflaming rumors of his Mob ties. Unpopular in victory, he was a pariah in defeat; a full quarter of his sixteen comeback fights had to be staged in Sweden, as if he'd become too suspect even for American boxing.

So it was odd, and not the least bit hopeful, that Liston took young George Foreman, the Olympic gold medalist newly turned pro, under his wing. Foreman, impressionable and vulnerable to strange epiphanies, had been lucky so far. He'd been a small-time punk in Houston's Fifth Ward, a takedown man for a gang that nightly converted stolen change—"the silver coin toll," as it was known in the neighborhood—into cheap wine. A virtual dropout, Foreman had an extremely small range of ambition, thinking a facial scar (he wore a bandage on his face for a time, to anticipate the delicious reaction) might stand him in good stead in the juvenile delinquent community, but long-term hoping for the bona fides of a prison sentence. He'd return to the Fifth Ward respected, perhaps even feared, someone "who maybe killed a man once." It was something to look forward to.

Then, hunkering in a crawl space one hot Houston night, smearing himself in dripping sewage to confound the police dogs the sirens were surely promising on his behalf, Foreman had a vision. It went hand in hand with a public service announcement he'd just seen on television, football star Jim Brown imploring him to be somebody, join the Job Corps. Suddenly, he needed to get out, and finally he had a place to go.

He fell under the sway of a boxing coach there, Doc Broadus, a crusty guy who favored berets, riding quirts, and supernaturally strong, if wildly amateurish, young heavyweights. It was not entirely smooth sailing, but Broadus did maneuver Foreman onto the 1968 Olympic team, more a testament to Broadus than Foreman, considering the tight two-year window. By the time Foreman had gotten to Mexico City, his amateur experience consisted of just twenty bouts, four of them losses.

One of the losses, coming on the undercard of a professional show in Oakland, California, was sufficiently dispiriting that Foreman nearly gave up boxing on the spot. If not for the offhand encouragement ("Keep it up, big man") of a floridly dressed ring announcer—the man wore a clown-like bow tie, in addition to an elaborate rig of tails and ruffles—boxing history might have gone quite differently. But Foreman assumed anybody dressed that splendidly had to be the arena's owner, somebody of importance for certain, somebody who knew what he was talking about. Foreman promised the peculiar-looking man he'd do better next time.

And he did, sweeping through the Olympics with a patriotic flourish. Hardly anybody realized that Foreman, in a stunt that made more news than the actual bout, was waving his little American flag out of spite, an in-your-face gesture intended for the ringside judges, who'd earlier jobbed one of his teammates. Instead, in that gold medal moment, he was recognized as the jingoistic antidote to the Games' earlier disruptions, when Tommie Smith and John Carlos raised black-gloved fists in the iconic pose of black protest.

That alone might have given Foreman all the traction he needed for a successful pro career. Normally, it was enough just to win a gold medal. Cassius Clay was the class of the 1960 Olympics, although he was fighting in the somewhat less glamorous light-heavyweight division at the time. Within months of returning from Rome, he had signed a contract with the Louisville Sponsoring Group, some Kentucky millionaires looking for a little fun. Clay received a $10,000 signing bonus and a monthly salary of $333, enough financial support to get him through a fighter's apprenticeship. Joe Frazier had won his at heavyweight in 1964, and he came back to Philadelphia with a similar appeal, maybe not immediately but eventually. Some of the locals, including sports columnist Larry Merchant, bought shares in Cloverlay, a corporate entity that would henceforth fund Frazier's career.

A gold medalist was a valuable franchise and had, in particular, produced many heavyweight champions of the era (Floyd Patterson came out of the 1952 Games; alas, Liston spent most of his Olympic year, 1956, in a Missouri workhouse). But Foreman wasn't interested in being syndicated, fronted, or otherwise owned. One thing he picked up from the Job Corps, something that had been drilled into him, was a taste for independence. He thought Frazier, with that Cloverlay insignia on his trunks, looked ridiculous.

But more than that, he had no intention of becoming a professional boxer. His plan was to return to the Job Corps, in Hayward, California, enroll in a local community college nearby, get his degree at night, and become a counselor. This might have fallen short of the traditional dream of wealth and celebrity, especially as practiced by previous gold medalists, but it still surpassed anything he ever envisioned as a Fifth Ward enforcer.

A life of community service evaporated in one of those financial crunches, or maybe it was just a shift in political winds (Richard Nixon assuming the presidency from Lyndon Johnson, the man who'd instituted the program), the kind that inevitably affects any public program, and Foreman was abruptly left without even that modest, if high-minded, future. So, running into Dick Sadler, who trained Liston nearby, Foreman came to a different, if inevitable, conclusion. Foreman suggested to Sadler that he might like to ease into the game, box a few exhibitions, "just to learn this boxing."

Sadler couldn't promise Foreman anything, certainly no signing bonus, no monthly draw. About all he could provide was a hotel room and three meals a day. Sadler's wagon was hitched to Liston, thirty-seven, past his prime and any hope of a big payday. That wagon wasn't going anywhere. But he could get Foreman valuable sparring time with the former champion, and maybe the odd exhibition bout here or there. Well, as far as that goes, Sadler explained to Foreman, why not take it one step further and get paid for your trouble? Any ideas of easing into the game were soon gone; Sadler got Foreman $5,000 for his pro debut the summer of 1969.

More important than that, though, was exposure to a veteran fighter. Liston may have been faded, may have been in disrepute, may have been without much of a future. He may have been reduced, in his professional twilight, to fighting in a Mexico bull ring for $12,000, stoned college kids from El Paso now his only fans. But, man, he could still punch. It didn't matter that Liston might disappear for weeks at a time, gone on some bender. If he happened, relying on some personal and mysterious urgency, to reappear in a ring, beware.

Foreman realized, gold medal or not, he was no match for Liston. Not at first. Liston would get that jab going, just a loaded piston, and Foreman was trapped behind it, no way out. The pneumatics of it were puzzling to the young pro; it just kept coming, a rhythmic pounding, short and powerful, no escape possible. That jab!

The rest of Liston was equally baffling. The two of them, the only heavyweights in Sadler's little stable, would take walks after dinner, Liston mostly silent and impenetrable. After a week, Liston began to acknowledge Foreman's existence, even speak. Liston didn't like or trust anybody and was always suspicious of slights. Once, the whole gang in Sadler's car, Foreman was rambling on about his horoscope, his latest preoccupation, and even thrust the magazine toward Liston in the backseat. Liston was suddenly ready to fight. "Get that out of my face!" he bellowed at Foreman. Sadler had to take Foreman aside later and explain the basis for the disturbance. "Big man can't read, George." But once Liston grew more comfortable with his young sparring partner, less paranoid, he began to assume the role of mentor, in the way he understood the concept.

"George," he said, stopping during one of their walks, "my grandmother always say, a man need two things." Foreman was more than ready to receive this wisdom. He gloried in the attention, the instruction of elders. Jim Brown, Doc Broadus, Pappy Gault, his Olympic coach—Foreman was fully formed by their inspirations. Liston continued: "A man need a haircut and shined shoes." Liston, it turned out, was hard-pressed to communicate much besides bitterness, the residue of so much shabby treatment. His biography, after all, was titled *The Champ Nobody Wanted*. Once Liston, in a pique of frustration over his limited respect as a champion, spat out his philosophy: "I don't care about nothing but the dough-re-me." Really, about the best Liston could do in the way of influence was show the young man his closet. Foreman was mightily impressed by the spoils of championship boxing. He counted the shoes—six, eight, ten pair!

But Foreman, bit by bit and round by round, was becoming his own man. He was scarcely aware of it. It wasn't too long before he figured how to get away from Liston's jab. It wasn't too much longer before he was giving Liston all he could handle. He was no more an agreeable punching bag, a butterfly pinned beneath Liston's jab. Once, the two sparring in New Orleans during one of Sadler's little caravans in 1970, Foreman hit Liston in the side and heard a slight *whoof*. Hit him in the stomach—*whoof*. It had happened that quickly. Sadler took him aside afterward and suggested he not push Liston too hard, and especially don't hit him in the head. It was just sparring, after all.

Others were noticing, too. By the autumn of 1970 he was 21–0, with nineteen knockouts, a glowering and fearsome brute at six-foot-four, 218 pounds. Everybody agreed, he had a lot to learn. But, everybody also agreed, there really is no substitute for concussive force. So a crowd of more than twelve thousand gathered in Madison Square Garden in August to watch Foreman fight that aging catcher George Chuvalo, a man who seemed specifically created to identify future champions, though never become one himself. Chuvalo, at thirty-two, was on the downward slope of a heavyweight's career, which included tough losses to Floyd Patterson, Ali, and Frazier. But he was still valuable as a metric of toughness, "the bum with a heart," they called him. In seventy-six fights, over the course of fourteen years, he'd never been knocked off his feet.

It took Foreman just three rounds, Chuvalo crumpling into a bloody crouch, the referee rushing to halt what appeared to be negligent manslaughter. Foreman had been landing punches at the rate of one per second, for roughly forty seconds, Chuvalo unable to lift a hand, before it could be stopped. It had been a horrible yet magnificent display of raw power.

That knockout, coming in the media capital, not only elevated Foreman into instant contention but also made him something of a celebrity. Jazz trumpeter Miles Davis, whom Foreman recognized only as someone who worked out in a San Francisco gym—"little mean guy, never did speak, just walk by you"—came back to the dressing room after the fight. "George," he said, "you feinted that guy right out of his shoes. So cool!" Foreman had just impressed the man who played with his back to the audience. Then, leaving the Garden, he was surprised to see a crowd waiting for him. "For me?" he thought.

The next day, awash in salutary newsprint (literally: "Salute the Grand Old Flag-Raiser" was one headline), George continued to exult in his new and improved status. He was sitting in a Manhattan coffee shop, chatting with some reporters, when he noticed heavyweight contender, and briefly champion, Jimmy Ellis sitting across the aisle. Ellis began with a story of how he'd bought his first Cadillac. "Walked into the showroom," he said, "and I said to the guy, 'Give me one of them.'" Both Ellis and Foreman slapped their thighs in shared appreciation of the audacity. Foreman, who'd just made $17,500 for the Chuvalo bout but could henceforth expect Cadillac money himself, made Ellis tell the story two more times, the New York scribes waiting patiently for their quotes.

Foreman was clearly the next thing in heavyweight boxing, talked up as a possible opponent for Frazier. Maybe not quite there, but coming hard and fast. "He's ready for the top fighters," Chuvalo himself said afterward. It was plain what Chuvalo meant by that. Ali had announced his return late that year, the Supreme Court offering a reprieve, with knockouts over Quarry and Bonavena, the quality of those opponents suggesting the exile had not materially damaged his contention. Frazier, having won Ali's vacated title, was more or less biding his time, waiting for the action to come to him. The three men, here at the end of 1970, seemed to have been set on a strange path, vague and uncertain at first, but ultimately sharply defined, single file.

Meanwhile, perhaps on the very last day of the year—the coroner could not be absolutely certain—onetime heavyweight champion of the world Sonny Liston, the man who more or less had taken Foreman under his wing, died in his Las Vegas home. His comeback was long since derailed, and he had been fighting on just for paydays. There was word on the streets that he'd taken up his old trade and was doing some enforcing on the side. He did not consort with angels in the best of times. The year 1970, one desultory bout to show for it, was not the best of times.

Liston's bloated body was discovered January 5, 1971, surrounded by drug paraphernalia, although the autopsy listed the cause of death as heart failure. Rumors of "hits" and "hot shots" were immediate. The autopsy further suggested that Liston's body, which had only briefly been put to purposeful and occasionally glorious use, had sat at the foot of his bed for five days.

1971

CHAPTER 4

VELVET HOT PANTS, TOUGH GOING IN LAOS, AND CLOSED-CIRCUIT DOPPELGÄNGERS

The plumage was magnificent. The pinnacle of the Peacock Revolution, according to one writer. Birds of every feather were represented. In fact, almost all of the animal kingdom was sampled that night, furred creatures in particular. Mink coats and hats, of course. Cowhide, certainly. And chinchilla, fox, beaver, and camel. But also rattlesnake, alligator, and . . . sharkskin? This was not, to survey the ticketholders, an ordinary event, the attire so extreme, so exaggerated that it resembled taxidermy far more than fashion. A man stepped from a horse-drawn carriage: He was cloaked in a white ermine, maxi-length cape, hemmed in chinchilla, the entire rig covering a gleaming silver-lamé jumpsuit. Atop it all, a matching ermine turban, a red feather the single demure touch.

The flamboyance was sharply exclusive to the black community. The whites in the swelling crowd were dressed extravagantly yet conservatively, as if to emphasize once more the racial separation in their sartorial contrast. Michael Caine wore a dinner jacket. Most all of them, celebrities and moguls alike, were in coats and ties, the most daring accessory a lit cigar. A few of the women acknowledged their sexuality (though not Eunice Shriver in her navy blue suit), one of them in a shimmering scoop-backed dress creating a stir as she passed along ringside, the titans craning their constricted necks behind her. And Barbi Benton, Hugh Hefner's date, caught some attention for a see-through blouse, covered here and there by a monkey fur coat. Among the men, though, it was quite a bit more formal, rather businesslike. Not even Frank Sinatra and Norman Mailer, who were working after all, risked popping a collar button. The rest of them, they might just as well have been attending the theater. The astronauts—and there were three of them in Madison Square Garden that night—couldn't have dressed with more dignity if they'd worn their NASA flight suits.

But the blacks at the Garden that night, good Lord! They might as well have been attending a carnival, or a masquerade ball even. Here was a woman with a huge horn of a hat, perhaps three feet tall. A man in a mink ten-gallon job, just about as wide as hers was high. Diana Ross was in black velvet hot pants. Miles Davis radiated cool in a dark jacket and open red shirt, his restraint almost radical in comparison. But everyone else chose a wild self-expression over moderation. There were leather coats of remarkable hues, none of which appear naturally on cows. It was kaleidoscopic, the range of color—yellow, purple, and green. Two men, in identical Walt Frazier–style muttonchops, wore identical yellow and black floor-length coats as well (and identical yellow hats), the symmetry of their appearance enough to induce a kind of self-doubt. Could this even be real? Could this occur in nature? The choice of textiles was various and just as mind-boggling, too, with brocades and velvets and suedes and shiny silks used in all combinations. Excess was the point: a mink apple cap, a wide and squat newsboy hat, might announce a patron in a white mink battle jacket, velvet pants, and laced boots.

It had been just a half century since women were legally permitted to attend a boxing match, turning subsequent events into a sort of mating ritual, the men using the occasion to preen ever more gloriously in their sexual urgency. But this occasion—Muhammad Ali versus Joe Frazier, finally—eclipsed all in terms of competitive display. One wonders how differently the crowd might have looked if the entertainment originally scheduled for March 8 had gone off instead. There was a hint: up near the rafters, folk rocker James Taylor, bought out of the gig for fifteen pairs of tickets when Garden officials discovered the scheduling conflict, sat with his raffish, stringy-haired entourage, all of them staring glumly at the shocking extravagance below them.

This was an eruption of pride, a show of self-satisfaction unequaled or, for that matter, unearned. There was nothing going on in America, not in the spring of 1971, that could possibly justify this sense of well-being, not to mention the sheer arrogance of it all. Not among whites, certainly not among blacks, repressed as ever, no matter the civil rights strides. This was, by any account, the beginning of a disastrous decade, racial and political divides threatening the progress of a nation, threatening its viability, really. No wonder a documentary of the time was able to so easily announce its intentions: *Approaching the Apocalypse*. The decade had begun with US troops abusing international privilege, marching into Cambodia, and then National Guardsmen, on their own soil, killing college students who might have voiced a righteous objection.

That, horrifying as it should have been, was mere preamble to the scandals, the institutional ugliness, the national mean-spiritedness that were soon to follow. Even for those who believed in America's agenda, the war in Vietnam, for example (if not historical segregation), it was a disappointing time. The week before this fight, *Life*'s cover story was "Tough Going in Laos," an account of a stalled US "incursion" that fewer and fewer agreed with in the first place. Nothing to be proud of here, whatever side you were on.

Yet the week after that gloomy news, here came *Life* again: "Battle of the Champs, Backstage with Ali and Frazier," the two of them wearing bow ties on the cover of the country's largest house organ. It was as if to say, we must interrupt the creeping gloom of these awful times for some old-fashioned foolishness, the kind of spectacle America used to be so good at. Here's a gladiatorial event between our two finest, best-conditioned specimens, bound to produce a conclusive and satisfying result, with maybe some fun along the way. Why wouldn't we pause?

The dynamics of the fight, if that's all it was, were heightened by the reemergence of one of the principals, Ali mainly. Ali had always enjoyed the power of disruption, but it was now amplified, or at least given weight, by his experience as a political hostage. No longer just a former champion, he'd become a symbol of defiance in a country that more and more appreciated the value of dissent. His views on religion and race, which had precipitated his exile, were now subsumed by the argument against foreign wars, an argument that was growing more popular. He had come to stand for any number of things, for that matter, all American agitations of the moment, whether it was for the youth movement, the antiwar movement, or even black empowerment. Besides that, there was the natural curiosity: what did this once marvelous athlete, still undefeated in the ring for all that goes, have left?

Also, there was that power of disruption, undiminished, apparently by three and a half years of legally enforced irrelevance.

So this was the response, a keening, multicultural, multihued crowd, a fantastic assembly representing a diversity that was by no means considered a national asset, certainly not yet. It wasn't just male and female jousting for attention, the normal (if heavily freighted) expression of sexuality, pantomimed in public. It wasn't only a racial war, blacks and whites testing the limits of a compulsory acceptance, the old violence now enacted in fashion one-upmanship. It wasn't simply a political referendum, either, the fighters handily representing competing ideologies. And it certainly was more than a boxing match—far more during these curious times—even if it materialized as a match of once-in-a-generation intrigue, a sports sensation in its own right.

It was all of those things, and the taxis disgorging the fans and celebrities and the movers and shakers, the whole feathered and furred lot of them, into an eight-block radius of pandemonium, the scalpers asking $600 for $150 ringside seats, pickpockets enjoying the national holiday, thieves running down dark city sidewalks with the rightful ticketholder in pursuit, mobs of people, all kinds of people, in all kinds of hats, iridescent under the streetlights, pressing forward, drawn toward something so big, so important, it no longer qualified as a sports event, but as some kind of cultural touchstone. The mob just engulfed the Garden.

It was more orderly inside, but not by much. Ali had decided to spend the day in a Garden hideout rather than risk another limo transit on New York City streets. His trip to the Garden for the weigh-in that morning had indeed been a colossal cock-up, the limo driver needing three laps around the facility to deliver him the one block from the New Yorker Hotel. So Ali hunkered down with his considerable entourage, about fifteen people, in the press lounge on the first promenade, killing time.

The Garden had provided Ali a folding bed, though not one adequate to his six-foot-three frame, and a kind of room service for his gang. That gang ordered up some $4,000 in food and beverages. Ali was not much for napping or eating during most of his sequestration. He wandered the empty arena, in search of an audience, seemingly terrified at the idea of being silent for so long a stretch. At one point he spotted workers tightening the ring canvas and launched into a tirade from the balcony. "Tonight is the night of truth," he boomed from above. "He ain't no champ. I can't wait. I want to fight now." Some food-service workers gathered, all in their white chef hats, as Ali continued: "Listen to me now: This will be no contest. I have a lot of speed, I have a lot of endurance. When I'm through with Frazier, he'll need more insurance." And then he returned to hide out for a bit.

And then he came back. The producers for the closed-circuit telecast were staging fight scenes, with stand-ins for the fighters, just to see how, or even if, they could capture the action. Ali was up in the rafters when his stand-in buckled, simulating a knockdown. "Ain't no way that Ali is getting knocked down," he shouted. "That is never going to happen." Protective of his closed-circuit doppelgänger, he shouted helpful advice from above. "Speed up! Float like a butterfly! Look pretty! Look pretty on them ropes."

Frazier's camp was suffering a different kind of hysteria, but not of their man's making. The week before the fight, Yank Durham had gotten two calls saying that Frazier would not live to hear the opening bell. This was in addition to two letters to the Garden saying the building would be bombed. Another letter, and a follow-up phone call, promised both fighters would be shot dead in the ring if a $75,000 payment was not made. And the morning of the fight, a caller told a New York talk show that Frazier was about to die.

Already there were 280 special police assigned to the event, in addition to 150 off-duty police hired by the Garden. But now, with credible death threats, Frazier was given his group of bodyguards. Also, while Ali was hiding from the crowds in the Garden, Frazier was hiding from assassins in the Hotel Pierre, in a room that was several stars above his previous room at the City Squire Motor Inn. Frazier didn't mind the detectives lounging around, but he was offended by the Pierre's presumed elegance. He complained that the scent of lilacs hurt his nose. Durham said it "smelled like a goddamned whore house" and that somebody better get up there pronto and "spray it." Also, "Get all those flowers out of here."

Still, Frazier relaxed in slightly more luxury, and certainly quiet, than Ali that Monday afternoon, choosing to return to the Pierre after the morning weigh-in and nap in his scented room, bodyguards all around him reading the morning papers.

As the fight drew closer, others finished their preparations, too. Archie Moore, a former champion and one of the fight's announcers, took it upon himself to school Burt Lancaster, another of the announcers, in the finer points of the snap jab. Lancaster was a friend of Jerry Perenchio, the Hollywood agent who'd put the promotion together, and was called in to provide some West Coast glamour to the telecast. Howard Cosell, who'd called many of Ali's fights and who felt he was instrumental in his return to the ring, was passed over and was miffed. But Lancaster, who'd once played a boxer in Ernest Hemingway's *The Killers,* was an upgrade in celebrity and a signifier that this was about more than just sports. Moore, petulant at Lancaster's progress ("When I say recoil, bring the knuckles back sharply—where you going?"), made Lancaster perform the exercise over and over. Lancaster grinned broadly.

The fight's true promoter, the man who fronted $4.5 million of the fighters' record-breaking $5 million purse, was likewise busy, entertaining celebrity guests in his apartment at the Waldorf Towers. Jack Kent Cooke, who owned the Los Angeles Lakers basketball team and Los Angeles Kings hockey team (as well as part of the Washington Redskins football team), gloried in such visibility and took advantage of his high-profile role in Ali-Frazier to dispense vast reserves of condescension. At his rather formal gathering (there was a noticeable lack of color, in every respect) that included actors Lorne Greene and Peter Falk, Cooke droned on and on for a TV interviewer. "Oh, the satisfaction is not at all in making money," he said. "Could have bought stock, could have bought debentures, could have bought certificates of deposit, more commonly known as CDs, and made as much money, with no risk. There's tremendous risk in this venture, don't you see." Finally, he ushered them out. "Leave your coats and hats," he said. "We can pick them up on our way back." The cars were all ready.

And still the fight drew closer. Part of Lancaster's role was to interview Ali in his dressing room before the fight. Lancaster asked Ali if he felt any fear. "No sir," he said, sitting on his rubbing table. "I feel mostly the pressure. It's a little worrisome until the first punch is thrown." Ali was wearing his red trunks and red tassels on his white shoes, attire that Ferdie Pacheco, his longtime doctor and cornerman, found wanting. "So the judges can see me dancing," Ali explained. Pacheco wondered, "What if they see you knocked on your ass and those tassels are dancin' in the air?"

Possibly the only truly sober moment in Ali's dressing room had been his short interview with Lancaster. When Butch Lewis, of Frazier's camp, visited the room to tell Ali's trainer that it was time for the customary exchange of trainers, where surrogates inspected the wrapping of their foe's hands, he was unmoored by the looseness there. "What Frazier doing right now?" Ali demanded of him. And then Ali proceeded to unleash a mock fusillade, driving one of his hapless cronies into a corner. "Frazier's down! Frazier's down!" Everyone was roaring with laughter. Lewis, badly shaken by the scene enacted on his behalf, retreated quickly to Frazier's dressing room.

That was a quieter, perhaps more nervous environment. Frazier had already knelt in prayer, asking, "Lord, help me kill this man because he's not righteous." He was in the same unforgiving mood when Archie Moore showed up to tape his part of the prefight show, giving the interlopers plenty of guff. "You guys just come in start shooting," Frazier said. "Nobody tell me nothing. Should be some consideration. What this for? Tell me that." He was wearing a sparkling green robe, still shooting jabs when he finally allowed Moore, ever dignified and still slightly petulant, to ask his questions. "Joe I know you don't like to talk at a moment like this," he said, "but you're getting $2.5 million. Is that going to make any difference in the way that you fight?" Frazier said it gave him a little more inspiration. Moore nodded and got out.

The arena was full now, Woody Allen and Diane Keaton in their seats, David Brenner having chased a mugger down to retrieve his ticket, now safely inside too. Former vice president Hubert Humphrey was ready, and so was Senator Ted Kennedy. Gene Kelly and Bill Cosby were settling in. Sinatra, on assignment from *Life*, was taking up his position at ringside, his Nikon strapped around his neck. Mailer, who would write the story for the magazine, was organizing his impressions. Across the country, at 350 closed-circuit venues, theater tickets costing $30 apiece, fans were likewise finding seats. Around the world, same thing, 300 million altogether.

Larry Merchant, the sports columnist, had dined before the fight with several like-minded writers, all young and irreverent, collectively known as the A. J. Leibling Chowder and Marching Band, and he was now at press row, too. He watched the fighters mount the canvas, dance around each other, Ali's red tassels flying. Merchant believed that Ali was singing, "Two and a half million dollars. Can you believe, two and a half million dollars?"

A 10:40 that night the two fighters were finally introduced. Merchant, who'd been complaining to his fellow band marchers that the new Garden was a soulless place, was now struck breathless by a guttural roar, a sudden rush of sound, a wall of noise that descended from the rafters, a crushing and disabling volume, almost paralyzing in its growing and frightening intensity. He thought, "I'm in the belly of the beast," not a feeling he'd ever had before. The noise just rolled down.

CHAPTER 5

LITTLE SISSIES, SOUL POWER, AND JUDY GARLAND'S SHOES

Once, in the spring of 1962, an aspiring fight publicist, a fight fan certainly, wandered into the Main St. Gym in Los Angeles, where Ali—Cassius Clay, of course—was training for a fight with George Logan. This young man, Bill Caplan, happened to be just as big a Dodgers fan, the kind who couldn't afford to miss an inning, no matter where he was. As he watched Clay bouncing around on the canvas, moving backward faster than he'd ever seen a heavyweight move forward, Caplan indulged his twin obsessions with the technology of the day, a red Zenith transistor radio plugged into his ear, the soothing tones of Vin Scully competing with Clay's patter.

It wasn't long before the young boxer, just twenty and only two years removed from his Olympic triumph and as easily distracted as ever, interrupted training to inquire of this new gadgetry. A transistor radio was fresh consumer electronics and was of far more interest to Clay than the work at hand. "What you got there?" he asked. Caplan told him. "That little thing a radio?" He climbed out of the ring to inspect it. Caplan introduced himself as a salesman who one day hoped to do fight publicity. Clay was doubly intrigued; here was a man who shared his same passions, the very latest toys and the arts of self-aggrandizement. "I got a thing that records," Clay told Caplan, inviting him to his suite at the nearby Alexandria Hotel. "Plus, I'll show you something about publicity."

Caplan, a stranger with a red radio just moments before, tagged along to the fighter's room, where Clay wheeled out a wire recorder, an enormous device. Caplan located a music station on his radio's dial, and Clay began recording, testing it, playing it back, recording some more. After a while, the novelty of it exhausted, he said, "So you want to be a publicity man" and went to his room, returning with a scrapbook that was, in format, the size of a coffee table and, in thickness, as big as the deli sandwiches Caplan favored. Caplan paged through it, twelve fights so thoroughly and painstakingly documented, the whole thing so organized, so complete in its coverage, that you just had to whistle at the ambition of it. But what struck Caplan hardest was not its comprehension, which was obviously total in scope, but the fact that subject and curator were one and the same. Not often, or maybe ever, has such self-absorption, such narcissism, been enacted beyond one's adolescence.

But that was Clay, to that point in his life anyway, a one-man PR firm, his most important client, himself. Only a year earlier he'd learned some important principles from the pro wrestler Gorgeous George, up to then the historical embodiment of conceit. Clay had been in Las Vegas for a fight when the promoter invited him to see Gorgeous George perform, a ritual of arrogance that even the young boxer had difficulty stomaching. The wrestler had paraded to the ring to the tune of "Pomp and Circumstance," his cornerman spraying a perfume before him, handlers fluffing his golden locks before the action. This was so over the top that even Ali had to boo.

Later, when he visited the wrestler in his dressing room—here was a conference of chaos—Gorgeous admitted his glorious effrontery, explaining that such comical self-confidence sold a lot of tickets, more than any half-nelson. Gorgeous advised the fighter to do the same. "You got your good looks, a great body, and a lot of people will pay to see somebody shut your big mouth. So keep on bragging, keep on sassing and always be outrageous." Clay took the lesson to heart, anointed himself the Greatest of All Time, proclaimed his prettiness, aggravating the public perhaps, but filling reporters' notebooks and, more to the point, arena seats, wherever he went.

As Gaseous Cassius, or the Louisville Lip, he'd become a ridiculous and, boxing purists were sure, temporary attraction. His talents for provocation were divisive only to the point they were taken seriously. And how could you take him seriously? The old guard among the press, the Jimmy Cannons and the Jim Murrays, were slow to forgive his immodesty. But in time, understanding that a good column trumped all generational bias (if in fact that's all it was), even they made allowances for his brand of buffoonery. If the young fighter was willing to drive up to Sonny Liston's Denver driveway at three in the morning, the bus painted out in "World's Most Colorful Boxer" (with "Liston Must Go in Eight" in subscript), just to goad the champion into a fight, well, how could you possibly take a stand against that level of nonsense? The young Cassius Clay honking the horn, a rattled Liston rushing to the curb in his satin robe, and Clay in a sudden panic gunning that bus out of there—ego must be excused for the sake of this kind of fun, these easy columns.

It was only during that Liston campaign, the securing of the fight and the ticket-selling turmoil, that Clay—for he was still Clay, after all—thought to include the opponent in his buildups. Up to then, he believed the effects of his own persona were sufficient to any event. He was not a particularly curious man, in any case, and had difficulty imagining a person, or even a group, as interesting as himself. In 1964, when he was training for that Liston fight in Miami, somebody thought to pose the Beatles, having just arrived for their first US tour, with him at the 5th Street Gym. It was a curious decision, crossing cultures, race, and even modes of entertainment. Yet it was also genius, gathering such like-minded imps in the small space of a ring. Clay, according to his instincts, lined them up and knocked all four down with one punch, domino-style. The result was classic publicity, a shot for the ages, advancing two different careers with one picture. Yet he had just one question after the gym cleared. "Who were those little sissies?"

By 1971, perhaps hardened by his exile or just a little less self-centered in his increasing years, Ali was ready to plug much more interesting narratives into his fight campaigns, taking into account personalities besides his own. He was still prettier than his opponents, still a greater boxer by untold magnitudes, but he was now more righteous, of a higher religion, more correct, a morally superior being, representing truths no mere opponent could hope to approach. Ali had, after all, spent the past several years honing his various messages, now incorporating the politics of the land, exploring the racial rifts in his country, ready to exploit them to his own rhetorical advantage. His doggerel was becoming more pointed, harder to take. In any case, he was receiving record purses.

As far as Frazier, this new opponent, they had been better friends than anybody had a right to expect. Frazier had additional motives in avoiding the unseemly scramble for Ali's stripped title—he'd been correct in guessing he'd make more money and eventually prestige by passing on that heavyweight tournament. But he'd been sympathetic and even supportive of Ali in his exile, and Ali was grateful for that. Of course, there was a natural wariness to their relationship, each sizing the other up for a big payday, sometime down the road. But mostly respect. Frazier especially had gone out of his way to show a kind of appreciation, never once criticizing Ali's explosive stand on the draft or his choice of religion. Frazier told his friend sportswriter Dave Wolf, "If Baptists weren't allowed to fight, I wouldn't fight either."

Frazier obliged Ali's need for the limelight, allowing himself to be dragged into some staged craziness here and there to keep Ali's name viable, had gone to Muslim services at Ali's invitation, mentioned Ali's unfair plight to President Nixon, and even loaned him money. They were colleagues in what happened to be a very strange profession.

In the summer of 1970, with Ali's chances for returning to the ring improving but by no means certain, never mind their own fight, he invited Frazier on a road trip from Philadelphia (Ali having moved there, the two of them almost neighbors) to New York, where both had business. The idea was that Ali would tape a conversation he could use in his just-signed autobiography (for a much-needed advance of $225,000). Frazier picked Ali up in his gold Cadillac, Ali commenting on the smashed grill, and the two commenced a somewhat wide-ranging and highly unlikely conversation that included not only contrary predictions for an eventual meeting (Frazier: "I'd tear your head off with a jab"), grudging compliments on style (Ali: "I gotta admit you're good, but I'm the fastest"), and diet tips (Ali: "Unsweetened grapefruits, man"), but also advice on dress and cars and a singing contest near the end that Frazier seemed to have won.

At one point, Ali even proposed himself as a sparring partner for Frazier, just in case his court case folded up on itself. "I mean, wouldn't you like to have a good sparring partner that could tag you?" Ali suggested. "And you can tag him, and he ain't gonna quit on you? I need a job." Frazier asked how much he'd want. "Couple hundred a week. That means eight hundred by the end of the month." Frazier whistled at that.

At the end of the ride, as the two approached New York, Ali wondered about a loan, since Frazier seemed to be carrying plenty. "How about a hundred?" he said. "I may stay overnight." And Frazier, amused, gave the former champion a hundred-dollar bill.

And now Ali was in a position to repay the debt. A court ruling in June 1970, while not overturning Ali's conviction, had made a ring return feasible, if rushed. To get ahead of a Supreme Court ruling the next summer, which still could go either way, Ali needed to fight Frazier sometime in the spring of 1971. And he needed to prove that, after almost four years of inactivity, he remained worthy of such a match. So Ali found a comeback fight in October with a tough Jerry Quarry in Atlanta, a bout that had generated surprising interest. Ali's purse of $1 million, the largest of his career, was fully justified by resulting ticket sales. The fight made $4 million, on a 70 percent buy rate among the two hundred closed-circuit locations. Madison Square Garden, one of twenty New York venues showing the fight, was packed.

Almost better than the payday was the social sanctioning. After the fight, civil rights leader Ralph Abernathy presented Ali with the

Martin Luther King Award, calling him the "living example of soul power, the March on Washington in two fists." King himself, who'd had to meet privately with Ali during those years lest he foul negotiations with President Johnson, was not around to vindicate him. But his widow, Coretta Scott King, did announce him as "a champion of justice and peace and unity."

Everybody was taking notice, it seemed. Veterans groups still opposed Ali's stand, but other hard-liners were softening. Perhaps they were following the lead of CBS anchor Walter Cronkite, who'd announced the "bloody experience of Vietnam" as a "stalemate" back in 1968. That repudiation caused President Johnson to famously say, "If I have lost Walter Cronkite, I have lost Mr. Average American Citizen." By late 1969, 250,000 antiwar protesters were demonstrating in Washington, DC. For that matter, Richard Nixon had been elected president on a platform of withdrawal. Ali was no longer out in the cold when it came to his objections to the military draft.

Even sportswriters, the older bunch as conservative as any veterans group, were coming around. Howard Cosell found it safe to trumpet Ali's cause (others, such as Robert Lipsyte of the *New York Times* and Jerry Izenberg of the *Newark Star-Ledger,* had been much braver, supporting Ali earlier and more forcefully). Jimmy Cannon, a longtime detractor and a known defender of the status quo, now pronounced Ali the "athlete of the decade," meaning the 1960s. "In him is the trouble and the wildness and hysterical gladness and the nonsense and the rebellion and the conflicts of race and the yearning for bizarre religions and the cult of the put-on and the changed values that altered the world and the feeling about Vietnam in the generation that ridicules what the parents cherish." He simply had to give it up for Ali.

His resurrection as a cultural icon, a man who had heralded change at his personal expense, announced him, more important for boxing, as a commercial property. Testing the waters in Atlanta, and then six weeks later back in Madison Square Garden in a December bout with Oscar Bonavena, he reensured that his draw had not diminished and might, with politics added to the pugilistic mix, even have increased. Promoters who'd found Ali toxic before—presumed poison had to be reintroduced in the boxing backwaters of Georgia—were now scrambling for the rights to a Frazier fight. The race was on to nail this down.

Because the business of boxing is largely a democratic enterprise, bowing to neither pedigree nor good sense, the only real barrier of entry was a letter of credit. In this case, according to the demands of both Ali and Frazier, who had both balked at the Garden's idea of a jackpot ($1.25 million per fighter, plus a percentage of the box-office gross), that letter of credit was going to have to be substantial. The fighters, or rather their handlers, had gotten the idea they should get $3 million per.

This ruled out a lot of the usual suspects, especially those with recent knowledge of the fight industry. Even if this was going to be the Fight of the Century, as many were already calling it, it was difficult to see how any investor could break even while permitting purses like that. The closed-circuit broadcast, which would have to do the heavy lifting in such an enormously scaled operation, would have to return at least $7 million to make it work. The closed-circuit record was $3.2 million for a fight in 1962 between Floyd Patterson and Sonny Liston. There was nothing to suggest this was remotely feasible.

The only way to make it pencil out was to salt the proposal with plenty of magical thinking. This was provided by Jerry Perenchio, a Beverly Hills talent agent who knew how to book Andy Williams in Salt Lake City but was entirely inexperienced when it came to putting two fighters in a ring. "I really don't know the first thing about boxing," he admitted. "This fight is like booking Andy Williams into 500 Salt Lake Citys all at once." But he knew show business and had been the first to realize this match transcended the usual notions of sports, and he was anxious to take part. "It's a show business spectacular," he'd decided. "A historic event."

Boxing does not hold anything against magical thinking; people of originality and ambition are always welcome. Still: that letter of credit.

Perenchio was surprised at how difficult this was to produce. Everyone had agreed that for purses of $2.5 million apiece, Perenchio could promote the fight. Who really cared if he'd never done one before? He just had to guarantee the money. He was in London at the time the agreement was reached, and he set about calling possible backers, easiest part of the job, he assumed. It took seventy-one calls, a long-distance tab of $16,000, before he reached an amenable party. Jack Kent Cooke, an entrepreneur who enjoyed high-stakes sports ownership as well as any limelight that went with it, had been toying with the idea of promoting the fight himself, possibly putting it in his Los Angeles Forum, home of his Lakers and Kings. Perenchio's proposal struck a chord, and he agreed to come on board, to the tune of $4.5 million, even if it was going to end up in New York.

Perenchio had plenty of plans for recouping Cooke's investment, not all of which struck the boxing establishment as sane. It was one thing to introduce some Hollywood glamour, remove the event from its normally tawdry circumstances. Replacing Cosell with Burt Lancaster on commentary was a bold move in that direction. But it was quite another to demand a 65–35 split from distributors when 50–50 had been customary. And to raise closed-circuit prices from $6 to as high as $30. It was all blue-sky stuff. Perenchio was banking on 2.5 million customers in 500 locations when the record holder, that Patterson-Liston fight, had drawn just 563,000 fans to 253 sites. Perenchio and Cooke somehow thought the gross would reach $30 million, when no fight before it had even gotten to $5 million.

The two were confident this event was greater by just such multiples, sure they would split as much as $2.5 million in profits. "It's potentially the greatest single grosser in the history of the world," said Perenchio. "It's like *Gone With the Wind*." But they were not so confident they were willing to overlook any possible income stream. Like the butcher who processes everything but the tail and the squeal, Perenchio was putting a figure on just about anything, and not just souvenirs, telecast commercials, and a feature-length documentary (planned for release sixty days after the fight) but fight memorabilia, including the fighters' trunks, gloves, and shoes. "If a movie studio can auction off Judy Garland's shoes," explained Perenchio, "these things ought to be worth something, too."

What even Perenchio and Cooke didn't dare monetize was publicity. There was so much of it, and so easily produced, it would have been a disgrace to claim its provenance. Of course, there was the usual fight-community interest, magnified by the notion of two undefeated heavyweights in the same ring. That doesn't happen often, and the mystery of a champ's inactivity, another champ's ferocity would have been plenty for any other campaign. This really could have been the Fight of the Century. But not all of the fifteen hundred applicants for press credentials (some six hundred were given out) could have told a haymaker from a haystack. There was a sense that a pageant was being mounted, a story being enacted, something about to be decided for the country, and you had better be there to make sense of it. This was larger than boxing: Literary lights such as Norman Mailer (for *Life*), William Saroyan (for *True*), and Budd Schulberg (*Playboy*) were among those given press access (representing two Pulitzer Prizes and one Oscar, two if photographer Sinatra is included). Alas, Abbie Hoffman, writing for the *Evergreen Review,* was not.

Throughout history, boxing matches have often been put in the service of issues larger than sports. In 1910, in the original Fight of the Century, Great White Hope Jim Jeffries had come out of retirement to meet heavyweight champion Jack Johnson, a man of a certain flamboyance and, most important, color. A Johnson victory by no means ensured racial equality—it probably arrested such progress, actually—but it certainly illuminated the divide in a country that still seemed mired in a civil war. And in 1938, Joe Louis, whose blackness was oddly incidental in the prewar preliminaries, defeated Germany's Max Schmeling for the heavyweight title. Louis, having met with President Roosevelt just weeks before the fight, understood that "the whole damned country was depending on me."

This fight was going to have political overtones no matter who was in it. Just by the circumstance of history, these diversions occurring at a time of such civic unrest, there were bound to be theses posited, symbols stretched, conclusions drawn. There was so much confusion—some young people dying in distant rice paddies but others marching and rioting in opposition to their cause—that almost any public event could be freighted with significance, a possible point of clarity. A fight? It had to stand for something, right?

No matter who was in it, *Life* would have likely done a cover story, if only to counterbalance a national misery. The event offered the country a chance to avert its gaze, if just for a week, or only a night. As it happened, *Life* did run a cover story on the upcoming fight: "The Battle of the Undefeated." It was, in addition to being a behind-the-scenes look at the two fighters, a publishing respite from the international indignity of Vietnam, although that too was incorporated in the issue. "Calley Takes the Stand" was the other big story that week, an Army lieutenant on trial for the murder of 102 men, women, and children during the massacre, of three years before, at My Lai.

It was interesting to think, if one let one's imagination run wild, that Ali could just as easily have appeared in the one article as the other. The only difference, unlike Calley and his troops and a shifting proportion of the American public, was that Ali had no quarrel with those unsuspecting villagers.

Ali had not, in the time of his exile, found reason to repudiate any of Gorgeous George's lessons of polarization. He sensed quite correctly that he was a symbol of the Left, any who opposed the war or the increasingly unpopular politics of the time. He was for the youth, for the disaffected, the persecuted, anybody whose principles had been abridged by patriotism. He was against tradition, entrenched policies, and authority. Although this incorporated a growing segment of America—by 1971 the antiwar movement was no longer the exclusive province of hippies and the otherwise disenfranchised—it still left a large portion, perhaps even a majority, who resented his presence. This was still a powerful population, still quite a vast territory on the American landscape. Ali, for the purposes of the promotion, assigned it to Frazier.

The idea that just because Ali stood for something, he must also, baffled Frazier. When did he pick sides? He'd never talked politics, race, or religion. How did he get involved in a national debate? Here was Ali saying, "That Joe Frazier, he's gonna get telephone calls and telegrams from folks in Georgia and Alabama and Mississippi saying, 'Joe Frazier, you be a white man tonight and stop that draft-dodging nigger.'" Frazier had a high tolerance for Ali's two-sided personality when it came to most fight publicity——he didn't mind terribly if Ali called him "chump" or otherwise disrespected him; Ali's stunts seemed mostly in fun——and he might have choked back his anger when Ali said he "was too ugly to be champ . . . too dumb to be champ." But this was outrageous. Frazier the white man? Frazier, of southern poverty, raised in discrimination, was far blacker than Ali was, a kid raised in middle-class comfort, more advantages than Frazier could have dreamed of. "He's the wrong kind of Negro," Ali said. "He's not like me, 'cause he's the Uncle Tom. He works for the enemy." Ali was actually calling him an "Uncle Tom"?

Ali dictated all terms of discourse, however, and neither logic nor good taste would interfere with his narrative. As Schulberg pointed out, "Ali was a recognized shibboleth. He divided sheep from goats, peaceniks from gung-hoers, leftists and liberals from conservatives and reactionaries." Ali, in his entrepreneurial cruelty, divided Frazier right out of his own race.

"Nobody wants to talk to him," Ali explained to some writers before the fight. "Oh, maybe Nixon will call him if he wins. I don't think he'll call me. But 99 per cent of my people are for me. They identify with my struggle. Same one they're fighting every day in the streets. If I win, they win. If I lose, they lose."

The rhetoric was so attractive that even the black press bought into the division. In its walk-up to the fight, *Ebony* admitted that Frazier "would be especially appreciated by the conservative blacks and, though probably not to his liking, by many Caucasians who see him, ironically, as some kind of 'Great White Hope.' They want to see Frazier whip 'that uppity loud nigger Clay!'" *Jet* called him an "unheralded white-created champion." The young editor of the magazine *Black Sports,* Bryant Gumbel, wondered, "Is Joe Frazier a white champion in a black skin?"

Frazier didn't know how to respond, how to reset the debate. Ali was talking about a mission "to free 30 million black people," explaining how he'd "win this fight because I've got a cause. Frazier has no cause. He's in it for the money alone." This was simply preposterous, that Ali wasn't in it for the monstrous paycheck as well. Frazier couldn't get over it. But he thought his enormous self-assurance would be enough to neutralize Ali's bluster. What more would be necessary? "I don't want to be no more than I am," answered Frazier, trying to restore the normal rules of the ring. His equanimity in public was impressive, but inwardly he was seething. "I ain't no Tom," he'd say in camp.

But there was no way to restore the conditions of a normal heavyweight championship fight. It had been more than that to begin with—nobody gets $2.5 million for a normal fight—and now it had escalated into some kind of national referendum, a spot check on civil rights, racial dignity, you name it. Ali, plumbing his talents for provocation, had spun this affair so far beyond the athletic realm that now playwrights, novelists, and screenwriters had to be ringside to properly interpret the results. This was, according to one essay headline published in the *New York Times,* "The All-Time Fascination Bout." Ali had been sassy, outrageous, shrewd, and unfair to a fault. And seats were selling out everywhere, in New York, San Francisco, Chicago, in London, where theatergoers were preparing for a 4:30 a.m. performance. They sold out in Los Angeles, where, to accommodate an overflow, fans were seated behind the screen, watching the action in reverse. More than five thousand fans bought tickets at Pittsburgh's Three Rivers Stadium, in eighteen-degree weather, some of them coming all the way from Buffalo, where the venues had filled. They sold out in French bistros, German beer halls, Italian hotels. The streets of Buenos Aires were empty. In Manila schoolchildren brought televisions to class. The world stood by.

CHAPTER 6

RED TASSELS, CELEBRITY SCRIBES, AND DUKE ELLINGTON

Whatever the moral disagreements, whatever the political quarrels, the racial accusations, the judicial injustices, the cultural arguments—all suspended in the seconds it took the comically underpaid Arthur Mercante ($500 for the third man, quite a drop-off) to recite his ring instructions. Now it became a fistfight between two large men, the very largest at hand, with such specific skills and such finely wrought determinations that anything short of annihilation would be, well, not necessarily a disappointment but certainly a surprise.

The sport of boxing, uniquely vulnerable to charges of corruption and cruelty, has long waxed and waned in national popularity. For many years, or at least as long as it had been legal, the heavyweight champion in particular has occupied a near-mythic position in American history. He is by occupation the remaining vestige of the pioneer spirit, of obvious independence and self-reliance, as well as fearlessness and ambition. The crudity of the sport, hand-to-hand combat in an age of increasing sophistication and refinement, was often attacked, with regular calls for abolishment. Yet boxing was always forgiven, its appeal as an institution for loner achievement always available.

Of course, the popularity depended upon the quality, durability, and excitement of the reigning champion. Even his appropriateness. America had been lucky to have such fistic totems as Jack Dempsey in the Roaring Twenties, not simply a good boxer but one of his times, flamboyant and ebullient. Gene Tunney, who succeeded him, was often characterized as a thinking man's fighter, and he became a convenient hero of a country that was undergoing enormous changes in aspiration and style. And then there was Joe Louis, arising out of the Great Depression, perhaps the greatest of them yet, transcending race and sports. Louis held the title for eleven years.

Decent-enough champions followed Louis, though none to threaten the Brown Bomber's dominance. There was Rocky Marciano in the 1950s, his plodding (and thudding) workmanship some comfort to his era. But until Cassius Clay sprang forth, winning the championship from Sonny Liston in 1964, the office had been in some disrepair. It was a commanding title even during this discontinuity, but its occupancy had been reduced to transients, exalted ones for sure, but transients nonetheless.

Clay's reign from 1964 to 1967 had been a lively one, even a distinguished one. As some other champions were lucky in their circumstances, he too was appropriate to his times, his high-energy recklessness metaphor enough for the forces that were percolating beneath American authority. But besides the force of personality he brought to bear upon the position—titleholders were expected to perform the obligations of celebrity, but none had ever executed them with such gusto—he'd also substantially changed the sport. There had always been style, to greater or lesser degrees, among the champions but never to the seeming exclusion of substance. His fights were essentially vanity projects, the eccentricities and inventions in the ring as much the point as an eventual knockout. It was maddening, but intoxicating, too.

Frazier, who now stood in front of him in the ring as Mercante reminded the fighters to protect themselves at all times, was of another piece. For him, boxing was a straightforward activity, an honest acceptance of give-and-take. Frazier's frightening advantage was that he didn't particularly care how much he needed to take in order to give. That disposition requires an abnormal self-confidence, that no matter how much punishment the opponent applies, there will always be a reservoir for rejoinder. Frazier's experience was that the opponent's resolve tended to vanish long before his own needle ever tilted toward empty. His were battles of attrition, although they were often hastened, perhaps mercifully, by a powerful left hook.

So as the two stood there, face-to-face, Mercante rattling off his conditions of conduct, questions of relative righteousness were replaced with far more immediate matters of survival. Never had two undefeated champions, their reigns separated by whatever strange circumstances, been matched in a ring during their prime. Never had two such similarly pedigreed fighters, Olympic champions, their skills proven and tested over a number of seasons, their titles defended over and over, reached this kind of elimination. And never had boxers of such extreme and opposite styles—Ali's loose-limbed filigrees of explosive violence and Frazier's horrifying mode of single-minded oppression—been set in motion against each other.

All around them were competing cries of anticipation, a near-riotous and keening mob looking for a satisfaction, whether of cause or even commerce. The peacocks groomed their plumage, the outrage of fashion a sort of stand-in for anger; the suits sat wreathed in their own cigar smoke, their smugness all the rebuttal they needed; the celebrities validated worldwide interest, their sponsored presence a reassurance of a momentous event. The broadcast operators, mindful of the unpredictable nature and tremendous investment of the occasion, bore down, overruling the catastrophic effects of chance: two backup generators whirred outside the Garden, lest Con Ed falter and interrupt a feed to 300 million souls.

And in this cyclonic eye stood, finally, two men of highly various temperament but identical purpose. Frazier heard the instructions, waited for Ali's reflexive rant to abate, and said, "I'm gonna kill you." Ali danced away, his red tassels shimmering under the ring lights, answer enough. The crowd—here in the Garden but also in theaters across the country and homes throughout the world—let forth a cathartic roar. Someone rang a bell.

Ali's plan was simple enough: let Frazier punch himself out while, sharpshooting, he peeled away that formerly impenetrable veneer, a layer of armor, really. This was not a new plan when it came to the puzzle of Frazier's squat implacability. But nobody had Ali's toolbox, either. Ali, though not on his toes, exploited his seven-inch reach advantage, jabbing, keeping that grinding, constantly swiveling tank at bay. In the first round, Frazier inched ahead in his tracks, accepting the jabs, bobbing constantly, a left and then a right to his head, sometimes finding Ali with hooks of his own—Ali shaking his head, "Nooooo contest." But Ali's jabs were finding their marks, mostly. Frazier was careless about the judges' points at this stage of a fight, usually was, just as he was careless of those jabs; he almost always lost the first round of his fights. He lost this one, too.

"That," said Burt Lancaster, when it was finally his turn to speak, "is one of the most exciting first rounds I think we've seen in a long time." Perhaps. It was at least instructive. Ali had not danced, perhaps no longer could. Whether it was the nearly four years of inactivity or just some extra baggage along the midriff, he had not been on his toes but instead fought flat-footed. Certainly, he could find Frazier with his punches. But although Frazier was hardly a piñata, his shoulder weave constantly reducing the target area, a lot of punches had found Frazier.

Ali continued to score, landing hard punches. "It's amazing that Frazier can stand up under that battering," ring announcer Don Dunphy told his audience. And it's true, this was not like any previous version of Ali, slugging away. But Frazier, undaunted as usual, scored, too. And he won rounds three and four on the scorecards, evening the bout.

The fight continued like that, the two men exchanging a tremendous volume of punches. There was no pause, no rest, just sustained swinging. In the sixth, when Ali had predicted a knockout, it was Frazier, now lunging confidently, who bulled him into the ropes, his aggression increasing by rounds. And it was Frazier who sounded concern, sensing something about Ali he just had not considered. "What's holding him up?" Frazier asked Durham after the sixth.

The Celebrity Scribes, the prizewinners who would have some time to digest these goings-on (or at least consolidate deadline accounts), decided that Ali could be in trouble for the first time in his life. "All through the first six rounds," William Saroyan wrote in *True*, perhaps a paltry contribution compared to *The Time of Your Life*, his Pulitzer play, "Ali informed the audience and the cameras that Frazier's blows were not hurting him." Saroyan was not convinced.

Nor was Budd Schulberg, the man who wrote *Waterfront* and *The Harder They Fall*, rather more boxing-centric. Schulberg, on assignment for *Playboy*, wrote, "Joe was as easy to hit as the side of a barn and Ali was tossing his stones at the barn but they bounced off like pebbles and grew into boulders flung back at Ali, which was not at all what Ali had in mind."

It was quite a bit more difficult to tell what Norman Mailer was thinking; his account in *Life* was filled with backstory, ruminations on ego—indeed, the title of the piece—and the ambiguities of twentieth-century man and did not truly address the action until the final fifth of a very long story. "It was obvious," Mailer finally observed, "that Ali was into the longest night of his career."

Among the working press, the *Observer*'s Hugh McIlvanney was more honest in his belief that Ali held the early, if only temporary, edge, "exploiting the anticipated clumsiness of Frazier's early moves with accurate jabs and right crosses. As Frazier pressed in close, Ali smothered his attacks, tangling up the arms and employing the advantage in height to lean on the smaller man's neck and shoulders. If the thunderous hooks got home to the body, Ali exposed his mouthpiece and shook his head in dismissal of their efforts, implying that the hitter was punching himself out. In fact, Ali was being hurt. He simply takes hurt rather well."

The hurt kept coming in the middle rounds, the crouching Frazier boring in, forcing Ali into the corner, against the ropes, so low that he was pounding away at the taller man's hips, occasionally uncoiling to fire a lurching hook. Frazier was doing this at some expense. When allowed the classic boxer's stance, usually in the middle of the ring, Ali used his greater reach to rifle jab after jab. But still, the two judges seemed to appreciate the effort, both scoring it 6–2 in rounds to Frazier's favor (the referee had it even, and many on press row had Ali ahead, attesting to the usual difficulty in assessment).

In the ninth round, Ali weathered a few more of those hooks and then suddenly, but briefly, mounted an attack highly reminiscent of his youth. His core followers were hugely encouraged. As Mailer wrote, "He snake-licked his face with jabs faster than he'd thrown before, he anticipated each attempt of Frazier at counterattack and threw it back, he danced on his toes for the first time in rounds, he popped in rights, he hurt him with hooks, it was his biggest round of the night, it was the best round of the fight."

Frazier may not have seemed to care—although Mailer thought he detected an "odd petulant concentration" in his ring rituals—but there was no mistaking his nonchalance for personal safety; Ali was raising welts on Frazier's face. Was it possible? Had Ali, as Mailer suggested, "weathered the purgatory of Joe Frazier"?

Ali may have been alarmed at the pace of the fight—this was lightweight action, from 200-pound men. This was no purgatory, but outright hell. Ali did not appreciate the level of exertion required, retiring to the ropes, trying to lean back over press row. And that was scant relief. Frazier just kept pounding at him anyway. Ali tried to reassure the crowd, or just himself, that his reserves were mainly untapped. His powers of persuasion were unequaled, but the laughing and mugging, the insults, were not terribly convincing, not to the fans and certainly not to Frazier. In the tenth round, Ali paused to help the ringside press with their copy: "He's out," he said.

He was not. In the eleventh, Frazier unleashed a series of left hooks to Ali's head—he was done with the hips now. Ali motioned

Frazier in, as if he welcomed the attention, as if it was exactly what he needed. Perhaps some boxers are affected by mockery, but Frazier was not one of them. Late in the round, suddenly unsprung from his compact ball of a stance, Frazier hit Ali a leaping hook to the head. Ali started to sink straight to the canvas—the power abruptly down—but immediately rescued himself, with hilarious bravura. He straightened and then, retreating to his corner in a comical sleepwalk, his jaw dropped in exaggerated effect and his arms hanging loosely, underplayed the whole disastrous exchange. Watching this, a neurologist might have concluded that capacity for play must be part of the lower brain structure, the same primitive part that rules on decisions of consciousness, so closely did one follow the other. Watching this, almost anybody else would have concluded Ali was in big trouble. Only the bell saved him.

So it was a kind of exhilaration to see Ali storm from his corner in the twelfth, rocking Frazier, the kind of comeback round that gave everybody watching pause. Could he truly restore the balance of power here? If Ali continued to demonstrate resilience, he might negate that catastrophic round, make his case for his more traditional mode of assault, for his clearly superior and vastly more pleasing style of offense. He might yet win on points, if not outright knockout. He was finding Frazier plenty, and would find him again. And, anyway, look at Frazier, blood drooling from his lips, swollen horribly, pulled back to reveal his mouthpiece, his face a terrible topography of lumps, his eyes narrowing. Frazier could project all the calm and determination he wanted, but the attitude of aggression, even as it flared to consequence in the eleventh round, was at odds with his increasingly reconfigured face. It was possible, maybe even probable, that Ali—shooting "straight left hands and spastic rights, probing the abysmal with spurts of kinesthesia," as Schulberg wrote from Ali's corner—could reclaim his title, reclaim his glory, reclaim his righteousness beyond any argument of government, history, or social condemnation.

It was highly likely even that Ali, displaying substance over style in these final rounds, might finally be appreciated as a man of importance, seriousness, of courage. This is what he'd been trying to impress all along, these past four years away from the ring. Now would they get it? Ali pressed on, into the fourteenth, his legs long gone, behind on all the cards, but Frazier worsening by the second. Frazier's right eye was all but closed now, his gallantry reduced by nothing more than wear and tear. After the fourteenth round, Burt Lancaster was speculating that his jaw was broken, so grotesque was the swelling. Even in the fifteenth round, Ali on his toes to start, the tide continued to turn. The cause had been just; it had been destiny. All Ali had to—oh, geez!

Frazier leaped off his feet, springing out of that crouch, and delivered the hardest hook of the night, perhaps his life—"sickeningly violent," McIlvanney thought—catching Ali flush on his jaw. And down Ali went, "dumped," Mailer wrote, "into 50,000 newspaper photographs . . . singing to the siren in the mistiest fogs of Queer Street." Ali remained on the canvas but for an instant, jackknifing right up, but the vision remained, Ali flat on his back, his right leg pointed to the lights, the red tassels dancing in their glow.

For the next two and a half minutes, Frazier, though wary and exhausted, employed Ali in the same way he did chilled steer back in the Philadelphia slaughterhouse, banging without possible retaliation. It was awful to watch. Yet there was a kind of magnificence in Ali's suffering, just taking it, as if it were his due for failure to fulfill his agenda. The fight, if it had ever been close (it was not, surprising many ringsiders and fight reporters—the *Daily News* had scored it a draw, Larry Merchant scored it for Ali—but Frazier well ahead on all the cards), was over with that knockdown, even if Mercante thought Frazier was "drowning" right along with Ali. Ali simply and dutifully needed to be present for its remainder. It was as if he felt he deserved this. He had to be there to represent a nation's disappointment.

Nobody could have designed a better entertainment, though. The activity of the bout had been phenomenal. Heavyweights generally marshaled their resources, mindful of their superior armament.

But Ali and Frazier had fully engaged, across all fifteen rounds. They had deployed every piece of weaponry, from small arms to nuclear megatonnage. And they had done it nonstop, only occasionally clinching, only occasionally mugging for the crowd. There had been no lulls, no intermissions. Just two of the largest, most skilled men in sport raining fearsome, perhaps deadly, punches upon each other.

"It was," wrote William Saroyan in *True,* "a great fight. It was a classic fight. It was an eccentric fight. It was as much a work of art in its accidental but inevitable style and structure as any liturgical ritual or any complicated choreography of ballet."

Again, perhaps. Of course, mostly thanks to Ali, it had been more than an athletic event anyway. He'd made it personal, political even. He'd turned Madison Square Garden, and venues across the country, into a kind of ballot box. Choices were made, votes cast. The bout had become a thing of significance, a way of picking sides. Whereas President Nixon could exult in the defeat of "that draft dodger asshole," others were bitterly disappointed. A black student leader at Cornell wrote in a piece published in the *New York Times,* "When Ali tasted defeat for the first time, I was crushed. Despite the fact that he proved to be more of a man in defeat than many of us are in victory, people everywhere who loved Ali also felt his defeat as a personal loss."

Its conclusion could never resolve differences, but, for the forty-five minutes of struggle that informed it, the fight had resonated powerfully in a nation that lacked conclusions of its own. At least there was a result.

Above all, it was a commercial bonanza. The fighters' immense paydays, however worrisome they had been at the promotion's start, turned out to be pocket change. The promoters certainly earned as much as the fighters, out of a worldwide gross of perhaps $30 million. The apparent folly of mistaking a highly local title for something of global consequence had paid out big. Perenchio and Cooke had demonstrated the far-reaching draw, not to mention income potential, of a sort of fight that had never before mattered very far beyond the ring ropes. A heavyweight title fight, it turned out, traveled rather well.

The fight fans, if that's what they really were, filled the streets around the Garden, many of them on their way to afterparties, where they had intended to celebrate Ali's victory. Yet they were conflicted. "I can't hardly party tonight," one of the peacocks told *Ebony,* sitting in the lobby of the Statler Hilton. The sounds of Duke Ellington's band drifted down from an upstairs ballroom. "I feel like I did that night Dr. Martin Luther King was shot." *Ebony* indicated in its pages that the feeling might have been temporary. Just then, the magazine reported, "a foxy young sister" in a white dress and mink coat coaxed the young peacock out of his funk. "I didn't wear this dress for nothing."

Celebrating with far less ambivalence were the promoters, gathered in Perenchio's suite at the St. Regis. It was a small gathering, and if they weren't actually counting their money, they were discussing it. Their party went on until two in the morning. It had been a good night for all. Mailer had some interesting ideas he wanted to explore in *Life* and would soon begin messaging them to the magazine, pages at a time. Sinatra's film was being processed, and one of the shots—"He held his camera at that angle on purpose," the editor assured in his notes—would make the cover. Less celebrated journalists, happy with the dramatic payoff, tinkered with their accounts, all of which would lead their sections.

But underneath the Garden, in the fighters' dressing rooms, it was a far different scene. It was a kind of carnage, the two boxers sprawled in their separate cubicles like so much battlefield debris. Frazier, in the winner's delirium, had spent some postfight minutes insisting that Ali crawl to him, as his tormentor had once promised he would. Frazier had circled the ring wildly, tears streaming down his face. "I want him over here. I want him to crawl to my feet. Crawl, crawl!" (Durham told him, "Leave that man along. That man hurt bad.") But now, in his dressing room, Frazier was gradually subsiding into his own pain.

A doctor felt among the cascades of his face for fractures, examined his eyes for signs of concussion. "Did he fall?" Frazier asked. Durham assured him he did, in the final round. "Yeah, yeah," said Frazier, remembering. "That's right." After a while Frazier went to a sink full of ice and water and submerged his face. He had the impression his body was shutting down.

Ali had been hustled from the ring by Bundini Brown, his loyal manservant, and was plopped on a rubbing table in his dressing room. Ali's parents visited, his father bitter over the decision. "Robbed!" he cried. "That is the question, truly." Diana Ross had come in. So had Gordon Parks, the Pulitzer Prize—winning photographer. His "guns" were loaded, but he took one look at Ali's puffed face and didn't feel he could draw either of the two Nikons in his coat pocket.

Ali was lifeless, for the first time in his life, a carcass, unable even to dress himself. He meekly complied when his handlers told him X-rays were advisable. Bundini put socks on his man's feet, then trousers, having to redo the process when he realized they were on backward. He zipped them up. "Must have been a helluva fight," Ali finally said, "'cause I sure am tired."

Ali's stay at the hospital was brief, just long enough for the X-rays. Dr. Ferdie Pacheco, of his corner, told him he should remain overnight, even though the jaw wasn't broken. But Ali did not want it recorded that Frazier sent him to the hospital. He was gone in an hour, back at the New Yorker by 1:30.

The next day Ali was sufficiently restored to hold court in his hotel room, having avoided the immediate postfight press conference on Monday night. He was remarkably sanguine, gracious even. He almost apologized for his prefight banter. "What I said before, that was to do with the fight. Just the fight." Ali said Frazier was a "nice man with a family, just another brother working to make a living." Additionally, "He's a good, tough fighter. Not a great boxer but great at his own thing." Finally: "I always thought of him as a nice fella."

Of course, he had excuses. "When you get as big as I got in this game," he said, "you get intoxicated with so-called greatness. You think you just have to run three miles a day. That's all I did for this fight. And I didn't rest properly, didn't train hard as I used to. You convince yourself you'll get by on natural talent, that it will all just explode in there on the night. But it don't."

When somebody interrupted to ask a question—"Champ?"—Ali immediately reminded, "Don't call me champ. Joe's the champ now." Anyway, he wondered, what was the big deal? It had just been a fight, that's all. "You don't shoot yourself. Soon this will be old news. People got lives to lead, bills to pay, mouths to feed. Maybe a plane will go down with 90 persons in it. Or a great man will be assassinated. That will be more important than Ali losing."

If he could just minimize the event, he could reduce the disappointment. On the other hand, the man who might capitalize on the result—maximizing its importance, thereby certifying his own greatness—was nowhere to be found. Frazier, his body and spirit emptied in the Garden that night, had been hustled off to a hospital in Philadelphia, where his bruised and depleted husk lingered off and on for three weeks. He was not there because of injury but because of extremely high blood pressure and a kidney infection, "athlete's kidney," according to his doctor, or perhaps the inescapable consequences of a forced march through hell. Frazier was in a state of physical and mental limbo, half-comatose at times. Doctors eventually stabilized him and sent him on his way. But the undisputed champion of the world—the winner!—had been mysteriously absent for his worldwide coronation, unexplainably unable to exploit his position.

Ali, however, was very much available. Six days after the fight, ABC's *Wide World of Sports* hoped to convene the two men for a taped interview that would run with the fight's replay. Only Ali showed, with Frazier's camp explaining to host Howard Cosell that he'd been "struck down with the flu," and, also, "Joe doesn't want his five children to see him until his face gets better." And so Ali began rewriting the story of that night. Frazier fumed as credit for his victory, which he had paid for in flesh, leached away. Ali, unopposed in the debate, meanwhile began nurturing the idea that he had indeed been robbed. "Look at my face," he said. "Forget the bruise. Then go look at him, and you'll see who really won." This was an inevitable turn of events; given a PR vacuum, Ali would fill it. The night may have belonged to Frazier, but by morning the glory would be returned to escrow. In any case, the narrative would always belong to Ali.

1972

—CHAPTER 7—

TECHNIQUES OF BALLYHOO, THE PITTSBURGH SYMPHONY, AND TALL TIMBER

George Foreman believed in the singularity of heavyweight power. By a law of the universe, it could inhabit no more than one person at a time. And, for that matter, it didn't necessarily have to inhabit any. Ali had been champion, had even been the Greatest for a while, but never possessed that supernatural force. He was many things, but never a knockout artist. Even Frazier, who'd nearly knocked Ali out, and who'd certainly KO'd twenty-three others in his twenty-seven fights, was without it. Nobody wanted to be on the business end of Frazier's left hook, but there was nothing especially surprising about its effect, either.

There was some mystical quality that turned an ordinary punch, however finely tuned by mechanics and muscle, into something beyond physical explanation. There were some punches—Rocky Marciano delivered them, Floyd Patterson did not—that were simply astonishing, even as they were concussive. The scale of impact could not be fairly predicted by comparative anatomy; the shock of such blunt force couldn't be explained by any study of physics. There was an element to this particular sort of heavyweight power that was, perhaps, even spiritual.

Foreman believed the last man so gifted had been Sonny Liston. He was a flawed, tragic character, but he had this one extraordinary talent, this rare ability—this "zip-punch-power-bang"—to neutralize the rest of mankind, at least inside a ring, though of course sometimes outside, too. It accounted for his rise from the St. Louis streets to heavyweight champion, an otherwise ridiculous transformation. There was no other reason for Liston's success, even in this one area, when so many impulses of self-destruction stood against it.

And then, at Liston's death, it had passed to Foreman, his eager disciple.

Foreman was not entirely comfortable with this new magic. It was fun to toy with at first. Like a young knight, who might pull Excalibur from the stone and then first use it to slice lunch meat for his friends, Foreman needed to more fully understand and explore the extent of his new powers, bit by bit. His trainers had told him there were spots on a man's head that were not vulnerable to concussion. Foreman trained his fists on those spots—top of the head, just to see—and knocked those men out. It was exciting to experience, a little bewildering, too. Nobody could stand up to him. But it began to feel slightly dangerous as well. These people, they were big people like him, strong, too. And they just crumpled. This was no parlor trick.

Whatever it was, it was beginning to draw attention. When Foreman had attended the Ali-Frazier fight, neither he nor his heavyweight power had yet been fully recognized. He was no secret. The novelty of the flag-waving gold medalist had endured, and, even with Ali and Frazier still head of the class, he was certainly a prospect. He was, after all, 26–0 with twenty-four KOs by the time of their bout. But he hadn't become very interesting. The night before Ali-Frazier, some promoters took him to a Harlem hot spot, where Foreman noticed a couple of his heroes. Walt Frazier, just months after helping the New York Knicks to an NBA championship, appraised him vaguely. "I've seen you do your thing," he said. "You've seen me do mine." Foreman was dismissed. He fared even worse when he approached Jim Brown, who, after all, was the reason he got out of Houston's Fifth Ward in the first place, the reason he wore those *100 Rifles* sideburns, the reason, if you wanted to know the truth, he walked the way he did. Brown gave him a limp handshake, didn't even bother to meet his eyes.

Yeah, but now in 1972, Frazier was becoming a heavyweight presence. He was becoming interesting. Since Ali-Frazier he'd fought eleven times, all knockouts, all but two of them within two rounds. None of the opponents had been of championship caliber; in fact, only four of them had winning records (one was 1–14, another just 1–2). But the blunt-force trauma of his fights was beginning to draw fans. *Ring* felt his career so far revealed "the techniques of ballyhoo" and that his knockouts "hardly merited entry into his record." The magazine guessed that manager Dick Sadler was "sitting on a golden egg . . . waiting for a hatching which will mean millions to Foreman, and merited financial rewards to himself." Yet it couldn't fault managerial caution or discount his prospects and nevertheless marveled at his results.

Few had arrived at this game as fully formed as Foreman had. He was a superbly muscled 215 pounds at twenty-three, whereas Ali had to grow into the division. Frazier weighed 205 pounds, but observers claimed they were unevenly distributed, his legs disproportionately thick. Foreman was a virtual Adonis, broad in the shoulders, thin at the waist, with huge arms. His power was only partly mystical. So of course, until proven otherwise, he was a prospect.

And why wouldn't he be, considering the disappointing aftermath of the Fight of the Century? Frazier failed to capitalize in any significant way, becoming, in *Ring*'s opinion, a "hermit." He returned to the canvas just once in 1971, as the front man for his eight-piece band, the Knockouts, performing eight numbers on the undercard of a fight at Madison Square Garden's Felt Forum. In fact, he seemed far more interested in a singing career, scheduling his band for shows— $4,500 per appearance—in Tahoe, San Francisco, nine European countries, and even back in Philadelphia, where, according to the *New York Times,* he would "appear on the card with the Pittsburgh Symphony." These were the only Knockouts he'd lined up.

These were traditional championship prerogatives. Having finally consolidated boxing's competing claims for glory under a single title, Frazier was able, perhaps even obliged, to indulge fantasies of recreation, retirement, and whatever the opposite of restraint is. So he immediately announced he might take a year off from the gym, would devote himself to more wholesome modes of entertainment, and would buy stuff—two Cadillacs, three Chevrolets (one of them a '34), "plenty of fancy clothes," and a swimming pool shaped like a boxing glove, built behind his $400,000 house.

One other thing he definitely wanted to buy was a piece of land for his mother, Dolly. Widowed six years, when Frazier's father had died of cancer, she had stubbornly maintained her old lifestyle; in the weeks after Frazier had earned .25 million dollars, Dolly was still climbing aboard trucks that took workers into the tomato fields, where they earned a quarter-dollar per bucket. She did enjoy some increased status, as mother of the heavyweight champion of the world, and was now allowed to sit in the front seat of the truck next to the driver. The new champion thought she could do better.

After a lot of negotiating, Frazier settled on a 368-acre plantation nineteen miles from where he grew up in Laurel Bay. The $157,000 transaction was seen partly as a tax shelter, but there was no question that Frazier enjoyed the idea of owning land where slaves once farmed rice. Dolly was not so enthusiastic about the move to Brewton. She packed along her dogs, a goat, pigs, and her flock of chickens in case her son's big plans—her son wanted cattle for "a little more class"—failed to work out.

Ali was in no position to threaten retirement, enjoy much recreation, or spend any money. Though the fighters' purses seemed astronomical, taxes in 1971 reduced them considerably. The state tax from the Fight of the Century alone was nearly $350,000 per fighter, on top of the $800,000 in federal taxes. Additionally, Ali had debts and liens to satisfy before he could see a single dollar from that record payday. He was not, in any case, fixed for life. Nor, as it turned out, for the rest of 1971. "We've got to get him right back in the saddle," Ali's manager, Herbert Muhammad, told Bob Arum, then Ali's lawyer.

One possible moneymaking opportunity was a fight with basketball great Wilt Chamberlain, an idea that had been floating around since 1967, mostly as a joke, but which now seemed a reasonable option. Ali was no longer marginalized by the government's prosecution, but he was no longer free from it, either, his court case still up in the air. So he was all for anything that might be quick, easy, and profitable. Chamberlain, who was thirty-five and finishing up his NBA career with the Los Angeles Lakers, was like-minded. He took it seriously enough that he began working with Cus D'Amato, Floyd Patterson's trainer.

A bout between Ali and Chamberlain, quite a physical specimen at seven-foot-two and 285 pounds, might have been an irresistible attraction, if not quite the Fight of the Century. And it was nearly made, for the summer of 1971 in Houston's Astrodome. But Chamberlain was not happy with the proposed purse, $500,000 tax free. Or else Lakers owner Jack Kent Cooke, rattled by his superstar's dalliance, rushed to renegotiate his basketball contract. Or perhaps, at the time of signing at the Astrodome, Ali should not have greeted Chamberlain, shouting, "Timber!" In April no less authority than Walter Cronkite reported on the *CBS Evening News* that the fight was off.

If not a great payday, Ali did get some good news later that summer. On June 28 the Supreme Court unanimously reversed his conviction for refusing military induction, thereby freeing him from a four-year legal overhang. The justices' ruling was based more on a technicality, and some furious compromising, than it was on the correctness of Ali's political stance. As such, it was hardly a vindication of his sacrifice, or a validation of his revolt. And it did not particularly suggest that America had done a U-turn on the subject of Ali. He remained as divisive as ever.

But he was legal. Ali recognized the difference, if the Court couldn't quite. "It's like a man's been in chains all his life and suddenly the chains are taken off," he told some reporters outside a

Chicago motel, hours after the decision was announced. "He don't realize he's free until he gets the circulation back in his arms and legs and starts to use his fingers." Asked if he intended to resort to any legal means to recover those lost years, Ali demurred. He had no bitterness. "They only did what they thought was right at the time. I did what I thought was right. That was all. I can't condemn them for doing what they think was right."

The decision would not alter public sentiment on its own. The country was like an ocean liner, slow to respond to even a violent wrench of the wheel. It did, however, remove all possible sanctions against his professional career; he was free to fight, free to make money. Just not, thanks to Joe Frazier, championship money.

Ali embarked on a hectic, if not athletically ambitious, tour, beginning with an old sparring partner, Jimmy Ellis, in July. He fought two more times in 1971 and six more times in 1972, ranging far and wide, from Houston to Dublin, from New York to Zurich. None of the fights was particularly inspiring and, some felt, were actually damaging to his prospects for a Frazier rematch. "Clay Stock Drops After Performances in Japan and Canada," *Ring* wrote, after Ali (still Cassius Clay to *Ring*) won lackluster decisions against Mac Foster and George Chuvalo. "Clay could very well be finished as a serious contender for the championship," it wrote.

At least he was fighting. Frazier didn't climb back into the ring until 1972, when he fought Terry Daniels in New Orleans. The event was somewhat less electric than his fight ten months earlier. But it was better attended than his European tour with the Knockouts, an act that drew almost no interest. Fewer than one hundred people showed up for one of his dates, forcing him and his Knockouts to sail back home. He didn't fight again in 1972 until five months later, when he engaged Ron Stander in Omaha. Frazier insisted he would eventually give Ali a rematch, if somebody would meet his $3.5 million price, but in the meantime he was husbanding his resources.

Part of the problem, a secret that only Frazier and his ophthalmologist shared, was that he needed to be as careful with location as opposition. His left eye was developing a cataract, possibly since the

1964 Olympics, and he needed state athletic commissions that were not necessarily compliant but in the low range of diligence. He was careful not to fight ever again in California, an important obstacle since Jack Kent Cooke had the rematch rights and intended the fight for his Los Angeles Forum. Frazier instead preferred places just like Omaha, where he could get away with the rather juvenile trick of changing hands—not eyes—when the doctor made him read the eye chart.

So for a number of reasons, Fight of the Century II remained on the back burner, as, for that matter, did Ali and Frazier. *Ring* was particularly appalled by Frazier's failure to promote the heavyweight championship. While conceding that Ali was at least active, and at least loud, it complained, "It is Frazier who hangs in the background, apparently content to play second fiddle and create a situation without precedent in the history of heavyweight competition."

But Foreman fought on, the opponents just disintegrating before him. He was becoming impossible to ignore. *Ring* hated to do it, given the lack of pedigree, but by the end of 1972 it put him at no. 2, behind Frazier and ahead of Ali. The magazine didn't think Foreman belonged in the ring with either of them, but neither it nor competing promoters could pretend he wasn't a viable prospect.

Really, Foreman himself wasn't so sure he belonged in the ring with either man, and certainly not Frazier. Ali, Foreman thought, might be a "cool boxing experience." Frazier, not very cool at all. Foreman thought, "I wanna be champ, but I don't wanna fight him." Even confident of that transfer of power, Foreman maintained reservations about a match with Frazier. Frazier could punch, of course. But what worried Foreman was his defense, all that weaving, the way he'd make you miss with the jab, him closing so suddenly, so violently, with that left hook. Man, you didn't want to miss with the jab. A fighter that misses with the jab is absolutely defenseless, a foolish abstraction of a boxer, naked. No amount of power, however otherworldly, protected a fighter in that case.

Plus, and this was peculiar to Foreman's concerns, Frazier was so squat. Foreman believed he was somehow vulnerable to shorter opponents. He'd amazed the press in Mexico City when he'd complained his opponent was too small, was scooting under him. Foreman didn't want anybody scooting under him, especially if he had a left hook that had been developed in a kosher slaughterhouse.

Make no mistake, he wanted to be champion. But he wasn't sure it could happen at Frazier's expense, or even should. Maybe Frazier would take that money—who'd even seen a sum like that?—and just depart the scene. That's certainly what he'd have done. But here's his manager, Dick Sadler, showing up every fight, selling his "woof tickets," calling Frazier out, saying he was afraid of Big George, issuing ultimatums. Frazier, Sadler declared to anyone who'd listen, simply had to fight Foreman. Foreman thought, "Who told him that?"

Foreman eventually did the sensible thing. He fired Sadler. It was actually over money, Sadler cutting strange deals, getting tangled up with Barbra Streisand's management team. Streisand? Foreman couldn't understand how this could promote his career. Plus, there was the Frazier thing, Sadler yapping it up every chance he had. On the advice of an attorney, Foreman turned to Archie Moore, one of the stranger characters in a very strange game, to get him ready for Frazier. Maybe.

Moore was many things, in addition to being a former champion. He was from an era when it was not entirely preposterous to wait until you were thirty-nine—as was Moore's case—to get a title shot. Moore capitalized, winning the light-heavy championship in 1952, defending several times before eating himself into the heavyweight division and a fight with the champion, Rocky Marciano. It was Marciano's last fight, and although Moore knocked him down in the second round, the Rock returned the favor five times. Moore eventually was in so much trouble that the ref visited him in the corner to stop the fight. "Let me try once more with a desperado," Moore pleaded, only prolonging the pain. In any case, Marciano managed to retire undefeated.

Moore, even though he was by then known as the Old Mongoose, did not feel similar stirrings of decrepitude, or even injury, and fought eight more years, until he retired at the age of forty-six. Alas, his penultimate fight, another payday to help finance his training facility in San Diego, an outpost he'd named the Salt Mine, was with an up-and-comer named Cassius Clay. This was an annoying, if profitable, proposition for the Old Mongoose, especially as he'd originally been hired as Clay's trainer when the young man was coming out of the Olympics. Ali—Cassius Clay then—was an enthusiastic rookie, taking an immediate liking to Moore and his odd camp (the gym, a barn actually, had a sign above the door advertising a Bucket of Blood). But he balked at the idea of chores. If he could not be instructed to hold his hands up, it was not likely he could be coaxed into doing dishes and mopping floors. The young man took the train back to Louisville for the Christmas holidays and never returned.

In 1962, when the two met again, it was for young Clay's 16th professional fight. And Moore's 216th. The outcome was more or less predestined, Clay even calling the round (Moore in four). The Old Mongoose surely knew what was up but found the poetry somewhat insulting, all the same. "I don't enjoy being struck by children," he said, chafing at the rhymes, but accepting all else, including the youngster's incipient, if still incomplete, greatness. "I view this young man with mixed emotions," he said at the time. "Sometimes he sounds humorous but sometimes he sounds like a man that can write beautifully but doesn't know how to punctuate."

Foreman was going to be a much more diligent and respectful pupil. And Moore, with his eccentric gab, would be a perfect fit. Discounting his experience as Burt Lancaster's silent partner during the Ali-Frazier broadcast—Moore was held to a few expert agreements ("That's right, Burt")—he was actually one of boxing's best talkers, colorfully obtuse. He could expound for hours on such practices as "escapology," "breathology," and "relaxism." He could hold forth on anything, really, in similarly confusing rhetoric. Once, explaining the arrest of one of his brothers, Moore said, "Louis was light-fingered by nature. Somehow a man's watch got tangled up in his hand and the man sent the police to ask Louis what time it was." That account, presumably, was not taken from the arrest report.

Moore was far more direct in his dealings with Foreman. Still capable of tremendous flights of fancy, he kept it simple, down to earth, for the big man. He'd traveled north to Hayward, where Sadler had been training Foreman, just outside Oakland, and began drilling him in basics. More than that, he began instilling in Foreman a new and even more violent urgency. After every workout, Moore wrapped Foreman in sheets and, the fighter mummified and immobilized, filled him with "this evil talk," how he should paralyze his opponent with a steely glare, how he should pummel him with the jab, how he should hit him on top of the head, "disturb his thoughts."

If Moore was a master motivator, Foreman was an ideal student. Accomplished adults had influenced him at every juncture of his life, and here was one more working his magic on this impressionable hulk. Foreman did everything Moore told him.

The results were quantifiable, at least in the gym setting. Sparring partners were growing desperate to get away from Foreman's jab and his thudding right hands. One of those sparring partners, Scrap Iron Johnson, a heavyweight who was known principally for his ability to withstand punishment, was particularly noticing the changes in Foreman. Johnson stood up to everybody. Johnson had stood up to Joe Frazier in their fight five years earlier, not quite giving the young contender a fright, but certainly pause. The crowd for that fight, if not Frazier himself, was somewhat mystified when Johnson began celebrating in the ring after the decision was announced. It was later learned, after Johnson began showing up at the gym in a new Cadillac, that he'd bet $2,000 of his $8,000 purse to go the distance.

Johnson had given Liston all he could handle, too, although only for seven rounds. For that matter, in their 1970 fight, Johnson had stood up to Foreman, not going out until the seventh round, and then only on cuts. Foreman was fully aware that Johnson was still coming at the stoppage. For a guy like Foreman, who required a sort of punching bag on legs for his daily deliberations, Johnson was ideal.

But he was barely surviving Foreman in the gym now. Moore told him to use the jab on Johnson, then instructed him further to put some combinations in after the jab. "Uppercut," Moore whispered from the corner. Foreman already had it. "Turn it, turn it," Moore whispered. Johnson sagged. The next day, more of the same. Johnson sagged. The third day, Johnson told Foreman he'd just received some bad news and he'd have to leave camp. His daughter was sick. Foreman, recognizing Johnson's usefulness, offered to pay whatever extra he needed, just so Johnson could continue sparring. He would send her to the Mayo Clinic if that would help. Johnson demurred. "She's daddy's baby girl," he explained. And he was gone.

Foreman realized that things had changed, that it was dangerous to be in the same ring with him. He stopped smiling, stopped talking, and walked around as if in a trance. There was something different about him, something new. The transfer of power was now complete.

CHAPTER 8

NIETZSCHE, A BLACK HOSPITAL, AND A PIRANHA POND

Don King spent enough time in the Marion Reformatory that he was unable to attend the Ali-Frazier fight—he listened to it on the prison radio—but not so much time he'd miss any possible rematches. Just four years, mysteriously brief considering the original second-degree murder conviction, ordinarily a life sentence. There had been no question he'd killed a man. He'd bounced poor Sam Garret's head on the sidewalk so hard and so often, his .357 Magnum held high in the air, that even the crowd outside the Tap Room was calling for him to stop. "Donald, don't kick him no more, he's hurt," somebody yelled. By the time the police got there, the beating still in progress, Garret was in bad shape. "Don, I'll pay you the money" were his last words. He slipped into a coma and died five days later.

What Garret owed was $600, a paltry sum considering King's finances at the time. As one of the biggest numbers bankers in Cleveland, "Donald the Kid" routinely grossed $15,000 a day from the belowground lottery. Some of it was earned on inside information, King receiving the possible combinations in advance and placing bets himself at more favorable odds. Usually, he exploited rival runners, but this time he'd placed the bet with Garret, one of his own. And Garret had not paid off on number 743 in a timely fashion. Still, it was small potatoes for King, who patrolled the streets in a new 1967 Cadillac, who owned the New Corner Tavern (where musicians such as B. B. King and his pal Lloyd Price often performed), and who lived comfortably in Shaker Heights, far from the East Cleveland ghettos where he operated his business. King just lost his temper and let a small-time beef escalate into a vicious beatdown. And now he had to pay for it.

The question was how much. He'd wriggled out of jams before, even got out of a previous deadly shooting, way back in 1954, on the grounds of justifiable homicide. The dead man was one of three who had invaded one of King's gambling houses. That was certainly justifiable. This might not go away quite as easily as that one—there were a lot of witnesses, including the police—but King was confident he'd never spend a day in jail. He bet $5,000 on just such a proposition.

King always enjoyed the advantage of inside information. And it was true, witnesses began changing their stories, or losing all recollection of the event. One of the best eyewitnesses for the prosecution simply disappeared. And at least one of the arresting detectives was told he could "make a lot of money" if he would just "do right." Altogether, it was learned by the city editor at the *Cleveland Plain Dealer,* King had spent "$30,000 already to knock out the testimony of witnesses against him."

That's a lot of inside information, but it still wasn't enough to override testimony from the two detectives who, after all, had arrived in time to see King in action, brandishing a weapon. The jury quickly found King guilty of second-degree murder, not acting in self-defense, as he claimed, a verdict punishable by life in prison. Yet in a meeting that was attended only by King's attorney, deliberating judge Hugh Corrigan entered an item on the docket, reducing the charge to manslaughter. The detectives were outraged, not only at the reduction but by the clandestine nature of it. "Judge Cuts Hood's Murder Penalty," sang the *Plain Dealer* headline when its reporter finally learned of it later in the summer. King was going to prison—he'd lost that bet—but not for life, and not quite for four years.

King did not come out of Marion particularly rehabilitated—he plunged back into the numbers business and was rarely without a briefcase containing $50,000 or more—but he was at least better read. His street smarts were now given the foundation of language from Shakespeare, Adam Smith, and Nietzsche. The tomes he checked out from the prison library, as thoroughly absorbed as they might have been, did not come with pronunciation guides, and he thereafter suffered the slights of self-educated men everywhere, mocked for mangling the names of his philosophical betters. Still, he left prison with a larger view of the world and with bigger ambitions, and a vastly improved rhetoric.

The first to be ensnared in these ambitions was an itinerant boxing promoter named Don Elbaum. He was a curious case himself, coming from a family of refined tastes (his mother was an accomplished pianist, and he'd been a bit of a prodigy) in upstate New York. But he'd been bent by a fascination with boxing (he had a short but undistinguished pro career, although he did acquire the credential of a squashed nose) and was promoting shows by the age of sixteen, forever ruined for a normal life.

Elbaum was of the impish sort, capable of insisting upon a policy of absolute honesty on the one hand, cheerfully explaining how he bamboozled the great Sugar Ray Robinson on the other hand. (A legendary story: he coaxed Robinson into a press event, promising him the same gloves he'd used in his pro debut at Madison Square Garden, twenty-five years earlier—"Ray, don't ask me how I got these"—then panicking as the former champ tried to pull on two left-handed gloves for the photographers.) But he was a fight guy through and through, and when King called him to help with a boxing show intended to help a failing black hospital—"You don't want a black hospital to go down, do you?"—Elbaum became a willing accomplice. Elbaum didn't even mind King bargaining him down from a fee of $5,000 all the way to $1,500. He was surprised, though, at how quickly King was able to do it.

This was all after King's release in the summer of 1972. King had already reached out to his old pal Lloyd Price, still a loyal friend from his Cleveland club, who in turn reached out to Ali, a friend of his going back to the '60s. Price and King together convinced him to box ten exhibition rounds—for a failing black hospital, of course. With Elbaum signed on for the nuts and bolts of the promotion, King was now in the boxing business, though, Elbaum discovered, not entirely out of the numbers game. King was always telling Elbaum to watch his briefcase while he was gone, then surprising him later by popping it open to show $100,000 in cash. It was a great joke. Elbaum had been around long enough to know that wasn't boxing money. Boxing money was usually tendered in envelopes, not briefcases.

As it turned out, the show was a remarkable success. Ali, of course, provided the promotional hook, earning King a lot of publicity with his appearance. And he came through on fight night, too, clowning, playing to the crowd, having a great time. Price was the cornerstone for an accompanying concert, gathering performers such as Lou Rawls and Marvin Gaye into the fold. Elbaum provided matchmaking and his customary chutzpah. When Gaye arrived at the airport in Cleveland, it was Elbaum who paid extras to pose as photographers, reassuring Gaye, who'd been promised front-page coverage by King. Still, the concert was a big-enough hit that it was allowed to eat into some of the bouts, shortened for time restraints.

The gate was $81,000, a record for a boxing exhibition. But there was some question as to how much Forest City Hospital ever received. Certainly not the $40,000 the papers said it would the next day. The hospital, in fact, might not have gotten any more than Elbaum did. There were expenses, of course. Ali was given $10,000 to defray his costs. The airport "photographers" had to be paid. And King and Elbaum were maintaining nice suites at the Sheraton. Boxing is an expensive business, if it's done correctly.

But a thoroughly exciting one. King was sold on this new line of work. For his part, Elbaum became sold on King. He was simply

"mesmerized" by the man, his wit, his bombast, his flair for business. He was tremendous fun. The two remained in their Sheraton
suites for some time after the exhibition, hatching plans, forging a
friendship, just enjoying each other's company.

King even invited Elbaum to his farm in the Ohio countryside,
a plot of land he'd purchased while still in prison. It was a curious
transaction and subject of newspaper investigations and one more
source of King's lore. He had managed to buy it from a Cleveland
lawyer for just $1,000, even though that lawyer (whose clients were
among those making a living in the numbers racket) had bought the
land for nearly $20,000 four years earlier. Elbaum was thoroughly
charmed by the rural atmosphere, no matter its provenance, even
though he'd been warned to stay far from King's pond. Word on the
East Cleveland streets was that it contained piranhas.

Elbaum was even charmed by King's wife, Henrietta, who
pleaded with Elbaum to get her husband out of the numbers business
and into boxing. Elbaum was amused, as Henrietta, even though she
was a "dynamite lady," had basically been a partner (arrested, never
convicted) in King's operation. But he agreed with her that boxing
was, by being largely legal, a good occupational alternative.

He thought so much of King's prospects that he became determined to take him to New York and introduce him to all the
important promoters, managers, and working press. Elbaum was
certain that Dick Young and Jimmy Cannon would go crazy for
this fast-talking hustler. It would be King's coming-out party. But
King wasn't so sure. "What are you talking about?" he said. "A black
promoter? There are no black promoters." King did not lack self-
confidence, but he was keenly aware of the black man's disadvan-
tages in twentieth-century America.

And it was true, there weren't any black promoters. The fighters were black, except on those rare occasions the press could build
up a white hope, but the business end was white. Even Ali, with all
the separatist notions of his Black Muslim teachings, reached out to
a white Jewish lawyer when it came time to promote his fights. King
doubted there was any possibility of overcoming this tradition. But

Elbaum, in a liberal glory, became livid at King's objections. "I don't want to hear it," he said. "You're equal to anyone. Look at me! This is America, Don. This is America!"

King was touched by his friend's insistence, swept up in his vision of an integrated country, or at least an integrated boxing business. "In America," he repeated, suddenly seeing a bigger future for himself, or maybe just a catchphrase. "Only in America."

Elbaum had one more favor for King, and it was an important one. Back in 1968 Elbaum had been among those who tried to get a piece of that hot young Olympian, the flag-waver, big George Foreman. He'd formed a group of backers from Detroit, offered him some cash and a new car to turn pro, as well as the tutelage of Detroit trainer Emanuel Steward. Foreman wasn't considering such offers and had chosen Dick Sadler instead. Sadler had the appeal of having no money and, thus, honorable intentions. But Sadler was having trouble maintaining so much honor on zero income. He'd phoned Elbaum, told him he'd sell off 10 percent of Foreman's contract for a quick and much-needed $5,000. Elbaum recognized a bargain when he heard one.

Of course, that would have been a difficult contract to enforce, and Elbaum understood it for what it really was, a promise of favors to come. So, by the end of 1972, four years later, with Frazier finally getting back to defending his title, Elbaum cashed that favor in and, in turn, started King on his own future.

For a variety of reasons, none of them reasonable on their own, Frazier had decided to make his next fight, in early 1973, in Kingston, Jamaica. Frazier had allowed his theatrical agent, Alex Valdez, the same guy who booked the failed European tour of Joe Frazier and the Knockouts, to promote his next fight. The Garden wanted the fight, of course, and even guaranteed Frazier a purse of $800,000, promising to reduce the New York tax bite to just 10 percent. But Valdez, through a China-born Jamaican named Lucien Chen, negotiated an even better deal with the Jamaican government, which offered $850,000 but no taxes. It was to be a grand and exotic fair, ushering in a new age of boxing, January 22.

As for the opponent, this is where Elbaum came in. Recognizing Elbaum's matchmaking talents, the closed-circuit operator—and, in place of the Jamaican government, suddenly the actual hands-on promoter—called him for suggestions for Frazier's foe. Elbaum had one. Hank Schwartz, president of Video Techniques, offered Elbaum a number of closed-circuit territories in Ohio and Pennsylvania if he could deliver on his idea, George Foreman. It would not be difficult to match Frazier with anybody. He was the heavyweight champion, and the challenger was guaranteed $375,000—untaxed—for a chance, however remote it might have seemed, at a title. But this was especially easy, a call to Dick Sadler, a reassurance that "Frazier was made to order for George," reminder of his debt, and an opponent produced.

One more thing, Elbaum said. He wanted to send this guy—"this black and powerful guy"—down to Jamaica for the fight. Schwartz was an electronics man. What Video Techniques mainly did was supply the technology to bounce the broadcast off satellites and into theaters. He didn't know boxing. Elbaum persisted, and he listened. "He's worth bringing into the group," he said. He's exactly what boxing needs right now, Elbaum continued, a black promoter, somebody who could relate to the mostly black fighters, maybe even control them, somebody who could continue to negotiate deals against Madison Square Garden. "He learns fast," Elbaum told him. He was going to be boxing's new "interface."

Schwartz agreed and said King could come down. What could be the harm? He didn't have a job for him, but he'd get him a room and give him the run of the place. Elbaum was pleased to help King, to do his new best friend the favor. "You won't regret it," Elbaum told Schwartz.

1973

CHAPTER 9

A TUNNEL OF LOVE, A RED RUBBER MOUSE, AND A VETERAN RUSSIAN

It felt unusual, maybe even wrong, to be traveling outside the country for a fight. It had been done before. Ali had fought in Great Britain, in Germany, and even in Ireland. But those visits were cynical concessions to a hometown contender, someone whose fans might plump the box office for an otherwise unimportant fight. Going to Jamaica, when neither fighter had an interest there, seemed almost treasonous. Although it was for the heavyweight championship of the world, it was understood that this was purely an American institution, to be enjoyed by Americans on American soil.

If anything, this was an era of global withdrawal, hardly one of exploration or advancement. The Vietnam War was spiraling to an end, with President Nixon, about to be inaugurated for a second term, announcing steady troop withdrawals until just twenty-seven thousand remained toward the fall of 1972. It had been a national disaster, the only consequence of a country's intervention being a thorough and perhaps irreparable polarization, not to mention fifty-eight thousand dead Americans. Nixon had been reelected by a tremendous margin, yet he remained a focus of antiwar protesters who couldn't get out even sooner. Even as he called troops back, even as he renewed peace talks, he continued bombing Hanoi, keeping the already flammable protest movement alive.

It just didn't seem a good time to be mounting expeditions, to be going places. This was a good time to be coming home. Yet, as has often been the case in boxing, the highest bid overcame all obstacles of reason. Boxing was interested in geopolitics only to the extent it specified currency conversion rates. Boxing would go anywhere if the price was right.

This happened most memorably back in 1923, when a growing oil town in northern Montana attempted to make a name for itself—become the "Tulsa of Montana"—by staging a heavyweight title fight. Jack (Doc) Kearns was agreeable to the Chamber of Commerce's proposition, provided he receive three timely payments of $100,000 on behalf of his fighter, the great Jack Dempsey. The citizens of Shelby, of whom there were about ten thousand, were uniformly enthralled by the idea of this event and met all conditions, including the construction of a wooden arena that would hold more than forty thousand people, as well as various devices of credit that would meet Kearns's needs. Kearns was nearly giddy at the attention and thereafter would say, "Whenever I am in Montana, I feel like a prostitute on a Saturday night."

Alas, forty thousand did not arrive, neither by rail nor by horse nor by any conveyance, and it was not Kearns who was serviced, but Shelby. The townspeople were basically the only potential audience, all those rail lines aside, and they stormed the wooden structure, most of them getting in for free. The bout was a financial failure, catastrophic, triggering a local recession and ruining at least three banks. Although not ruining either Kearns or Dempsey, who escaped on a caboose in the dead of night with, Kearns was able to report, $201,000 of Shelby's remaining money.

Jamaica could hardly hope to improve its image by becoming a boxing destination. It did not need to become the "Tulsa of the Caribbean." It was already well known for its natural beauty, its white sand beaches, its Tunnel of Love. When the *Los Angeles Times* sent its man down to scout the location, he was almost apologetic for the invasion of so much barbarism. "It is an island that a man, with the heart of a poet and the ways of an idler, might come to beach comb. Or if he were young, and newly wed, an Eden he might share with his bride." And this is going to happen?

Jamaica was about to be busted, was what was going to happen, at least to the tune of $500,000, maybe even more. Like the Sack of Shelby, the so-called Sunshine Showdown was distinguished by much civic ambition but little regard for reality. National Sports, Ltd., which was promoting the fight on the government's behalf, was boldly promising a profit even as the local newspaper was reporting that only about eight thousand tickets in the forty-three-thousand-seat National Stadium had been sold. At as little as $5 a seat (but up to $110 at ringside), that was not going to do much to defray an outlay of close to $1.5 million for the fighters' purses.

Unlike Shelby, Jamaica could write it off as a promotional expense. It would be good for tourism. Otherwise, it was a totally implausible idea. The two million people on the island——Kingston itself had a population of about six hundred thousand——may have been sports fans, even boxing fans, but with an average monthly wage of around $25, they were not an ideal demographic for a boxing extravaganza. In fact, the whole affair seemed to be working against the hope of increased prestige. It was backfiring, if anything. The visiting press, instead of trumpeting the blue lagoons, was raising alarms about safety, noting that seven hundred militia and another seven hundred police had been assigned to the stadium. The townspeople weren't so confident, either. "Come to fight," one of the local radio ads announced. "You will be safe."

The only participant who seemed insulated from the looming fiasco was the man who put it together, Lucien Chen. Chen was not only a Kingston restaurant owner but the proprietor of 140 betting shops in the city. Chen told the visiting press that he was doing great business. Better, certainly, than National Sports, Ltd.

The fight crowd did not particularly care where it was. It was a movable mob, circulating here and there, reconvening at assigned sites, resuming old narratives. Location was of little consequence.

Just so there was a gym, a hotel lobby, a bar, and some kind of atmospheric window to accommodate a satellite signal. Anyplace would do. All the regulars were showing up in Kingston this time. Here was Red Smith from the *New York Times,* George Plimpton from *Sports Illustrated,* even Howard Cosell from ABC. Once again, Cosell had been overlooked for the closed-circuit broadcast (those duties went to Don Dunphy once more, although this time his color commentator would be singer Pearl Bailey). But he would provide his braying expertise for the *Wide World of Sports* delayed telecast and would inform and annoy his print brethren in the meantime.

"Take a gander at these limbs," Cosell commanded Plimpton, the two of them enjoying a drink on a hotel balcony during the week before the fight. Cosell was not often in Bermuda shorts and seemed delighted at the chance for such exposure. "At the PSAL [Public Schools Athletic League] championship held in 1931 at the 168th Street Armory in Manhattan, these legs carried me to a second-place finish in the standing broad jump." Plimpton made no record of a reply.

Others were making this scene for the first time. Don King, a man without apparent portfolio, busied himself in both camps, striking up friendships, making acquaintances. Among them was Roy Foreman, the fighter's seventeen-year-old brother, who'd tagged along with the rest of the family for this strange road trip. Once King recognized the connection, he latched on to him, started introducing him to his new friends, even Pearl Bailey. Suddenly, he was appearing at George's training.

Roy, who was largely agog at his first international experience, met someone else, and it was even more unnerving. He was trying to negotiate passport control upon arrival when he received a horrifying jolt, recognizing his brother's opponent in line with him. "Joe Frazier, sharp as a razor," the man said, shaking young Foreman's hand, just going up and down the line, greeting everybody. Whatever camp confidence had existed vanished in that instant. Foreman struggled for a proper description, running through a number of geological properties. Finally, he hit upon one. "He's like a boulder with a head!" This was just awful. He'd had no idea what they were up against. "What's one loss," he thought. "Lots of great fighters have one loss."

Frazier's superiority was the prevailing opinion, and young Roy needn't have apologized for any doubt. Frazier had all the experience, all the pedigree, and that left hook. Not to mention the heavyweight title of the world and that win over Ali. He was as much as a 4–1 favorite to retain his title and move on to the real money, a rematch with Ali. Frazier had put that off as long as he could and, even with a hard-punching youngster at hand, found himself dreaming of the day when he could silence Ali for good, and reap a considerable windfall while he was at it. He could barely wait. "I want him real bad," he said. "I might buy another plantation."

Money—Frazier-Ali money—seemed to dominate the prefight chatter. "I want a percentage," explained manager Yank Durham, talking about an Ali fight, even as Frazier was appearing with Foreman at a prefight press conference. "They're talking about $20 million, $30 million, I want a piece of that." Referring to Jack Kent Cooke, who had fronted the first fight and consequently held the paper for the rematch, Durham said his offer of $3 million, especially as it was for a fight in Cooke's Los Angeles Forum, was simply not enough. "I asked Mr. Cooke if any promoter was entitled to as much as the athlete. He said that's a matter of opinion."

Ali was definitely looking forward to the rematch, too, having been remaindered in their 1971 fight, without a title and without alternative prospects. He'd fought nine times since the Frazier decision and was growing desperate for his redemption. "Don't let nothing happen to Joe Frazier," he'd said the week before the Foreman fight. He wanted some of Cooke's Los Angeles money, too. He'd dispatched several from his considerable entourage to the fight to look after his interests.

There were a few among the fight crowd who did give Foreman a chance. One of them was heavyweight great Joe Louis, who'd been lured from the golf course to come to Kingston and help promote the fight, presumably to encourage the notion of a competitive bout. "He's always in front of you," said Louis, describing Frazier, "and he's easy to hit." Angelo Dundee, Ali's trainer, was another. He was on hand, as if to safeguard his investment, but he was growing increasingly worried as the fight drew closer. "I'm rooting for Frazier," he said, "but I've got this feeling Foreman will win. Why? Because he has all the attributes to beat Frazier's style. He's got a jab like I've never seen on a heavyweight since Sonny Liston. He has a strong left hand. I mean strong. He can stop a man in his tracks."

Dundee seemed to be getting depressed at his own analysis. "I don't know why, but I feel this 'dream match' between Ali and Frazier is going to go up in smoke. I feel like it's going to blow up." Dundee said he wouldn't be surprised if "Foreman puts some hurt on him before the fifth."

Another lonely voice, though considerably louder and more aggravating, was Cosell's. By 1973 Cosell had become almost bigger than the sports he broadcast. He'd been a fixture on much of the fight coverage, had come to be identified with the political left that had freed Ali from his exile, and had reached through to even bigger audiences as the self-styled and highly self-absorbed intellectual on *Monday Night Football*. Probably half of America hated him; probably half loved him. But there was little question that he was a knowledgeable and important asset to sports entertainment, possible even an authority when it came to boxing.

Here in Jamaica, Cosell was once more telling it like he thought it was, reminding listeners that he'd "been with George in Mexico City when he took out the Russian, Ionis Chepulis, on a TKO [technical knockout] in the second round." That was all he needed to have seen. He advised, "There are going to be some shocked people in the world."

Finally, there was Lucien Chen who, like many Jamaicans, had jumped on Foreman's roomy bandwagon. "He hits like a tornado," he said, coming away from a training session. Odds on Frazier had dropped to 2–1 at Chen's betting shops.

Foreman himself had not gotten over his initial wariness of Frazier. You would have thought he'd be at peak confidence. He had just turned twenty-four, had learned of the birth of a daughter the week before the fight, was about to make the biggest money of his life in front of the whole world, and was assured of that mysterious transfer of power. He was undefeated, knockouts galore, as feared as any man to enter the ring. Things were clearly going his way. But, truth be told, he had just about the same opinion of his chances as his little brother. He was going through the motions of the big-talking challenger, building himself up, telling reporters how he was going to "dry-gulch" Frazier, all the while wondering if he'd freeze in the ring at the introductions.

"I'm worried none," he told one of those reporters, with a bravado that might not have been false, but was certainly exaggerated. "I thought I would be, but I'm not. Last couple of times I saw Joe fight, he was just looking for that one good punch. It's the matter of a blind man trying to get somewhere. Keeps tapping his stick around. But I ain't gonna be waiting while he's tapping. I'll be punching. If I throw 10 punches in a row, I'll get him with 6. Can't anybody stand up to that."

Archie Moore, on board as a "technical adviser," even though Foreman had retained Sadler after all, understood just how delicate the big man's psyche was. He had stood at Foreman's shoulder during a particularly tense showdown at a press conference, Foreman surprising himself and telling Frazier to shut up. "You can't tell me to shut up," yelled Frazier, more in surprise at the audacity of this young pup than in anger. Moore whispered from behind: "Look him in the eye. Look him in the eye." Foreman tried.

In Jamaica, Moore had devised another confidence-building exercise, built around their post-training ritual of table tennis. Moore would announce at critical points in the game that they were now playing for possession of a red rubber mouse. The loser of the point would have to pick up the mouse and squeak it—"man or mouse," Moore explained. "I like a man who puts priorities in perspective," he said. "I like a man who wants to win the championship of the world."

Yet it took all of Moore's ministrations to even get Foreman into the ring that night. Perhaps thirty-six thousand were in attendance, many more than were anticipated, and as Foreman walked through the warm evening air he began to recognize just how foolish this enterprise was. He had no business being there with Frazier. Frazier was 29–0, twenty-five knockouts! He truly was sharp as a razor. Foreman began to dance around a little, afraid his knees could be seen shaking if he stood still. It occurred to him, they might even stop the fight if his real condition was realized.

Moore, wearing another of his strange woolen caps, prodded him to the center of the ring, where referee Arthur Mercante was giving instructions. Good Lord! There was Frazier, too! "Look at him," Moore said from behind, rubbing his neck. "Look at him." Foreman tried.

At ringside the reporters were settling in for what they imagined would be a long evening, Frazier eventually cutting this poor young man to ribbons, his steady onslaught taking a tremendous toll, round by round. Cosell turned around to Plimpton and said, "Boyle's Thirty Acres, Jack Dempsey vs. Georges Carpentier. 1921. But you know that. You were there." Plimpton wrote this down but, again, did not record a response.

And then, entirely against Foreman's wishes, the bell rang.

There are few events, in life and even in sports, that have the same capacity for surprise as a boxing match. A heavyweight bout, even one for a title, can be dull, inconclusive, a plodding affair as two tacticians struggle for the smallest of advantages, each mindful of terrible consequences that are natural to the game. Sometimes there will be flurries of abandon, as the combatants briefly reach beyond their comfort zones. Or, on the rarest of occasions, it can detonate in a sudden explosion of surprise. It can happen in less than a second: long-held values vacated, a bias corrected, the surety of opinion canceled, a whole foundation of belief instantly subsumed, swallowed up in an instant. What was once a strictly choreographed dance becomes a blast sector. All in the time it takes a man to swing his arm.

No sooner had that bell fallen silent than Foreman, as instructed by Sadler, rushed to the middle of the ring and threw a wild, looping right hand. It appeared to be a ridiculous haymaker, amateurish, born of desperation. It was not confidence inspiring. Dunphy, at ringside, said, "Foreman's a little tense looking." But it was actually a calculated move. Sadler, who was still trying to regain Foreman's trust, had told him to swing once, not two or three times, but just once. Don't even try to hit Frazier. Just swing. That maneuver, which took up a lot of space, established a danger zone. Frazier was not used to people setting boundaries, and he wasn't likely to respect them. But, even if subconsciously, he now recognized an area that probably wasn't safe to be in.

Foreman kept up a brisk pace, determined not to let Frazier in his chest, and to never back up. Several times he used both his mitts to simply push Frazier back. Or else used that left jab to keep him at a distance. "Now," Dunphy admitted, "Foreman looks a little looser."

Cosell had an alternate view. Broadcasting simultaneously, if for a delayed telecast, he immediately sensed something was different. "There's another left hook by George. He's getting into Frazier's head. We'll find out tonight how much the Ali fight took out of Frazier, if anything. And we'll find out just how good George Foreman is at giving and taking a punch." Seconds later, Foreman shuddered Frazier with a left of his own. "I think he hurt Joe Frazier," Cosell said with mounting urgency. "I think Joe is hurt."

From the corner, Moore competed with the ringside commentary and yelled, "Uppercut!" Foreman threw an uppercut.

It was the single most shocking sight in the world, so totally unexpected. The punch caught Frazier flush, and he simply capsized. Nobody was prepared for this, not this soon and, probably, not ever. It didn't even take a second, destinies altered, fortunes reversed. "Down goes Frazier!" Cosell screamed. "Down goes Frazier! Down goes Frazier!"

In truth, Frazier was up before Cosell finished the call. And, in truth, Foreman was not that much encouraged by the damage he had just wrought. Frazier had gotten up, after all. In the next thirty seconds, Foreman backed Frazier into the corner and delivered a succession of thudding right hands and then, perhaps responding to Moore's screams of "Underneath!," one more uppercut. "Frazier is down again," yelled Cosell. "And maybe, no, he is rising. He is game." And then, at the bell, Frazier's corner becoming hysterical, Foreman clubbed him to the canvas once more. At ringside Frazier's twelve-year-old son, Marvis, was slapping the canvas. "Daddy, quit playing around."

The second opened, and Foreman again forced him into the ropes, just pounding away. Frazier fell again. Cosell: "He is down for the fourth time in the fight. George Foreman is doing to Joe Frazier what a 19-year-old did to a veteran Russian, a fellow named Ionis Chepulis, in October of 1968 in the Mexico City Arena."

There were two more knockdowns—six in all—before the fight was finally called at 1:35 of the second round. None of the knockdowns was conclusive in itself; none showed the neural disconnect, a man going suddenly vacant, as if a switch had been flipped. But each showed a steady degradation of the nervous system, Frazier in less and less control of his body, his legs almost palsied, wobbling, as he attempted to keep his ground, assault after assault. Knockdown by knockdown, he was being reduced from heavyweight champion to a clumsy and helpless husk. It is a sad corollary. A fallen fighter is not simply defeated; he must look ridiculous as well. "A pitiful sight," the local paper proclaimed. It was only after the sixth that Foreman, forever wary of Frazier, a kind of undead the way he kept getting up, allowed himself to believe he'd won. It was only after the sixth that Mercante stopped it.

"George Foreman," screamed Cosell, "is the heavyweight champion of the world!"

There was chaos in the ring, even with more than a thousand police and militia to patrol it. Not only had sports artist LeRoy Neiman, with his signature mustache gleaming in the ring lights, gotten to Foreman's corner, but so had Don King. King had come to the arena in Frazier's limo but was now grabbing Foreman by the shoulders. "My man!" he kept repeating. The chaos followed Foreman to his dressing room, only partially restricted by law enforcement.

By the time Roy Foreman got there, bringing up the rear, he saw a rather remarkable sight, King spread-eagled against the door jam, one leg in and one out. "I'm family!" he screamed.

The tumult was actually going to reverberate much further and much longer, boxing's world order totally disrupted. This was going to take a while to sort out. Even Foreman seemed to have misgivings. Back at the hotel he appeared on his balcony, celebrating with his arms aloft, a crowd below cheering him on. He really had been a favorite of Jamaica. But then he looked to the balcony next to his and recognized Frazier's sister—she looked just like Joe—and he was immediately chastened. He waved an apology in her direction. He was apologizing for winning the heavyweight championship of the world.

"Don't feel bad, Mr. Foreman," she said. "We've had many victories."

He waved back and returned to his crowd.

CHAPTER 10

A SHORT TRIP,
A WHODOYOUCALLUM,
AND OLD HEROES

Almost one month later, Frazier appeared on *The Dick Cavett Show*. Cavett, the cerebral alternative to Johnny Carson on late-night television, was not booking particularly high-brow this night, having already presented comics Bill Cosby and Jack Benny. They had each done their ritual riffs and were lighting up various tobacco products—Cosby ignited a tremendous cigar, Benny a pipe—by the time Cavett waved Frazier in from the wings. "Do you know where you are?" Cavett asked him, the audience howling.

Frazier was so genial, so agreeable, so glad to be there, you'd have thought he'd just battered Foreman to the canvas, not the other way around. Once the laughter died down, Frazier owned up to the beating, admitting he'd lost "fair and square." He was so gracious about the whole thing that Benny was driven to interrupt, pointing his pipe at him and saying, "I just want to say, you're one of the nicest fellas I've ever met." He may have meant that he wasn't Ali, or Cassius Clay, as Frazier was still calling him, or maybe he was just moved by the presence of that rarest thing in sports, a good loser.

While the panel pestered him about why he kept jumping up, only to get knocked down again, Frazier gamely explained the fighter's overwhelming impulse, which is to fight back in such situations. Perhaps, he agreed, his timing could have benefited from a mind-clearing eight-count. To tell the truth, he admitted, he had felt like he'd taken "a short trip," not that he knew anything about LSD. But this is what fighters do. They get back up. "He hadn't tasted my punches," he said. Then, with timing that might have been borrowed from Benny himself, added, "Though I did taste his."

Benny was impressed with Frazier's ability to take a punch, and not just those he'd just seen on the clip Cavett showed to introduce the fighter. Frazier had additionally been required to answer questions of possible embarrassment ("Not really," as if it had never occurred to him) and to watch Cosby arise from his chair and do an impersonation of a man—say, Frazier—who'd been comically wobbled. "Well," said Benny at the end of the segment, trying to make his new friend feel better, "we have also laid eggs."

This was one for the ages, though. The stunning upset cost Frazier and Ali one high-dollar rematch, a fight that Jack Kent Cooke, the moneyman behind the first outing, thought would do more than $18 million, outgrossing the original. Cooke had previously made offers of $3.25 million to the fighters. Now? After Frazier had spent five and a half minutes, mostly crawling around on the canvas? "Only fractional," he admitted.

Whatever fraction Cooke believed it was worth was about to be halved again, maybe nullified altogether. It turned out there were even bigger eggs to be laid.

Ali, who'd been scornful of Frazier's performance in Jamaica, wondering if his loss to Foreman hadn't been ordained by their match nearly two years before, had been on a whirlwind schedule. Since their fight at the Garden nineteen months before, Ali had fought ten times, traveling to Japan, Switzerland, and Japan. If Frazier had botched a rematch, Ali at least had been doing his part to keep it alive. He'd even recovered his talents for the fight rhyme. Before a Valentine's Day fight with Joe Bugner, less than a month after Foreman-Frazier, Ali was handicapping in couplet form. "Since when can a bug handle a bee," he said, "a bee that's as pretty and quick as me?"

The bee prevailed over the bug, in a rather ordinary affair that lasted all twelve rounds. Except for Ali's dazzling robe, a gift from Elvis Presley—"People's Choice" spelled out in rhinestones—there had not been much to see. Ali had not been much inspired or worried by the fight, interested primarily in the $275,000 payday. And he worked accordingly. The bout concluded, he was on to the next opponent six weeks later, this time for a $200,000 payday in San Diego. Talk about fractional, this was less than a tenth of what he made for Frazier. He was making up for it in volume, though, rushing through the calendar a fight every month or two, conscious of being thirty-one years old, time running out.

Had Ali and Frazier maintained a civil relationship, the two might have shared a conversation about Ken Norton. Frazier had been paying Norton, a former Marine who'd come to boxing late in life, $400 to prepare him for the Foreman fight. That Frazier was not prepared was not Norton's fault; by his own admission, Norton had been giving him all he wanted in sparring.

But outside of Frazier, nobody knew a thing about Norton. He'd boxed a little in the Marines, mostly to get out of the 5:00 a.m. reveille (not to mention a trip to Vietnam), and upon his discharge had turned pro in San Diego to absolutely no fanfare. Norton was raising a son on the $100 a week his backers were paying and was getting nowhere and growing desperate enough that he daydreamed about sticking up liquor stores. In the six years since his pro debut, he'd fought thirty times, losing once. Yet, at the age of twenty-nine, he was getting just $300 a fight.

Ali would change that. Having exhausted the list of name contenders, all in hopes of keeping his Frazier rematch alive, he was now dipping into the ranks of has-beens and nobodies or, rather, in the lingo of *Sports Illustrated,* "whodoyoucallums." Norton, in recompense for simply being available, and ranked seventh, would get a massive check for $50,000, and Ali would get a walkover, a "tune-up," he called it. The bout was so unpromising that, for the first time in six years, Ali would be fighting on network TV, Howard Cosell (with Frazier at his side) reluctantly doing the call in real time. And not as a stand-alone broadcast either but as part of the *Wide World of Sports* anthology. Nobody but Norton was especially happy about any of this. Cosell thought the fight was a "farce" and beneath his dignity, if not necessarily Ali's. Ali might not have thought of it at all. He spent some of his camp time on the golf course, where he may have sprained an ankle running up to the tee, in a version of speed golf, "revolutionizing the game," he told reporters. And he spent the night before at a party. But people were getting paid, which was the important thing.

So this was the night, March 31, that Ali laid his egg. It's never easy to isolate any one element of defeat. There was overconfidence, of course. And maybe a sprained ankle. And Norton may have been one of those late bloomers, only just now coming into his own, his time with Frazier finally enlarging his vision for himself. Or was it Eddie Futch, Frazier's assistant trainer? Futch had come over to help with Norton, and he had a few ideas on how to neutralize Ali. "The minute you hit him with the jab," Futch told Norton, "step in and jab him again. Two, three moves like that in an 18-foot ring should force Ali back against the ropes. When you get him to the ropes, work both hands to the body and make him bring his elbows to his side to protect his body. When he does, his head will drop, his chin will be there for you. Then hit him with the right."

There was no sudden deformation, no telltale *crack!* There was no especially damaging punch or exchange. So it was impossible to tell exactly when it happened. Some thought the first round, some even the tenth. But most, including Ali's physician, Dr. Ferdie Pacheco, agreed that Norton broke Ali's jaw in the second. That is a horrible thought, that it happened as soon as that, because Ali then must have fought ten more rounds with a jaw that was a "very bad break . . . three or four jagged edges," according to the surgeon who wired it up later. "The edges kept poking into his cheek and into his mouth." For ten rounds?

Pacheco knew during the fight that the injury was plenty seri-ous enough to throw in the towel. But he also knew that the sight of a white man bursting forth from a mostly black corner might be an incendiary sight. Any Ali fight was a politically and racially charged event, and a "draft dodger" fighting a former Marine in the politically conservative San Diego, basically a naval base with some surrounding amenities, was especially provocative. He hated his complicity, but he felt there was little he could do. Besides, Ali was insisting that he continue.

There wasn't much question who won, even though the deci-sion was split. Ali heard the judges' cards read, 2–1 for Norton, pulled a brush through his hair and went over to congratulate Nor-ton, and then left without speaking a word, even to Cosell. "Mu-hammad Ali cannot talk!" Cosell screamed, in the same elevation of excitement he'd used in Jamaica. In fact, the one condition was probably as unexpected as the other.

The idea that Gaseous Cassius, the Louisville Lip, was now rendered mute—his jaw clamped shut, per surgical procedure—may have been a cause for ironic amusement, certainly for funny headlines. He was now a national joke. Once more, it is not enough to be defeated. There must be personal insult as well.

But, actually, it was plenty to be defeated. Frazier had done much to torpedo their high-value rematch, but now Ali, losing to a 5–1 underdog, had truly sunk that ship. The fact that Ali could not explain his defeat, to put a proper spin on this unusual development, was the least of their problems. Eggs had been laid. There were now serious questions, not just about a rematch, but whether Frazier and Ali were through. Each had lost to underdogs, and in fashions so convincing that it was reasonable to ask if they should even con-tinue. "Right now," *Ring* wrote, sizing up the "jigsaw puzzle pieces" of the heavyweight division, "nobody knows."

Foreman remained removed from this fray. As the heavyweight champion, young and dominant, he was now free to enjoy the of-fice's spoils, without the urgency of an immediate title defense. He'd come back to the States as a father and was exulting in his paternity. But he soon realized he was not as agreeable a husband as he was a father, and it wasn't long—well, it was actually immediately, starting in Kingston—before his rampant infidelity began threatening his marriage. What was the point of being champion if you couldn't enjoy it? He indulged himself at every opportunity, and not just with women. He bought clothes, for sure. He'd already been named to the top-ten list by the American Fashion Foundation. He bought cars, jewelry—whatever he wanted. He paid $21,000 for a German shepherd.

None of this behavior penetrated public opinion. The initial coverage of the new heavyweight champion leaned heavily on biography—"Foreman a Gentle Giant," ran a *Ring* profile, observing that the "Heavyweight Champion Pulled Self Up By the Bootstraps." It conformed to the popular notion that heavyweight champions proceeded from poverty and, with the luck of intervention, some noble institution like the Job Corps, for example, went on to hit the jackpot. This is just the kind of story that, even if it has the benefit of truth, can obscure greater realities. Foreman certainly played along. In his one outing, a Las Vegas exhibition three months after the Frazier fight, Foreman said all the right things—"I'm so lucky, because lots of guys deserve to be the champion"—and did them, too. He described some charitable efforts and explained how he wanted to work with kids and "inspire them to high goals."

He did let slip that he and his wife, Adrienne, would be divorcing after a marriage of two years. Asked if he'd become a target now that he was single, he said, "From time to time there are ladies that are impressed." Some of them, he agreed, "are overly impressed by things like a title." He gave the impression that he wasn't.

Close up, nobody mistook him for gentle. He had reverted to his surly self, going back to the public persona of Liston, his early role model. He adopted a steely glare that made approach all but impossible. He was not a pleasant man. But who knew that for sure? Since winning the title he'd become scarce, hard to reach, hunkered down in his small house in California. "An invisible champion," the *New York Times* complained.

In other words, the heavyweight division, which had just re-claimed its position as the most exciting and glamorous game in the country, had been blown up. This was a violent upheaval. Two box-office draws, reliable generators of publicity, had been put in retreat, their championship pedigrees perhaps a matter of history. Foreman's complete destruction of Frazier now had fans wondering if they hadn't been crazy to place stock in such a squat specimen. As far as Ali, the man Frazier had beaten—and Norton had beaten!—it was fair to wonder if he'd been unfit for a comeback in the first place.

Teddy Brenner, the matchmaker at Madison Square Garden, was forced to historical analogy. "Thirty years ago," he said, "Henry Armstrong was the Cassius Clay of his generation, a champion of champions. He was 10–1 to beat Fritzie Zivic and Zivic beat him. No one could believe it. So they were rematched and Henry was 5–1. This time Zivic knocked him out. Henry was all gone and no one knew it." Brenner reminded, "Old heroes die hard." This was in the tradition of finding premature exits for athletes, as if a pre-science of doom was an important aspect of boxing coverage. Ali, his jaw wired up, was now being groomed for retirement. "Ali's sun is setting fast," wrote Red Smith in the *New York Times*.

He had become a sorry sight, maybe as sorry as Frazier had been after his Kingston calamity. How sorry? By April, assured that he could work that mouth again, Cavett booked Ali for a show, along with Jean Stapleton and Elliott Roosevelt, FDR's son.

CHAPTER 11

A ROPE BED, UFOS, AND
THE DATING GAME

If this was going to become something more interesting than the Return of Sonny Liston, a hard-punching and glowering youth laying systematic siege to the remnants of the heavyweight division, Ali and Frazier would need to rehabilitate themselves. Ali would have to prove the Norton fight was a fluke, and Frazier would have to find someone he could remain upright against for longer than six minutes. They were still the marquee names of the sport and could still attract a worldwide following. The Fight of the Century hadn't been that long ago. But they would need to abort the growing suspicion that they were closer to the end of their careers than the beginning. Work had to be done.

Ali repaired to Deer Lake, his training compound in Pennsylvania. He'd bought the six-acre tract overlooking the Poconos in 1972, partly as a cost-cutting measure and partly to realize his dream of a rustic, old-time fight camp. "When you picture a training camp for a fighter, you picture this," he told a visitor, of whom there were legion. "Going up a hill, a dirt road, trees and woods. This is what I always thought of when I was a kid. Not hotels. No going into a fancy hotel lobby with chandeliers and pies and cakes. That's not a training camp."

He justified the development of this plot, which included a gym, a mess hall, cabins for himself and for his parents when they visited, a mosque, as well as a bunkhouse for his sparring partners, as training-camp economy. Expenses for the Frazier fight, with all the pies and cakes, came to $250,000. "I'm saving money this way," he said. "This is an investment."

In fact, it was a bare-bones operation, physically anyway, its only amenity a huge fireplace outside the mess hall. Ali's cabin, in particular, was rustic. He slept on a two-hundred-year-old rope bed, warmed himself in front of a coal stove, read beneath a coal oil lamp, and drank water from a hand pump. At 4:30 each morning he rang a hundred-year-old church bell to gather the fighters for road-work. There was nothing on the property to distract a fighter from his gladiatorial routines. Even the countryside was reconfigured for inspiration. Massive boulders lined the roads, many of them painted out in the names of former champions. There was a Rocky Marciano rock, of course. But also Jack Johnson, Floyd Patterson, Sonny Liston, Jersey Joe Walcott. The road was a virtual hall of fame.

This is not to say Deer Lake was quiet, or in any way monastic. It was, despite the spartan accommodations, a rather lively place, probably more like a frat house than a retreat. Aside from the principals—the fighter, the sparring partners, the trainers, the cooks—there were likely to be as many as forty others in attendance, most of them with very vague duties, except for cheerleading.

Ali was not the first fighter ever to have an entourage, although he was among the first to pay a man (his brother) $50,000 a year for "driving and jiving." The concept, and even the term, was invented by middleweight great Sugar Ray Robinson, a man who tried to reproduce the fun of a touring jazz band, the kind that played his Harlem nightclub, in his training experience. Robinson traveled with his own barber, secretary, dietitian, and even a dwarf mascot, all in addition to the usual throng of trainers, assistant trainers, and any sundry characters who might be called upon to service a boxer. Robinson also required a hairdresser, a voice coach, and a man who whistled while he worked. Also a golf instructor.

Robinson did not originally have a word to describe this portable population, calling them his attendants when he was forced to put a name to them. Friends was a better, if less satisfying, description. Really, that's what they were. It wasn't until his legendary ocean voyage to France in 1951 that a better term was produced. One of the French stewards on the *Liberté,* wrestling with the cast's fifteen suitcases and thirty-two trunks (the pink Cadillac had been stowed separately), was moved to awe: "The boxer, Sugar Ray Robinson, and his entourage." That, thought the fighter, overhearing it, "sounded classy."

The term has persisted and, even though Ali's retinue was rarely classy, certainly described the mob at Deer Lake. Some of them, an inner circle, had definite, or mostly definite, job descriptions. There was Ferdie Pacheco, the Miami ghetto doctor, who'd come along for the ride. He'd been recruited by Ali's trainer, Angelo Dundee, way back at the beginning. Pacheco loved the glamour and excitement of this circus. He loved it enough that he never asked, and never received, one dime for his services in the corner.

Also with specific and necessary duties: Lana Shabazz, the longtime cook; Luis Sarria, Ali's masseur; and Pat Patterson, the Chicago policeman who became Ali's bodyguard.

More prominent in the entourage, but less easily explained, were facilitator Gene Kilroy and motivator Bundini Brown. Kilroy, one of the few white men in Ali's camp, had left the marketing department at MGM to be a sort of right-hand man to Ali. It wasn't so much that his job description was vague as it was all-encompassing. He fixed things. If somebody needed a doctor, Kilroy got one. An interview? He got that, too. If a sparring partner needed a new mouthpiece, he went to Kilroy. At fights Kilroy slept in a room adjacent to Ali's, his presence comfort enough. It was Kilroy, in fact, who came up with the idea of camp in the first place, even finding the acreage.

Bundini, on the other hand, resisted occupational definition altogether. He called himself the assistant trainer, and, it's true, he seconded Dundee in the corner. But he had very little to do with actual training. Ringside, he was more of a prop man than tactician; when Ali fought Patterson, whom he called the Rabbit, it was Bundini's task to shake lettuce and carrots at him. Pacheco took a bigger view and pegged him as a "spiritual witch doctor," a clownish fellow of nebulous talents who nevertheless had peculiar access to Ali's psyche and grew ever more important.

He'd come to Ali in 1963, delivered by Sugar Ray Robinson himself. Robinson had worried about the young boxer, seeing him read poetry in Greenwich Village. "That was no way to train for a fight," he thought, and he sent Bundini "to watch over him, somebody to keep him happy and relaxed." Robinson could always promote from within; the early Cassius Clay did not yet have a proper support group and needed all the help he could get.

Once Ali converted to the Nation of Islam, Bundini's position immediately became tenuous. He was a womanizer and a drinker and steadfast in his own religious beliefs—his god happened to be called Shorty. Plus, he had the occupational tendency toward theft. When he was caught selling Ali's championship belt for $500, he was banished. But after an exile of his own, Bundini was eventually brought back and became a camp fixture, its most colorful and voluble member.

At times he seemed little more than a helpless foil, often reduced to tears by Ali's teasing. More often he was court jester, exhorting Ali to "Flail the Whale" in his fight with the portly Buster Mathis. Yet, at others, he became the source of Ali's genius. "Float like a butterfly, sting like a bee." That was Bundini. "If you gonna tell him something," he'd once explained, "you got to have a memorable and pleasing way to put it."

This bunch, along with "50 hard charging followers," as Pacheco called Ali's strange chorus, people who would simply show up and invent a task, such as dusting the gym or calling "time" between rounds, constituted a remarkable village. But even this large group swelled during the afternoon, when the visitors began climbing the hill up to the gym to watch Ali spar and then declaim from the ring. Most fighters ran closed camps, but Ali encouraged attendance, turning Deer Lake into a tourist destination. Once a camp member, perhaps thinking he'd just developed a new job and hence lifetime employment, strung a rope across the camp, dividing the gawkers from Ali. "Never put it up again," Ali barked.

And certainly never divide him from children and especially sick children. As word of his consideration went out, the site became a kind of Lourdes, with groups of youngsters, stricken with leukemia or cerebral palsy, showing up, bringing all proceedings to a halt as he stooped to kiss them, one by one.

But it didn't take much to get Ali's attention. Just as celebrities or other noteworthy personalities might pop in—Tom Jones or Richard Harris—so did the journalists who all knew they could count on an interview just for showing up. Ali was surely the most accessible personality who ever lived, and he was always available if a New York writer wanted to visit him for an easy column. But he was available for anyone. He refused to discriminate by circulation. A television reporter from nearby Reading would get the same treatment as Howard Cosell (or Dick Cavett, who got into the ring with him there). Many a high school sports reporter filled space with a sit-down with Ali.

Deer Lake, then, was a comfortable place to be, especially for a fighter coming off a particularly ignominious defeat. Ali had never been especially diligent in training, but he'd been embarrassed by Norton and was newly driven. This time, with the rematch set for September, he'd shown up fourteen weeks ahead. He'd trained just three for Frazier, about the same for Liston. He bragged to visiting reporters that he'd chopped down eighty-five trees—"They not pine, they oak!"—breaking one ax and ruining the edges on five more. His weight, he said, was down to 211 pounds, about what he came in for Liston, about 10 less than for Norton. Remember, no pies or cakes here.

He was rewinding his clock, all right, but not just to the Liston days, when he was in his athletic prime. He was going back centuries, this entirely modern man now buying up antiques—"old antiques," preferably—throughout the Pennsylvania Dutch countryside. Everything had to be ancient. He cleared benches, replacing them with "real logs." When his wife, Belinda, visited, they often spent an after-dinner hour sitting in a wooden surrey, another "old antique," watching for UFOs in the clear night sky, every once in a while claiming to identify Elijah Muhammad's mother ship. Even as his bus and Rolls-Royce gleamed in the moonlight nearby, Ali could exult in this pioneer authenticity, certain that his sacrifice would restore him to his former glory. He was a man who could comfortably accommodate any number of personal discrepancies.

Of course, there was still some curiosity about that jaw. Clearly, it worked, but could it stand up to the pounding of Norton again, and even Frazier and Foreman down the road? There was no medical reason it couldn't heal, the bone strong as before. It had not been compromised, just broken. But still. In August, a month before the Norton fight, *Sports Illustrated* sent its boxing writer to Deer Lake to determine whether that famous mandible was sturdy enough to invest further coverage.

Mark Kram, the writer, meant to watch some sparring there, see Ali catch a few shots to the puss, and report back on the fighter's rehab. And he did. But first he was forced to observe—this led the story—that Ali had added yet one more remarkable position to the entourage, a man whose primary duty it was to read from the *Guinness Book of World Records,* thus lulling the fighter to sleep in his old antique rope bed each evening. "The tallest race in the world is the Tutsi," the man read, Ali slowly drifting away.

But, yes, the jaw was fine. "Look, no headgear, no protection," Ali shouted from the ring. "Nobody telling sparring partners to hold back." As instructed, the sparring partners let forth, and several did reach Ali's jaw. It did not shatter.

Ali was not the only fighter getting back to business. In July Frazier—"Haunted Frazier," according to the *New York Times* headline—finally returned to the ring, meeting Joe Bugner in London. Not a lot had gone right for Frazier the past year. First Foreman, followed by a not-so-successful singing tour, then the silly Superstars decathlon in February when he tied for last place with Johnny

Unitas (pole vaulter Bob Seagren whipped him in the weight-lifting event!), and now a fight in London where Bugner, a former circus strongman who had somehow gone the distance with Ali, had become the crowd favorite. All anybody wanted to ask there was why he'd fallen down so often in his fight with Foreman.

Still, Frazier was not the kind of man to suffer ghosts. He was hardly haunted. He'd been assured by Foreman, who was working through some contractual difficulties, that he'd get his rematch. Things would be different this time. A bout with Bugner would restore credibility, profitability, and maybe even some confidence throughout the boxing community. In fact, Frazier narrowly outpointed Bugner, having knocked him down just once. Afterward, Frazier said he'd been sufficiently in charge of the action that he "could have killed" Bugner. But he "didn't want my mama to think of me as a naughty boy." Others, mulling the closeness of the decision, weren't as sure that Frazier was all the way back. Foreman, who was watching the fight at ringside, initially said Bugner had won and then, remembering his payday lay with Frazier, not Bugner, backtracked a bit. "Both fighters have an equal amount of heart," he decided.

But invincibility had gone out the window months before, for everybody except perhaps Foreman. Frazier just needed viability. And, with the victory, he had at least reclaimed that much. He hadn't fallen down; nobody broke his jaw. He was back in action.

Foreman, meanwhile, waited nearly nine months before demonstrating his talents for destruction. Like Frazier, he'd toyed with less demanding sidelines than boxing. But his exhibitions were drawing about what Frazier's Knockouts had. He'd also been bedeviled by Sadler's contract shenanigans (he was out as manager, though remained as head trainer), as well as divorce proceedings, which were turning increasingly ugly. Also, Frazier and his rematch demands. So maybe it was time for a real fight, an actual championship defense.

For the occasion Foreman chose Joe (King) Roman, an undersize heavyweight, maybe even 50 pounds lighter than Foreman, with an unimpressive record of 46–7–1. Foreman additionally chose Tokyo for the site. He was led to believe the tax bite would be more favorable there. In other words, Foreman was scheduling yet one more exhibition, with faint overtones of championship boxing.

To the extent that anyone noticed, the fight proceeded predictably. Foreman used the occasion to experiment with his new powers of concussion, more or less adding to his growing literature of ring violence, plumping up his database of cruelty. He now wanted to see if he could knock somebody out without hitting him on the chin. How about up by the ear? Poor Roman went down in the first round, corkscrewed at Foreman's feet. So you could apply catastrophic injury in the ear area. This was good to know.

A little more than a week later, September 10, it was time for Ali and his rematch with Norton in Los Angeles. Ali had impressed everybody, especially those in his own camp, coming to the fight in such great shape. "There's no way you can eliminate the ravages of time," Dr. Pacheco said, "but he has his weight down and he is mentally recharged." Ali agreed that this had become a desperate time and understood that his constituency, dwindling or not, felt he was at a crossroads. "They are all talking about Muhammad Ali like it's his life or death on the line," he said. "There is a very great deal of interest in Muhammad Ali. Is he through, or is he not? Is he still the fastest and most beautiful man in the world, or is he growing old and slow?"

The fight, as it happened, did not prove either contention. Ali meant to punish Norton for the predicament he'd been cast. "I took a nobody and created a monster," he said. "I put him on *The Dating Game.*" Norton had not only beaten him, broken his jaw, and shut him up, but absorbed some necessary limelight. Yet Ali did not punish him. Norton had been emboldened by their first meeting and was convinced Ali could not hurt him. He continued to give him trouble in this fight, too, attacking him. Ali's legs, toughened by all that roadwork, were not toughened enough. He became flat-footed in the later rounds, yielding the offense to the younger fighter. The fight was up for grabs going into the twelfth and final round.

It's hard to imagine how boxing history might have veered, had Ali chopped down even one less oak tree back at Deer Lake. It took a furious rally in that last round, Ali jabbing and dancing, standing in to slug when it mattered, to earn him his split decision. It took everything he had to get out alive.

But like Frazier that summer, like Foreman the week before, he'd won. All three were alive for the moment. They could sort it out later.

1974

CHAPTER 12

TWO PASTY MEN, A BAD AND UGLY SCENE, AND ICE CREAM ON A STICK

Not even a half hour had passed before they were wrestling on the studio floor, a dozen or so handlers from the fighters' entourages pouring from the wings to try to separate them. Only Cosell, sitting there in his yellow *Wide World of Sports* jacket, remained calm, as if obliged to report even this action with a professional detachment. "Well," he said, as the scuffling at his feet continued to draw yet more participants, "we're having a scene, as you can see."

Well, that was the idea, wasn't it? The two men had been jabbing at each other from a distance ever since they'd agreed to a rematch back in October. By then their stars had fallen far enough that their guarantees were worth barely a third of what they'd received three years before—$850,000 each. And publicity was required. "There was no title on the line," said Tom Kenville, the Madison Square Garden publicity man. "There was a sense that both of them had slipped a little." Something else would have to goose the box-office take.

Ali had done his part, in an unrelenting attack on Frazier's intelligence. He never missed an occasion to call his opponent "ignorant." For Frazier, who lacked the verbal ability to counter (his basic comeback was to insist upon calling him Cassius Clay), not to mention the natural inclination, this was a stinging and lasting insult. Frazier looked at boxing as more of a fraternal enterprise, two men in the ring trying to make a living. He was as puzzled as he was hurt by Ali's taunts. And as the fight, scheduled for January 28 in New York, drew closer, the taunts grew uglier, the discourse dictated by Ali's requirements of humiliation. Whereas he was Uncle Tom for the first fight, now he was without even the significance of a racial implication. He was just dumb.

Ali had just belittled Frazier anew on *The Dick Cavett Show* filmed six days before the fight, not only calling him ignorant, but mocking his diction as well. The show was meant to be a comedy set-piece with filmed segments from each fighter's camp. Cavett had shown up at Deer Lake to spar with Ali, and the BBC's Mike Parkinson had gone to Frazier's Cloverlay gym in Philadelphia. The sight of the two pasty men lifting their oversize mitts in the same ring as former heavyweight champions might have defused the situation enough to prevent any rasslin'. Indeed, their bit ended on a bit of a high note, with Ali and Frazier coming together to lift Cavett high in the air between them. "I feel like an Oreo cookie," Cavett said.

But now, just two days before the fight, those spirits of cooperation had departed. Eddie Futch, who had become Frazier's principal trainer when Yank Durham had died the previous fall (and had been chief Ali tormentor during the Norton fights), did not like the way *The Dick Cavett Show* had gone and had resisted Cosell's invitation for the *Wide World of Sports* segment. Cosell promised all they'd do was review the replay of the first fight and that everything would be conducted at the highest levels of decorum. He pledged that he would cut off Ali at the first disparaging remark and would restrict him to comments about the first fight, allowing nothing more. Further, he'd sit between the two fighters, establishing a somewhat physical barrier to insult.

Futch allowed the stunt on those conditions. Yet when Frazier appeared, he was seated between Ali and Cosell, not what he had hoped. Still, the broadcast did not get off to a bad start, and, for that matter, Ali appeared to be in a magnanimous mood. As Cosell unspooled the video, beginning in the tenth round, Ali easily and completely took control of the show. "One billion watchers waiting for this fight," he said. "I think we deserve a hand. We done a lot of work to accumulate one billion, which is bigger than the Rose Bowl, the Super Bowl, the Kentucky Derby, the Indy 500 and . . . "

Cosell tried to get Ali on point. "All right," he said, interrupting. "But let's get back . . . "

Ali rolled over him, not missing a beat. " . . . the World Series! Them two men you're watching right there, beats everything America ever produced. Two black brothers . . . "

Cosell: "So what was your feeling at this point?"

"Get off that mess," Ali said. "I'm talking about something now. These two black men can command more attention than anything America can produce. Now you can finish talking."

"I want you to get back to the fight," Cosell said.

"The whole planet earth," said Ali, before allowing his attention to be diverted to matters at hand.

Frazier might have been mollified by Ali's attempt at inclusion, but he clearly was nursing a grudge from *The Dick Cavett Show,* and any other appearance Ali had made to his detriment, which was all of them, now that he thought about it. He was poised for rebuttal, whether it was needed or not. And he delivered it in the strangest possible way. As soon as Ali made a reference to Frazier's hitting him below the belt—"Ref didn't see nothing," Ali said. "Got hit there ninety-five times"—Frazier sprang to the offense. "That's why he went to the hospital, Howard."

It was an odd, even inappropriate, thing to say. Yes, Ali did go to the hospital. But it was well known by now that it was Frazier who had stayed there. When it came to points of debate, this was not one that Frazier would ever own. But Frazier, unbeknownst to the audience, was flummoxed by more than Ali. Off in the wings, where the entourages were milling around, Ali's brother Rahaman had been narrating the filmed fight action within Frazier's earshot. Every time it showed Ali landing a punch, Rahman, his well-paid jiver, sang out, "Amen! Praise Allah! There it is again!" This was ordinarily a routine annoyance, the cost of doing business with Ali. But coming on top of their recent history, this constant chirping was simply too much. So he mentioned a hospital visit.

Ali was startled, but not quite to the point of silence. "Don't talk about no hospital. You know you wrong about bringing up the hospital. I wasn't gonna talk about the hospital. Everybody know I went to the hospital for 10 minutes. You were in the hospital for a month."

"I was resting," Frazier shot back. "In and out."

"How dumb is that," Ali said. "He brought up the hospital! How ignorant that man is!"

That was Frazier's trigger word, and it was here that he stood up, yanked his earpiece out, and stood over Ali. "Sit down, Joe," Ali said, but he didn't like the look of Frazier standing on top of him. Neither did Rahman, who immediately rushed out. Futch rallied from his side. "Sit down quick, Joe," said Ali, rising and putting a headlock on him, everybody going to the floor in a pile, providing Cosell with a nice little melee. "It's hard to tell whether it's clowning or for real," said Cosell, the only man still in his seat at this point. "This kind of thing has been going on all along in terms of promotion of a fight but this time it seems to be really real, because Joe Frazier is really angry."

The fighters were separated, and Frazier was led away, Cosell calling after him, "Sorry, Joe." Futch took one last look back at Cosell and said, "You are a corrupt individual, do you know that?" Left alone in the studio with Ali, Cosell, not the least bit chastened by his role in the ruckus, summed it up: "a bad and ugly scene."

It had not been done in terms of promotion, though, the fight having long since sold out. It didn't hurt closed-circuit sales, the footage leading most newscasts that night, the whole thing getting big headlines. But Cosell was right. This was not clowning. It was real. Also, it was bad and it was ugly.

Up to then it had been merely silly. Frazier had engineered some prefight publicity when he showed up in New York to get fitted for an ankle-length mink coat. He was, the press seemed to approve, acting every bit the aspiring champ. He flashed a solitaire on his pinkie finger that, by his count, contained nineteen diamonds. Ali, meanwhile, was manufacturing some modest intrigue by claiming a hand injury, the proof being that he didn't use his right hand in sparring. "I never seen a guy train that way," said former featherweight champion Willie Pep, after a visit to Deer Lake. "He's not throwing no punches."

Ali and his camp could generate this kind of nonsense standing on their heads, if it meant getting an extra column inch of newsprint. "I taste Ali's sweat now," Bundini told the visiting press, "and it's got salt in it. The last time it was like water. But the salt means he's got his body juices working again." Nobody dared inquire under what conditions Bundini did his sweat tasting. This was news enough.

But now the event had become personal. Ali, who'd been left with Cosell to describe the remaining five rounds of that first fight from his point of view alone, had joked, "It was just the way we rehearsed it." He added, "Every theater that isn't sold out is selling now. I can see two guys down in Waycross, Georgia, one of them is saying, 'Ernie, we got to see this fight now.' Yes, sir, it'll help." But off the telecast he registered his surprise at Frazier's anger. "His eyes meant it," he said, of Frazier's sudden and very real fury. "When he was standing over me, I didn't know what he was going to do." Frazier was hurt, anybody could see, beyond the possibility of reconciliation.

The fact was, their animosity was about all that drove the promotion. They could still draw—were drawing—but their meeting no longer mattered, not in the same way it did in 1971. Race, politics—it was all in question for that bout. Now? Joe didn't like Ali (or, as he still called him, Clay). That was about it.

Time, which had put the two on its cover for their first meeting, had severely downgraded the rematch. "Perhaps the fight will be as dramatic as their last clash," the magazine wrote in the walk-up to the fight. "But by any measure the stakes are not." The article, titled "Picking Foreman's Foe," said the fight was little more than a qualifier for the winner. "The loser is likely to pass into frustrated retirement."

Was it possible? This was a single-elimination bout? The winner may be the real loser, just cannon fodder for Foreman? Ali was thirty-two now and had never recovered the magic of his championship years, not in the ring anyway. Frazier was thirty, but that Foreman beating had put his future in doubt. The two could still carry an event, but there was a sort of melancholy about their meeting, too. Even the fighters seemed to feel it. Between his manic bursts, Ali could fall to gloomy introspection. What was he thinking about these days? "Age," he said. "People dying." Frazier wasn't much happier. "People look and say, 'My, my, look at that boy, he has a $125,000 house, a motorcycle, big cars.' But nobody thinks of the aggravation, people don't know about the gym and the rooms with walls just looking back at you."

Fight night at the Garden drew the same sold-out crowd, the same peacocks, though the celebrity quotient—Barbra Streisand, but also George Jessel and Milton Berle—was much lower. It was an event, just not like the first. And similarly it was a fight. Just not like the first.

No amount of time could dull the fighters' memory, and each was properly wary of the other, mindful of the toll that first one had taken. And so Ali fought a savvy fight, not a reckless one, doing more clutching than jabbing. He did not mug in the ring, and only once did he do his shuffle. And so Frazier rested his head on Ali's chest, his hook willingly nullified by the embrace. If this was a strategy, it was abetted by referee Tony Perez, who refused to step in and separate the fighters. On they danced for twelve rounds.

Ali did little more than punch for show, "pittypat punches," in Frazier's mind, and flashed power only once, in the second round, when he shook Frazier with a right to the head. Frazier had a tough time regaining his senses and might not have withstood another punch. But Perez thought he heard the bell and called time. By the time he realized his mistake and drew the fighters together, Frazier was back on his toes.

The rest of the time Ali, having learned to stay off the ropes in any fight with Frazier, closed in and grabbed him around the head, reducing all chances of damage. "You gotta stop this," Futch complained from the corner. Perez said after the fight that there was nothing wrong with Ali's holding, as long as he wasn't hitting, too. And besides, Frazier was hardly struggling to get away himself. But it was not fun to watch. Even Emile Griffith, the former welterweight champion, was yelling from ringside. "Let go of his head!"

Ali didn't, nor was he told to. Perez continued to allow the clutching and grabbing—133 "holds" in all, when Futch was able to count them up—and to allow Ali to pile up points. It was just as Bundini had promised back in Deer Lake. "Champ ain't gonna try to hose him down this time. He's gonna pick the backdoor lock."

It was not a bad fight; it had good pace. Ali showed some of the glide and pop from his prime, and Frazier delivered some classic menace, especially in the final round, when even he realized how desperate his situation was. But it was certainly not the fight of the century, the fighters putting everything on the line. They'd put just enough.

Afterward, having scored a unanimous decision, Ali preened in the dressing room, eating ice cream on a stick and demanding, "Answer me. Do I look like I'm thirty-two years old? Did I fight like a thirty-two-year-old?" But he was uncharacteristically modest when it came to his opponent, disavowing any "bad feeling between us."

Seated next to Frazier on a postfight dais, Ali said, "I can't say nothing bad about him. I actually thought Joe was finished. He isn't. He had me out on my feet twice." He promised he'd "give Joe another chance. I'm not gonna duck him."

In his opinion the two had delivered another masterpiece, "another fight that can't be topped," he said. "We drew more people than any event in the recorded annals of earth. And I'm glad the people got their money's worth." He had done exactly what he wanted: "No clowning, a little slugging and a little boxing, a little dancing. A good fight."

Of course, it wasn't all ice cream on a stick. What had really just happened, anyway? Foreman's next foe had been picked, that's all.

CHAPTER 13

MARLENE DIETRICH, A ROBOT, AND AN INTERNATIONAL SMASH AND GRAB

Foreman was not happy, but then why should he have been any different? Nobody was happy. The war in Vietnam had been a drag, and it still was. And now there was the idea that the president of the United States ought to be impeached. Plus, long lines at the gas pumps, where the energy crisis was hitting home in most inconvenient ways. And there was inflation. As 1974 dawned, it was clear that America was one depressed nation.

This turned out be something measurable; it wasn't just a feeling in the air. Polls again and again demonstrated a plunging confidence in leaders, institutions, and even the future. One survey found negative feelings about Nixon, just as you'd expect of somebody who seemed more and more likely to have engineered a small-time burglary in his reelection campaign. But respondents felt the whole government seemed "paralyzed, inept and impotent." In ten years of the survey, confidence had never been so low.

"This kind of malaise," a Princeton historian told *Time*, "atrophies the will of the people." And nobody thought it was going to get better soon. More than half of the people thought that the quality of life in the United States had deteriorated over the previous ten years, and only 11 percent thought it was going to get immediately better.

But what was Foreman's problem, exactly? As heavyweight champion, he was now apart from the rest of America, elevated beyond their mundane concerns. He didn't have to worry about any odd-even rationing to fill up his many automobiles. He had cars and license plates to accommodate any situation. He'd be okay whether Nixon stayed or went. What did he care which way America went? He was now a world citizen. And as far as inflation, Foreman wasn't so much suffering from it as he was contributing to it. He'd made about $70,000 as an overlooked challenger in Jamaica and, the title well in hand, was being offered $700,000 to fight Norton in Venezuela. And, under a secret agreement, he'd just been assured he would get $5.5 million to fight Ali, assuming he got past Norton. Which was worth assuming.

If he was unhappy, it was for far different reasons than his fellow Americans. Becoming champion at the age of twenty-four had delivered more misery than joy. His life had become a morass of legal entanglements, of competing influences and constant criticism. He'd assumed he'd be instantly popular, looked up to. Instead, everybody was getting a piece of him and disregarding him at the same time, even complaining about his competition. What did he have to do? He'd almost murdered the one man who'd beaten Ali—he was about to murder the second—and still Ali was considered the People's Champion, growing ever more likable in his old age.

He retreated to a reliable persona, modeling his old mentor, Sonny Liston. At first he channeled Liston out of ignorance; Foreman simply thought that's how champions ought to comport themselves, aloof and disdainful. But as the lawsuits and double-crosses piled up against him, and especially when his dog was killed by a car (bystanders had to carry a crying Foreman, who'd been found slouched on the curb, to his mother's house after the accident), the assumed bitterness began to suit him. He no longer was acting angry. He really was angry.

He was still furious with Sadler over that contract debacle with Marty Erlichman, Streisand's manager. Every time Sadler was in a personal financial jam, which was often in those early days, he sold off a chunk of Foreman's future. The Garden's Teddy Brenner joked at the time that Foreman's archives might be more valuable than Nixon's, certainly more voluminous. Sadler had once given a woman in Houston, the owner of Texas Boxing Enterprises, exclusive promotional rights, unbeknownst to his fighter. He was lucky he could invalidate that contract, beating back a $1.2 million lawsuit. But more troublesome was that paper with Erlichman, a ten-year deal that gave away half of his ancillary rights—the bulk of his income—for just $500,000. That had gotten Sadler in the doghouse before the Frazier fight, even though Foreman continued to use him as his trainer. The aftermath of the contract, which his lawyers were furiously trying to undo, continued to reverberate. Foreman had yet to be paid for his title defense in Tokyo, which he'd selected in the first place as a tax dodge, when a group in Philadelphia, claiming Erlichman had sold them part of the contract, attached his purse.

Then there was the divorce. It had barely been civil, and it was going to be costly. If his wife's attorneys were to learn of a pending megafight with Ali, with a purse upward of $5 million, it would be costlier yet. Foreman was determined to keep news of the possible payday to himself and to keep the divorce damage to a minimum.

Jerry Perenchio, who'd put the first Ali-Frazier fight together, had already approached Foreman about a possible Ali bout, the logical super-event now that both men held a win over Frazier. The number of $5 million was tossed about. Foreman liked the figure, and he liked Perenchio. But here came Don King, trying to tie up the fighters before Perenchio and gain control of the promotion. King arrived in Foreman's camp outside Oakland, where he was training in the Minerals and Gems Exhibition Hall of the Alameda County Fairgrounds, and gave his pitch, telling Foreman it was a chance to help a fellow black man. King told him he could deliver $5.5 million and Ali with his agreement.

Foreman suddenly recognized an angle and, in King, a possible coconspirator. He didn't care that King was black—he actually preferred the clean-cut Perenchio—and he didn't really care about an extra $500,000. Would King, Foreman wondered, be willing to postdate the contract past his divorce decree? Would he ever! King had killed a man over a $600 debt. This was not going to be a problem. So without ever consulting lawyers, and certainly not Sadler, Foreman signed three blank pages, giving King the fight. The divorce settlement, which was unable to acknowledge the looming and postdated bonanza, came through shortly after. Foreman would pay a onetime cash award of $235,000, plus $400 a month in child support, not a lot for a man about to become a multimillionaire.

Even this didn't do much to cheer him up. Everyone who visited him reported him as "sullen" or "glowering." Nobody needed a Harris survey to gauge Foreman's mood.

He was even worse once he got to Caracas, a site that had materialized with the help of Alex Valdez, the same Paris theatrical impresario who had arranged for the Foreman-Frazier fight in Jamaica. Valdez felt it was a natural. "I know Caracas well," he said. "I have put Maurice Chevalier there, Sammy Davis Jr., Marlene Dietrich, people like that." He had not, however, put anybody like Foreman there. Foreman had gone there without his new pup, Caracas reneging on that condition at the last moment, and without sex. He'd decided to give up women for seventy-five days of training instead of the normal fifteen before a fight.

He had gone past cranky into a dangerous area, saying just the most alarming things. "I want to hurt him so bad," he told some press, "he'll just pass out, just won't be there anymore." He wanted to hurt Norton so bad, "it's embarrassing." One writer came away from the meeting shaken, but at least recognizing the references. "All week," he wrote, "he seemed to be auditioning for the ogre's role that was left vacant when the late Sonny Liston shriveled to mortal proportions before the iridescent talent of Muhammad Ali."

Somebody did manage to get a smile out of him that week, and it happened to be that iridescent talent himself. Ali, who'd been brought down as a color "analyst" for the broadcast, had invited Foreman to his hotel in downtown Caracas for a little sit-down. It was a puzzling and remarkable meeting, especially considering the two had a secret agreement to share their blood lust just a little down the road. Ali took Foreman to a private room above the hotel lobby and instructed the young man in ways of championship behavior. Do not, for example, let anybody talk you into opening a restaurant or bar. Don't buy too many cars. Ali continued to administer such practical advice in gentle and even tones, Foreman nodding his head, gratefully absorbing the counsel.

When the two had finished, Ali ushered Foreman to the railing of a mezzanine above the lobby, where a throng of Ali fans had remained. Ali pointed to Foreman, a switch suddenly thrown. "You see this robot? You know what I'm gonna do? . . ." It was the one time in Caracas that Foreman laughed.

Norton, for his part, was talking a great fight. He'd helped columnists with their angles before the Ali bouts, explaining how his success had been ordained by a regimen of hypnosis. Now in Caracas he was espousing the benefits of "autosuggestion," something he'd picked up from a cassette course from the Napoleon Hill Academy's Philosophy of Success. "Many times a day," Norton said, "I repeat instructions to myself, and after a while they become conditioned reflex. Say Foreman pins me in a corner: I throw a hook or a right hand and spin out. Or say I get knocked down. I tell myself I won't rush back in. I keep repeating these things, to get them embedded in my subconscious mind."

In sum, he said, he was not at all afraid of Foreman, whom he regarded as a "cheap imitation" of Ali and Liston, a conclusion that many were arriving at simultaneously.

Told of the remarks, Foreman glowered, predictably by now. "It's really best he imitate Houdini," he said, "and disappear." Foreman had already decided he was probably going to kill Norton in the ring.

As for the fight, this little impediment to a $5.5 million paycheck, neither autosuggestion nor sleight of hand played much of a part. Nor did Ali, who was shouting encouragement to Norton from ringside, as if to sabotage his own payday. Foreman, having studied Norton's head during ring instructions, picking out possible knockout points, stalked the challenger the first round, nibbling patiently. The striking impression was that, while Norton was actually the same size—really, just ten pounds lighter—as Foreman, and much better muscled, he seemed dwarfed by Foreman's menace.

Ali, in his role as expert commentator, did not convey the same impression. Rather, according to his remarks, Foreman seemed just a "good amateur," while Norton was obviously "a great fighter," having "gone twenty-four rounds with me."

Then in the second round, a minute gone, Foreman knocked Norton into the ropes with a succession of right hands, the referee rushing in for a standing eight-count. Seconds later, Foreman spun him from one ring post to the other, finishing him off with two uppercuts, one of them lifting Norton off his feet. There was nothing Norton could repeat to himself now, even if he'd had the brain waves to manifest it. He sank clumsily to the canvas, struggled to pull himself up on the ropes, but only further entangled himself, the referee once more rushing to his rescue.

"It's like magic when I lay my hand on these guys," Foreman marveled. He had gone over to his corner to see whether he'd killed him after all and was more relieved than disappointed, surprising himself, to find Norton alert and communicative. "What happened?" Norton kept asking.

Yet even the ease of the fight, the satisfying concussion of another challenger, proved scarce relief for Foreman. He didn't even enjoy a single day of pride before he was once again plunged into his funk.

Anybody else in Caracas might have told him what was coming. What was meant as a publicity campaign for the new regime—a new president had taken office the week of the fight—became more of a cautionary experience, visitors learning firsthand the necessary arts of bribery. Nobody's hotel room was ready, the reservation confirmed or not, until $50 could be produced at check-in. Broadcast equipment had been seized just days before the event and held for safekeeping. Press photographers did not get their cameras back until just hours before the fight, after paying "taxes."

Did Marlene Dietrich and Maurice Chevalier go through this? It became clear that the government was not hosting a sporting event as much as it was an international smash and grab. Of the ten

George Foreman plays to his patriotic reputation, handing out flags before his 1969 pro debut in New York City. The summer before, in Mexico City, he captured America's attention by waving a similar flag after his gold medal win in the Olympics. Hard to believe, only a few years before this, he was the scourge of Houston's Fifth Ward. Or, for that matter, that a few years hence he'd be the scourge of the heavyweight division. This would be the last time he'd be seen in public with a straw hat. (Associated Press)

Muhammad Ali may have been out of a job but he was hardly out of mind. Here, in typically manic fashion, he greets students at St. John's University in the spring of 1968. During these years of exile from boxing he managed to remain relevant, and financially afloat, giving speeches on campuses across the country. (Getty Images)

Joe Frazier strikes the pose as Eddie Futch, who had just come on board as his trainer in early 1968, looks on. Futch, a one-time sparring partner for Joe Louis, would become something of a problem for Ali, creating game plans for two of his defeats, one by Frazier, another by Ken Norton. Alas, he'd become more famous for Ali's greatest victory, when he kept Frazier on the stool in Manila. (Getty Images)

Frazier didn't always appreciate Ali invading his turf, but he understood his genius for promotion. This, Ali mugging outside his gym in Philadelphia before their first fight in 1971, was acceptable. But characterizing him as an Uncle Tom, a preposterous claim that stuck all the same, was not. That, as much as their violent wars in the ring, fed his lifelong bitterness. (Getty Images)

TRAINING HDQTS.
FOR
JOE FRAZIER
HEAVYWEIGHT
CHAMPION

Ali-Frazier I was as much a fashion show as it was a heavyweight championship fight. The men turned out in an astonishing display of unusual textiles and animal hides, but the women were hardly outdone. Here, posing in the lobby of Madison Square Garden the night of the 1971 fight, the ladies flout their furs. (Getty Images)

Despite defeating Ali in their 1971 bout, **Frazier** was largely unable to capitalize on the win in the media, as he was mostly holed up in a Philadelphia hospital. Frazier claimed he was in and out, being treated for high blood pressure, but this kind of photo, hobnobbing with elderly invalids in his supposed time of triumph, did not make him look particularly invincible. And he knew it. Thereafter, "hospital" became a kind of trigger for Frazier and may have set off a later melee with Ali. (Associated Press)

Not even **Foreman**, despite his growing record of vicious knockouts, thought he had a chance against Frazier. But Archie Moore, a veteran trainer and former light-heavyweight champion, was not called the Old Mongoose for nothing. Eccentric to the max, he knew every trick in the book and imparted more than a few to his young pupil for his 1973 title bid. (Associated Press)

It's not enough to lose, but you must also look ridiculous. Here, **Frazier** goes down yet again, one of six times in his loss to Foreman, wobbling dreamily, almost comically to the canvas. **Foreman**, who had been wary of Frazier to begin with, was terrified at the way Frazier kept getting up. He didn't breath easily until the referee finally called it. (Associated Press)

Foreman made a poor initial impression in Zaire, disembarking with Daggo, his prized German shepherd. The dog was a reminder to the citizens of their recent Belgian occupation, when they were often routed by such animals. Ali, arriving earlier for their Rumble in the Jungle, had already cast Foreman as the villain, telling onlookers that Foreman was a "Belgium." (Associated Press)

Don King, the man who made the Rumble in the Jungle and then kept it together through a long postponement, rambles on at a press conference in Zaire while **Ali** grooms Bundini Brown. Bundini, who had been sprung from Sugar Ray Robinson's entourage to serve Ali, was a man of mysterious duties, more often given to hysterics than tactical advice. Still, Ali seemed to rely on him for motivation, at least when he wasn't abusing him. (Associated Press)

Foreman often thrilled onlookers with his concussive work on the heavy bag, usually lifting lead trainer Dick Sadler off his feet as the bag swung wildly. Norman Mailer, on hand in Zaire for the Ali fight, was especially amazed at dents the size of "half a watermelon." They didn't have a similarly amazing effect on Ali, though. (Associated Press)

Foreman was mostly inaccessible during his pre-fight preparation in Zaire. Often his only public appearances were at poolside at his hotel in Kinshasa where he held daily table tennis matches. Moore, who carried his paddles in a wicker basket, made sure to lose in their matches. Bill Caplan, Foreman's frustrated PR man, made sure to win. (Associated Press)

If you do not want to be called a gorilla, given Ali's talents for rhyme, you should not agree to a fight in Manila. Frazier learned this too late, as **Ali** barges in on his press conference in New York before their third fight, wearing his themed shirt. Frazier found this characterization even more odious than Ali's Uncle Tom taunts. (Associated Press)

Philippines' president Ferdinand Marcos became the next ruler to fund a heavyweight championship fight, hoping for national exposure in general and a more favorable understanding of martial law in particular. Marcos, standing between **Ali** and **Frazier** several weeks before their 1975 fight, ended up doing more for marital discord than martial law when he inadvertently drew attention to Ali's traveling mistress. (Getty Images)

Foreman may have been the trio's real success story. Not only did he come back to win a title in his forties, but he also went on to a fabulously successful career as celebrity endorser. The Foreman Grill made him far richer, and happier, than boxing ever had. (Associated Press)

Ali and **Frazier** never really reconciled, although Frazier could occasionally be coaxed into a feel-good photo, such as this one at an awards show in 2002. Frazier may have softened toward Ali closer to the end of his life but he never really forgave Ali for a career's worth of promotional slights and insults. He gleefully took credit for Ali's Parkinson's disease. (Getty Images)

photographers and officials (including a member of the US Embassy) to rush into the ring immediately after the fight, eight had their pockets picked.

Worse was yet to come. The next day, as Foreman tried to retrieve his tickets at the Pan Am counter, he was told he couldn't leave the country until he ponied up somewhere between $150,000 and $200,000 in taxes, even though the whole idea of staging it in Venezuela was to escape taxation. That had been in the original agreement. Foreman's publicist, Bill Caplan (yes, the man with the red transistor radio and Ali's scrapbook), managed to create just enough of a scene at the counter that agents agreed to give them their tickets home. But even Caplan's bellowing could not save them at passport control. "You'd better cool it," Foreman finally said to Caplan. "These guys have got guns."

Everybody was getting shaken down. Norton was also detained, unable to travel until he forked over $40,000 to cover taxes and posted another $40,000 bond to cover any income from the broadcast cut. Video Techniques was effectively given a ransom note of $50,000, in case it wanted its equipment back.

Foreman returned to the city and tried to enlist the US Embassy in his cause. For five days the ambassador tried to reach a settlement with the government, but he had very little bargaining power. Venezuela held the largest oil reserves outside of the Middle East and was a tentative supplier to the oil-strapped United States. The ambassador had very little clout. "My bosses," the man told Foreman, "tell me we can't intercede."

But Foreman wouldn't budge on Venezuela's demands. He wasn't paying. Of course, by now there were people heavily invested in his future and eager to see him somewhere other than Caracas. Video Techniques came to the fighter's aid and made up the difference, allowing Foreman to come home with his purse intact and perhaps fight again. Come home, he did. But, boy, was he mad.

—CHAPTER 14—

A LEOPARD-SKIN HAT, A MONSTER, AND MR. TOOTH DECAY

It had been more than just a sports event for several years now. Ali, able to weave personality and politics so seamlessly, had turned each of his fights into a kind of national argument. And then, given proper competition, he made a heavyweight championship fight even bigger than that, more important, too important, really, for its normal presentation. His accumulated charisma, coupled with whatever heightened jeopardy this new far-deadlier sort of opponent could bring to bear, was now enough to excite international fascination. And this fight with Foreman, who'd shown over and over an almost obscene capacity for obliteration, had almost certainly become a geopolitical affair.

After traveling the franchise to places such as Jamaica and Venezuela, it no longer seemed appropriate to stage a title fight in anything as mundane as Madison Square Garden or the Los Angeles Forum. That was never even a consideration. Ali might not be able to beat Foreman, or even survive a bout with him, but his growth as a worldwide figure demanded a bigger stage, a global venue. And it would draw more than just boxing fans. An Ali fight was available for hopes and dreams that went far beyond any idea of athletics. These were contests of global interest and maybe even consequence.

The scramble to acquire this property, quite possibly a vehicle of international improvement, was concluded quickly, when an African dictator named Joseph Mobutu, corrupt and maybe even homicidal, advanced $9.6 million from the national coffers to secure the promotion. This was an odd extravagance for Zaire, which was as often as not described as backward and impoverished (the average annual wage was $110). But Mobutu saw his involvement as a way to rebrand himself as something more than a run-of-the-mill postcolonial African dictator, or, as the French called him, "a bank vault in a leopard-skin hat." Someone more important than that other corrupt and homicidal dictator, Uganda's Idi Amin.

Mobutu had come to power during a 1965 coup, when the Belgian Congo was still enduring anarchy, civil war, and bloodshed. The country, which became known as Zaire under his rule, entered a period of stability, although its economic gains from vast reserves of natural resources tended to be channeled to his personal Swiss bank accounts, not capital improvements. He had palatial residences in each of Zaire's eight provinces, as well as in France, Belgium, and Switzerland. He had the biggest swimming pool in Africa, which gave him a bit of an edge over Idi Amin in their imaginary rivalry. And he had his own national airline, Air Zaire, to ferry him and his family to Paris shopping trips (which proved disruptive to the airline's schedule).

He was a man of some vanity, as you'd suspect of someone with nicknames such as "le Guide" and "le Clairvoyant," not to mention one moniker that translated to "the all-powerful warrior who, because of his endurance and will to win, will go from contest to contest, leaving fire in his wake." So alignment with an event of this stature would confer much-deserved fame and respectability. To personally host an event such as this, in other words, would put a feather in his leopard-skin hat. Even if it was coming at personal sacrifice. Because, face it, whatever money he was paying for the fight was being diverted from his Swiss bank accounts.

Still, it would never have happened except for Don King. He had remained at Video Techniques, the promoter-for-hire during all these international escapades (it fronted for the governments of Jamaica and Venezuela), as a "black presence." He had no title or, really, definite job. When the Zaire fight was announced, one day after the Foreman-Norton fight in Caracas, King's name wasn't even on the press release (which caused him to wad it in a ball and throw it across the room). But he had been far more than just a "black presence." He'd signed the two fighters, after all.

Ali had been the first order of business, and he required all of King's flaming rhetoric, separating him from his longtime promoter, Bob Arum. At the time, Arum was negotiating for another Ali-Quarry fight, which would have paid $850,000. But King was promising a far greater, if somewhat mysterious, sum. It was hard to believe he could produce a letter of credit for $5 million in just one month. And where was Zaire, anyway? "This isn't just another fight," he boomed to Ali, during their meeting in Chicago. "Consider the monumental magnitude, the symbolic impact. Your regaining your title would do more for the cause of freedom and justice and equality than anything."

Ali and his manager, Herbert Muhammad, probably didn't think he could come through, but nevertheless gave him permission to try. Just get Foreman aboard. "Here's an opportunity to re-gain what was stolen," King boomed anew. "Your crown." Fine, they said. Just get Foreman. You have two days.

King flew to California and found Foreman far more practical than Ali, less moved by his oratory than the possibility of an under-hand contract that would shield his payday from divorce lawyers. The two shook hands on that sneaky little ploy in an Oakland park-ing lot at midnight. He had gotten Foreman. The fight was on.

Nobody really inquired of the promotion, wondered why the jewel of American sport was being transported to darkest Africa. It made no sense, not a bit. Did it really matter that one of the coun-try's most important sporting events—the most, if one went by Ali's numbers—would be held in Mobutu's empire of cruelty and deceit? It was best not to ask. Back home in the United States, the citizens were recovering from the single most wrenching upheaval in their civic history. President Nixon, no longer able to withstand the repercussions from Watergate, his entirely needless and paranoid exercise in burglary hobbling his presidency, resigned in early August. It was unprecedented, but inevitable. A country's own corruption had to be accounted for and, if possible, corrected. Still, it was reasonable to ask, could things get any worse than this? The United States was suffering an "economic migraine" to go with the political nausea; inflation was raging so high that many felt the country was about to plunge into a depression, the economic jumping-out-of-a-window kind. A Gallup poll found that nearly half the respondents thought America was about to revisit the economic disaster of the '30s.

The fight at least offered the opportunity, no matter where it was held, for a fairness that just didn't seem available politically. Whatever happened in the ring would be just, transparent, and conclusive. Say what you will about boxing, but it does offer a moral clarity.

Still, the fight, which was scheduled for September 25 in Kinshasa, was an oddity all around. Nobody in Africa cared about boxing. Nor, probably, did anybody care about American music. King's idea to add a three-day music festival in advance of the fight, with performers such as James Brown and B. B. King, felt well intentioned but widely off the mark. Not many in Zaire would be attracted by the Spinners. And it seemed terribly optimistic that thirty thousand foreign visitors, as King was predicting, would be buying any of the $2,500 flight-fight packages the promoters were offering. It's true, most of the money would come from closed-circuit TV. But still, this was, all in all, a mainly artificial production, the staging just a way to produce the paydays the fighters demanded, and the publicity Mobutu needed. Otherwise, it was an altogether inconvenient exercise. The fight needed to go off at 3:00 a.m. to accommodate the real viewers, the ones in the rest of the world.

And, really, what kind of fight were we talking about? Ali had been talking about retirement anyway, hanging his gloves up at the age of thirty-two. He told a visiting reporter at Deer Lake that he'd go through with the Foreman fight and believed that "God has set him up for me." But he no longer seemed that enthusiastic about boxing, or a continued career in it. It no longer seemed worth it. "People bet and lose their houses on me when I fight and lose," he said. "It's a fact that people die of heart attacks every time I fight. It's not right. Too serious. No fun. Whole countries, sad. The women in Egypt cry. Me, the greatest fighter of all time, losing. How could I lose. Me losing? The king of Egypt said it was the second worst thing that ever happened to him."

He seemed, even as he pronounced Foreman easy prey, to be anticipating one more loss, another bad night in Egypt. Certainly, everybody else was. Foreman was a huge favorite off the Norton performance. When the Ali fight was announced in Caracas, a reporter asked Foreman's trainer, Dick Sadler, how he saw the upcoming fight. "Briefly," he said. "I've had a chance to mold and create a monster."

This was the prevailing sentiment. The *New York Times*'s Dave Anderson had written that "sooner or later, the champion will land one of his sledgehammer punches, and for the first time in his career, Muhammad Ali will be counted out. That could happen in the very first round." The view was seconded on the West Coast, where the *Los Angeles Times*'s Jim Murray was writing, "He doesn't fight you, he mugs you. His fights are as one-sided as a shark bite. Whatever he hits, clots."

Even Ali's pal Howard Cosell thought it was shaping up as a mismatch. He led off one of his shows with a commentary that, if you just happened to be passing the TV and were uncertain of context, you would have assumed was a eulogy. "The time may have come to say good-bye to Muhammad Ali," the yellow blazer was saying,

> because, very honestly, I don't think he can beat George Foreman. It's hard for me as a reporter to be totally objective in this case because Muhammad Ali has been a significant factor in my

own career. I thought, before he was idled for three and a half years, he was the best fighter I've ever seen. I still think he's a remarkable athlete and one can never put anything beyond him. Maybe he can pull off a miracle. But against George Foreman, so young, so strong, so fearless? Against George Foreman, who does away with his opponents one after another in less than three rounds? It's hard for me to conjure with that.

Even the Ali camp was wary. Dundee had brought in Eddie (Bossman) Jones from Foreman's camp as a sparring partner. This was done all the time, sparring partners circulating from camp to camp, so interchangeable there was never a hint of treason or of covert operations. Ali often sparred with Larry Holmes, a near doppelgänger in the ring. Frazier recognized as much and hired him away from Ali for their second fight. Ali had no problem with that. But Bossman, he might just have some interesting intelligence. The day he got to Deer Lake, the camp crowded around him for a scouting report. "George is the first I been with in the ring I know can kill you," he said. This was exciting news. Furthermore, he said, Foreman possessed a particularly brutal weapon in his "anywhere punch." The way Bossman described it to the group, Foreman would throw a punch he wasn't "aiming anywhere," but "anywhere" it landed, "it breaks something inside you."

They all went to Africa anyway, the fighters to get their share of Mobutu loot, the press to enjoy another expenses-paid caper. And, in a sense, the world went along with them all. Some acclimated quicker than others. Ali made an early gaffe when, in some trademark diatribe, he'd promised Stateside reporters that any doubters, as soon as they got to Africa, "Mobutu's people gonna put you in a pot, cook you and eat you." Zaire's foreign minister called Ali at Deer Lake immediately, reminding him that "we're not cannibals" and that "we're doing the fight to create trade and help our country, and Mr. Ali's remarks are damaging our image." Left unsaid, but understood all the same: and we're paying you $5 million.

Ali got onboard quickly. He departed from New York—where he told a TV reporter, in a strange aside, that the most pressing job at hand was "to whip Mr. Tooth Decay"—and immediately began extolling the beauties of African culture. By the time he was on the Air Zaire flight into Kinshasa, he was rounding into form, marveling at the idea of black pilots. "Strange to the American negro," he said. Stranger, they could speak three languages. French from the time of Belgian occupation, English just because, and, of course, African. "We can't even speak English that good."

Ali joked to the mob of reporters, all veterans of many such campaigns, that while he was glad to see those black pilots, he was sure that, once they got the plane in the air, a white pilot came out of a closet to do the real flying.

Once on the tarmac, arriving in the predawn hours, well before Foreman was scheduled to land—Ali was shrewder than that—he surveyed the massive crowd there to greet him and became determined to use his time advantage over Foreman and establish new ground rules. As usual he was surrounded by nearly fifty of his "hard-charging followers," but the one he counted on most was right by his side, Gene Kilroy. "Who do blacks hate most?" he asked him. Kilroy said, uncertainly, "Whites?"

Ali thought. "I can't say George Foreman is a white man," although he had more or less said that of Joe Frazier in their previous meetings. "Who else they hate?" Kilroy thought again. Remembering the Congo's history of bloody occupation, police dogs routing the citizens, he offered, again uncertainly, "Belgians?"

Ali got off the plane, and in the twilight he greeted the masses below him. "George Foreman," he announced, "is a Belgium." And the crowd went wild.

In fact, Zaire was not originally interested in taking sides, even if Ali did have the higher profile. It was enough that two black men had returned to the source continent and were about to spread the word of black glory. Signs along the roads in Kinshasa made the point, careful to suggest who the real architect of world understanding was. "A fight between two blacks in a black nation organized by blacks and seen by the world: This is the victory of Mobutuism."

Ali was Mobutuism's greatest spokesman, articulating his home country's presumed surprise at such advancement. "All we see of Africa is a bunch of natives leading white men on a safari, and maybe one of the white men is trapped by a gorilla and the natives save him," he said. "We never get shown African cars and African boats and African jet planes." He added, "I used to think Africans were savages. But now that I'm here, I've learned that many Africans are wiser than we are."

Foreman, for his part, had good intentions, just poor instincts. Plus, as any of the previous foes might have reminded him, he was not Ali. Whereas he normally gave no indication that crowd support mattered to him, he appeared this time unusually anxious to win over the locals. This was a welcome and surprising diplomacy, coming from him. In interviews leading up to the fight, he emphasized just how appropriate the site was, especially for two black fighters. "Africa is the cradle of civilization," he said, trying to beat back the notion that Ali ought to be installed as the hometown favorite. "Everybody's home is Africa." He wasn't quite as enthusiastic as Ali on the topic, but it seemed that tiny heart of his was at least in the right place.

So what did he do? What initial and insurmountable impression did he make? How did he forfeit the entire public relations campaign and do it within a minute of arrival? With a crowd gathered to meet him, a band of tribal dancers banging away on drums, and Don King in what would become his African uniform (a brightly colored dashiki) shouting from the tarmac, Foreman stepped forth to greet this wonderful nation with a huge German shepherd at his side, the kind of animal that was once used in crowd control, a vicious reminder of their occupied past. The crowd gasped as Daggo pranced into their midst. Was it possible? Was it just like Ali had said? Was Foreman a "Belgium"?

CHAPTER 15

NUCLEAROLOGY, A PICNIC BASKET, AND JUDGE CRAVEN

Whether it had been the offense of the dog, or just the necessary logistics of finding so many places for so many people, Zaire officials settled the Foreman camp in a military encampment well outside of Kinshasa. Well beyond even the presidential compound in N'Sele, where the Ali camp was stationed in relative luxury. It was not the squalor to which so many of the citizens were accustomed. But it wasn't championship splendor, either. Guards stared down upon the entourage from towers, the whole thing ringed in barbed wire, nobody in or out unless a large military pike at the road was raised for them. A public address system broadcast native music or military announcements at all hours of the day. There were no showers in any of the five little houses assigned them. And nobody in their right mind would endure a bath; lizards hung from the tiled ceilings above them.

Also, the food was bad. Foreman's cook, try as he might, could not find the necessary ingredients for a decent cheeseburger. Even as Foreman was telling people he'd returned to his birthplace, he was realizing, to considerable discomfort, that he was very far from home.

Foreman was falling into the same trap that eventually collected all Ali opponents, stung by his words, their images warped beyond recognition, and entire populations turned against them. Now everything seemed a slight of massive proportions. And there was no way to fight back perception. That was a condition of fighting Ali, it seemed. You no longer had a voice. Everywhere he went, children were marching through the streets, chanting a new national anthem: Ali, *bomaye*! Ali, *bomaye*! Foreman was disheartened to learn that they were exhorting Ali to kill him. Kill him? It was absurd; he was the killer. More than that, it just seemed inhospitable, impolite.

There wasn't anything he liked about this country. That any among them liked. Sadler, as soon as his feet hit African soil, hinted at the party's general distaste for the experience. "I'd rather be in a hospital bed in Hayward," he said. It might as well have been the camp slogan.

Foreman could not arrest the rolling movement for Ali. That advantage had been seized early, and there was no getting it back. But he could at least get better digs. A week into his confinement, he marched into the Intercontinental Hotel, Kinshasa's newest, where the press was staying, lolling about a vast and serene lobby, comparing their notes. He invited himself up to Don King's suite there, where the "black presence" was more and more passing himself off as the promoter of record, surveyed the accommodations, and calmly announced, "This is mine."

If he was any more comfortable, he was no happier. Now he was simply closer to the swelling Ali sentiment, surrounded actually. Amateur bands collected in the hotel parking lot, the steel drums sounding rhythms that Foreman began to regard as a national mockery. To the extent that the people of Zaire were against him, he was now face-to-face with more and more of them. It was dispiriting.

But endurable, of course. He might be suffering in this strange and unfriendly land, but it wouldn't be much longer before he retired the Ali myth and could move past these constant affronts. Foreman understood that, while he was the undefeated champion, he could not truly expect much in the way of popularity or even attention until he'd disposed of Ali. And even then, Ali would never be absolutely gone. "I can beat him and knock him out in the first or second round," he said. "But that doesn't mean that people are going to follow me with the same enthusiasm as they did him. It's just something God gave him to have."

Nobody attending his workouts in N'Sele, where the two camps shared training quarters, doubted whether Foreman would knock Ali out. Ali would always have his charisma, but it would be useless against Foreman's brute force. Writer Norman Mailer, who'd come over to give the bout some literary sheen, marveled at the sight of Foreman on the heavy bag. "One of the more prodigious sights I've had in my life." He couldn't believe the indentations the slugger was leaving—"dents the size of half a watermelon," he reported. Everybody was remarking on the experience, especially enjoying the work of Sadler, who clung desperately to the bag, lifted off his feet with every punch, to swing helplessly from the same chain.

But that's what Archie Moore had been saying all along, right? "He not only has TNT in his mitts, but nuclearology as well. Even if Foreman misses with a punch, the whoosh of air will lower the temperature in the air very considerably."

All Foreman had to do was stay the course, remain patient, take what was rightfully his. It was just a matter of days. He could scratch them off a calendar, like a man doing time. Ten more to go. Nine. Now . . .

With just eight days to go, James Brown and his Revue already on their way, the five hundred workers polishing up the sixty-thousand-seat outdoor arena, the weedy median along Kinshasa's main boulevard planted with flowers, new streetlights installed and city buildings scrubbed and painted, Ali promising how he'd dance and dance, a flight of late-arriving sportswriters just then changing planes in Luxembourg—with eight days to go, the fight was postponed.

Foreman was sparring, a sight only slightly less spectacular than pummeling the heavy bag, when his partner had thrown up his elbows in self-defense. Foreman rushed right into them and collected one of those elbows on his right eyebrow, opening a long gash. It wouldn't have mattered—the gash was that long—but Foreman, afraid of needles (he'd screamed, "Oh, mama!" when the doctor had given him his shot for international travel back at the Minerals and Gems Exhibition Hall), insisted on a butterfly bandage. The only true repair would come with rest, so much rest that the fight had to be rescheduled for October 30, six weeks out, at the onset of the monsoon season.

The repercussions were immense. The most immediate among them, the Telex lines went down and journalists were unable to transmit the news for hours. "You must not publicize this," insisted Bula Mandungu, the man whom Mobutu had put in charge. "It will be improperly understood in your country. This cut is nothing. I suggest you forget about this story. Go for a swim."

The story eventually got out, the journalists back from their swim. Those late-arriving sportswriters, including the *Los Angeles Times*'s Jim Murray and the *Washington Post*'s Shirley Povich, got the news in Luxembourg and beat a path back to the gate for an immediate trip home. They were not cub reporters. But nobody else was so smart or so lucky. The performers continued in for Zaire 74, as the concert was called, and gave the show as scheduled, to a sparse and somewhat perplexed crowd. Tourists who'd already made the trip were stranded; tourists who hadn't yet deferred departure. And neither Ali nor Foreman, by national decree, was allowed out of the country. If they were so much as to cross the Congo, confidence in this already surreal promotion would be destroyed.

Misery ensued. Ali continued to campaign, rallying even more people to his cause, but privately he was grousing about the enforced delay. At first he wanted Foreman to go ahead with the fight anyway. Then he thought of flying Frazier in, giving him $1 million as a substitute. Nobody was buying any of it, of course. He reconciled himself to Foreman and the postponement but was never happy about it. "I'd give anything to be training in the United States," he told members of his camp. "They got ice cream there, and pretty girls and miniskirts."

Foreman wasn't sure he could take it. He'd been going day to day anyway and now, six more weeks. Like Ali, he missed his sweet treats: "ice cream and snow cones." He lobbied to go back to Paris and train there, but Zaire officials were having none of that. They were sure if they let him out, he'd never come back. They were right. In fact, to make the point that the fight was still on, Mobutu delivered a radio address that night and announced a rally, which both fighters would attend, for the next day. About seventy thousand showed up for one of Mobutu's two-hour speeches.

The fighters settled back into their routines, preparing for a long haul. Ali continued to hone his shtick. "George Foreman is nothing but a big mummy," he told his crowds. "I've officially named him the mummy." Whenever Foreman worked out, Ali made sure to heckle him through the concrete lattice. Foreman never took it seriously. He had adored Ali growing up and still thought he was nothing but fun, when the two could get together outside the ring. But Foreman never considered Ali "that swift," and was always able to shrug off the poetry, the comedy, anything Ali tossed at him. Ali wanted to be great; Foreman wanted "to earn my money and go home."

Now that he was residing in the Intercontinental, where the remaining press mingled, he was a source of more or less daily interest. Ali gave press conferences at the drop of a hat, but Foreman refused almost all interview requests. He told his PR man, Bill Caplan, that he might—might!—do interviews on Tuesdays and Thursdays, but he shouldn't count on it.

In fact, he not only was not talking to the media, but wasn't talking to Caplan, either. Caplan would jot down interview requests on a piece of paper—"Be at the Intercontinental at 9 a.m. for a press conference. Signed. Your press agent"—and attempt to get it to Foreman as he passed through the lobby. Sometimes he'd read it; sometimes he'd crumple it up unread and just throw it on the floor.

The curious thing, apart from Foreman's insistence upon impersonating Liston in the first place, was that Caplan and Foreman, without much of a working relationship, still maintained a daily table-tennis date. The whole entourage was crazy for it. Archie Moore was a strange presence anyway, in his wool yachting cap, bright trousers, the legs tucked into his socks. But, on top of that, he was always carrying a wicker picnic basket—Little Red Riding Hood style—that contained his various paddles. He'd play Foreman on the table by the pool and was careful to let the champion win.

Caplan, however, showed no such consideration. He'd been Foreman's biggest supporter, never mind his official duties, and now was embittered by the treatment he was getting in return. He didn't deserve this. He beat Foreman every day. "Let the big man win once in a while," Moore pleaded with him. Caplan refused. And every day Foreman met him at the pool, in each case their fury and resolve redoubled.

The number of writers was growing again as they started to trickle back to Africa. A few had remained during the postponement. Some of them were foreign correspondents, for whom one dateline was as good as the next. John Vinocur of the Associated Press had stayed and filled the otherwise uneventful evenings with yarns of exotic places. Horst Faas, the AP photographer who'd done much to document the horror of the Vietnam War, stayed on, too. He was another welcome raconteur.

Also in attendance was Hunter Thompson, whose book on the Hells Angels, and later the classic *Fear and Loathing in Las Vegas*, had propelled him into a career of counterculture journalism at *Rolling Stone*. The editor there, Jann Wenner, was always on the lookout for a suitable assignment for his star writer, and he was sure the so-called Rumble in the Jungle (though never called that in Zaire) was just the ticket. Thompson mostly seemed bored by the assignment and amused himself by composing fake messages for the bellboy to strut through the lobby. Thus, calls had apparently been made to such guests as "Martin Borman" and "Judge Craven." Sometimes, though, he was stirred to industry. Thompson gave his colleagues the impression he was conducting many adventures that were possibly unrelated to the fight. They would see him setting out for someplace with purpose, yet never saw him at press conferences or training sessions.

One writer who hadn't returned was the *New York Post*'s Larry Merchant. He'd actually been on the plane with Ali the first trip over, Ali telling him, "If he doesn't get me in seven, his parachute won't open." Merchant wasn't sure what to make of the comment and never got around to asking in Zaire. Instead, he'd done a couple of columns critical of both King and Mobutu, a "bread and circuses" column, ridiculing Mobutu for thinking this is what nations do to increase tourism, and then Foreman got cut and he went home. He wasn't sure which column did it, but when he tried to board his flight at JFK Airport in New York for his return to Africa, somebody from the US Embassy approached him and told him he wouldn't be welcome in Zaire. He could get on the plane, but he wouldn't get off. He didn't get on.

A lot of others did and, once back in their headquarters at the Intercontinental, were finding Foreman almost delightfully inscrutable. He was almost more interesting when he didn't talk than when he did speak. Whole columns were spun from scenes of Foreman reading a Superman comic in the lobby. A stray comment, if one was lucky enough to catch one, might verge onto a multipart series. One time a writer came face-to-face with Foreman and, obliged to take the opportunity for a sudden Q&A, asked him what he had been dreaming about. Foreman, equally surprised by the encounter, was uncharacteristically civil and answered that he recently dreamed he was teaching a dog how to ice skate. The writer took this information back to the lobby, and the press corps chewed it over for a long time.

It was far easier to talk to Foreman's entourage. Sadler was a reliable quote, but nobody was better than Moore. The writers felt it was a shame that Moore wasn't a principal, because he delivered his observations in the form of finished paragraphs. For example, he dismissed Ali's winning rhetoric in one fell swoop: "It had become timeworn, an act as thin as a Baltimore pimp's patent leather shoes."

If Foreman wasn't recounting fugue states, or if Moore was unavailable, there was always King. He was everywhere, it seemed, as if his availability certified his role as acting promoter. In fact, he was the man holding this together, controlling the crisis while the official promoters were back in New York. In any case, his personality was in full flower, as was his hair. For this promotion he had groomed his previously large Afro into an even more voluminous and subsequently signature upsweep—Mailer decided he looked like a man who had just dropped down an elevator shaft—and was modeling a vast wardrobe of bright dashikis as well. That alone would get most writers a column. But his ready reiteration of the classics also proved endlessly fascinating.

He dismissed the postponement in Shakespearean terms. "We must look at the bright side of things," he said. "Adversity is ugly and venomous like a toad, yet wears a precious jewel in her head." Everybody wrote that down. King was predicting that the fight would now escalate from merely "colossal" to "supercolossal." They wrote that down, too.

Here was a promoter, after all, who was delivering copy-ready quotes, at the merest provocation. Nobody could characterize an event as routine as a boxing match with such grandiosity. "Two prodigal sons returning home to the land of their heritage," he began, "the womb from which they sprang, which would be of symbolic impact around the world—a black promoter, two black gladiators fighting on a black venue." Quite a bit more important, in other words, than a heavyweight title fight.

Even Mailer became a target of his rhetorical extravagance. Meeting the novelist, King said, "You are a genius in tune with the higher consciousness, yet an instinctive exponent of the untiring search for aspiration in the warm earth embracing potential of exploited peoples." Normally, Mailer made up his own mouthfuls, but this one he wrote down.

And, of course, there was Ali. Nobody could make the time pass like Ali. He was as impatient as anybody but understood his role fully and delivered, his poetry now grown from previous limerick length to epic form. For one press conference he unspooled a quite long ode called "A Bad Morning Shave." Shorter ones appeared in more spontaneous circumstances: "You think the world was shocked when Nixon resigned? / Wait till I whup George Foreman's behind."

He may have had other, less well-known, preoccupations in Zaire. Ali had been a slow starter in the romance department. Reportedly, his first kiss sent him into a deep faint. He was sixteen. Singer Lloyd Price remembers meeting the young man in Louisville about the same time. He introduced himself as the Golden Gloves champion of Louisville and asked the singer how to make out with girls. Even after his Olympic gold medal he was too shy to make a proper advance toward US sprinter Wilma Rudolph. She thought he was the most bashful boy she'd ever met. Since becoming heavyweight champion of the world, however, he'd become more confident.

As part of the promotion, a Los Angeles radio station had run a contest to pick four poster girls for the trip to Zaire. Ali had already picked out Veronica Porsche, having spotted the tall Creole at a press conference in Salt Lake City. In Zaire she had been one of the two girls assigned to Foreman's camp, a condition he meant to remedy. Word came to Foreman that Ali wanted to work a trade. "Please," Foreman told the PR man, "leave 'em all over there." He couldn't believe Ali was "idiot enough to mess with a woman" in the weeks before the fight. But he'd seen Ali in action before, how a pretty girl could just render him senseless. Foreman couldn't get over it. "Like he wasn't used to pretty girls," he thought. "A good looking guy, but a pretty girl drove him nuts."

Ali's affair with Veronica, who was most definitely a pretty girl, was driving his wife nuts. Belinda was a stolid type, a Muslim wife more in the homemaker mold, who'd grown to tolerate her husband's wanderings. But while in Zaire, with the family livelihood on the line, here was Ali messing about with a Los Angeles poster girl. She caught her husband coming back to the Intercontinental late with Veronica. She scratched Ali up a bit and might have done the same to Veronica if she hadn't fled so quickly.

Didn't he have a bigger fight than this coming up?

CHAPTER 16

CHICKEN CLAWS, MOZAMBIQUE, AND A CONVERTIBLE CADILLAC

One person, maybe the only one in all of Zaire, who didn't see the Rumble in the Jungle was Hunter Thompson. He'd heard that Mobutu was going to watch the fight at one of his presidential palaces and had decided his *Rolling Stone* readers would be better served by an account at such a royal remove. He told George Plimpton, who was on assignment for *Sports Illustrated* again (but who would watch at ringside), "That's the place to be. Hobnobbing with his nibs, and the generals all standing around, scraping, and mixing drinks and so forth, and the president and I rocking to and fro on our heels and looking at the TV and conversing about things in general."

It never happened. And as the other scribes began making their way to the stadium in the midnight hour—the fight was now rescheduled for 4:00 a.m.—Thompson, who had long since given his credential away, gathered the tools of his trade, which were a bucket of ice, a bottle of liquor, and a pack of Dunhills, and retired to the hotel pool.

Except for the spectacle of sixty thousand moonlit people, including the *feticheurs* who led their clients in humming incantations and who dangled chicken claws and other tools of sorcery, in the huge outdoor arena (an immense picture of Mobutu hovered above it all; he was indeed watching it at a palace), Thompson did not expect to miss much. Even with Ali at the controls of the propaganda machine, and for an extended period at that, the sentiment that he was doing little more than a ring walk to his execution could not be nudged. The tourists, uninspired by such a one-sided match, never materialized (about a hundred out of an expected fifteen thousand had arrived, their seats given at reduced rates to the locals). Foreman's youth, his brute force, his record against such opponents as Frazier and Norton qualified him as a one-man epidemic. There was nothing that could survive him. "As we go to the stadium at that unreal hour," wrote Hugh McIlvanney, sounding a somber note in his prefight column, "we shall be hoping for a miracle but dreading a calamity."

Ali, perhaps pandering to the opinion that he had only one hope of beating Foreman, had been reminding his fans, and even his vast entourage, that he intended to dance the night away, until Foreman simply collapsed from the effort to engage. "Lean, step in, pop-pop-pop, and then step out," he'd promised. It seemed a relatively safe strategy, if not a plan that could actually return his championship. In fact, the writers had announced him as a 3–1 underdog. However, if he could devise a tactic that might save his life, his fans and entourage, and all the witch doctors who had been retained on his behalf, would be much encouraged.

The mood in his dressing room in those predawn hours was so gloomy that he finally had to address it. "What's wrong around here?" he asked. "Everybody scared?" They were. "Scared?" he said again. "A little thing like this? Nothing much scares me. Horror films scare me. Mummies scare me. I also fear Allah, thunderstorms and bad plane rides. But this is like another day in the gym."

It was comforting to his clan to see him this way. He even conducted a sort of fashion show, preening in his new white robe. "Look how long and beautiful it is," he'd said. "It's African. Everybody can look at it and tell it's African." This was true, but it was also true that Bundini derived additional income from his own robe designing, usually selling it afterward, once its appearance in the ring transformed it into a collectible. Bundini's loyalty could be clouded by only one thing, the possibility for profit. He'd already made a bundle on thousands of Ali buttons he'd had made for 14 cents and was retailing for $6. The robe—his robe, the one with a map of Africa on it—ought to sell nicely, too, but here was Ali modeling this new, other, outfit.

Which he preferred. "Look how much better this one looks," he commanded Bundini. Bundini, feeling like his pocket had just been picked, refused to look. "You look when I tell you," Ali said, slapping Bundini once, and then again. This had happened so many times in periods of stress, nobody in the room paid much attention, except to experience a reassurance that all was normal after all. "Now," Ali said, prefight conditions restored to the default mode, "let's rumble in the jungle!"

Foreman was enjoying his own version of calm. He had been badly shaken two days before the fight by a dream, one that did not involve either ice skates or a dog. In the dream, all the people of Africa were chasing him. In the dream, he had lost the fight. It was unnerving. First the cut, testing his notion of invincibility. And now this dream. The people chasing him seemed to be from Mozambique, which struck him as odd and frightening and full of mysterious portent. He'd never heard the word before in his life.

But here in the dressing room, with Sadler and Moore messing about, he was more relaxed than he'd ever been for a fight. For previous bouts he'd been so scared and so nervous—"like having a nightmare"—that he wondered if such a career could be for him. He'd be scared the opponent "could do this, or that." The fear was unendurable. He'd think, "I'll never box again." He'd go through with this fight, but never again. "Can't live like that." Yet on this night, for the first time in his life, he was completely without anxiety. He felt nothing at all. He stretched out on a rubbing table, completely still. "This is the way I want to feel," he thought. "If I can feel like this, I'll box forever."

There were no corresponding histrionics among the Foreman camp. It was full of confidence. When Dr. Pacheco finally got into the dressing room to inspect the opponent's wraps, he was surprised to see Foreman just lying there, covered in towels, the only thing visibly human beneath them his eyes. Nobody was worried about this fight.

Ali tried to renew his psychological advantage at the introductions, peppering Foreman with various warnings. "Chump," he told him, "you're gonna get beat in front of all these Africans." He didn't let up, talking over the referee's instructions, just mouthing away. "He's doomed," he said finally. This did not seem to have any effect on Foreman and probably none on Bundini, who stood behind Ali, rubbing his shoulders, doubtful as ever. His whispered appraisal of Foreman was not meant to inspire. "That's some mean looking man," he told Dundee.

And, then, finally it began. After nearly two months in Africa, after the postponement and the enforced stay, the fight was here. It seemed a miracle it was even happening after all that. Certainly, it was a miracle it was happening before the rainy season, an African storm sweeping off the Congo River and knocking the whole promotion out. Tourist interest had never recovered after the interruption, and who knew how many had stayed away, worried about the change of seasons. But for those who'd crammed the Stade du 20 Mai, even if most of them were from Kinshasa and not the keenest of boxing fans, there was definitely a charge in the night air. Two big men, one of them lethal and the other a former champion of irresistible charm, were now facing off in the middle of a ring.

At the bell Ali behaved as expected, trying to box a bit but taking some shots, too. Foreman, too, behaved as expected, shrugging them off and just plodding forward, winging those "anywhere" punches. He was indiscriminate in their delivery, as if he had plenty to spare. Large, round punches. It would take just one.

Ali seemed to realize that standing in the middle of the ring with Foreman was not a long-term proposition. The "pop-pop-pop" offense might have to be reconsidered. Coming out for the second round, he first roused the crowd into their "Ali, *bomaye!*" chants, then almost immediately retired to the ropes, leaning way back, as if consigned to his fate. It was horrible to watch. It was suicide by boxer. Foreman stepped forth, obligingly, and whanged away, no fear of reprisal. Why couldn't he have dreamed this? That Ali, that charismatic butterfly, would undergo a reverse metamorphosis? He'd turned into a heavy bag, and Foreman punched him side to side, Ali seeming to swing from a chain. The picture couldn't have been more complete if Sadler had been hanging onto Ali for the pendulous ride, just like in training.

For anybody truly paying attention, this was a remarkable turn of events. Plimpton shouted "It's a fix!" to Mailer next to him.

The Ali corner was similarly dumbfounded. "What you doing?" he was asked between rounds. "Why don't you dance? You got to dance."

Ali told them all to shut up. "Don't talk," he said. "I know what I'm doing."

Dundee didn't fully understand the strategy. His plan had been for Ali to dance for five or six rounds, then take a tiring Foreman apart with his jab. Seeing this, he "felt sick." But he largely shut up. Bundini continued to scream for Ali to "dance," but that just wasn't happening. Ali backed into the ropes and submitted to Foreman's pummeling. By the third round the Ali camp was willing to see how this might play out. After all, the big man's punches had not killed him. "They're not that bad," Ali said.

The Foreman camp was as pleased as could be. They had trained the big man, expecting it to take big effort, to maneuver Ali into just such a place. Cutting off the ring, overpowering Ali—the whole idea was to get Ali on the ropes. Sadler surveyed the situation and liked it. "A bird's nest was on the ground," he thought. The only thing that remained? "You tuck your napkin under your chin."

By the fourth round, no deviation in the plan, if there ever was a plan, Ali began yapping at Foreman. "Show me something," he said. "That's a sissy punch." But he was looking less and less like a bird's nest on the ground.

Foreman faced a growing prospect. Every barrage that failed to destroy Ali was returned to him as a failure, a predictor of his own collapse. That power he'd inherited from Liston and had groomed so viciously as a champion was gone. The cut! That's what did it! "The magic was gone," he thought. "I've been deserted." The man with an "anywhere" punch, the man whose practiced cruelty had always been a given, was naked in the ring. Ali would not succumb to his power, easily absorbing the punches with his arms. And he had no alternative plan. What was he going to do? Box? Jab? Hold? He'd never held anybody in his life. He wouldn't have even known where to grab.

Archie Moore watched this from the corner, recognizing the very same defense he'd used in his long career. He knew about conserving energy, blocking shots, until the opponent had finally depleted his arsenal, and then striking. "Oh, no, you beautiful thief," he cried from the corner. "I know what you're doing." Ali had deployed Moore's old "turtle shell" defense, which he'd shown Ali all those years ago in San Diego. He even understood the use of the ropes, Ali tall enough to remove his most valuable target, his head, well over ringside. "Ali swayed so far back on the ropes," he realized, "that it was like he was sitting in an old convertible Cadillac. The '54 model."

Dundee started to get a handle on the strategy as well. So this is what Ali had meant on that plane trip. Foreman's parachute wasn't opening. He was plunging into exhaustion, falling, falling. He was throwing a punch at a time, no longer even moving his head. He had not taken a beating at all, not really tagged, yet he began to look slightly dazed as he continued to whale away, a windup toy whose sprung coil was slowly giving out. It looked as he'd suffered all that punishment, not Ali. Robotically, he moved forward, Ali grown smug in his strategy, just taking it.

By the eighth round even the most casual observer understood what had happened. Foreman was so completely out of gas, so punched out, that it appeared he might simply pitch forward out of his own exhaustion. Still, he continued his assault, even though he realized it had grown harmless. And then, toward the end of the round, Foreman fell slightly off balance—he just seemed to be staggering around at this point—and Ali caught him flush with a right hand.

It was important to remember, and few had, that Ali was a big and powerful man himself. Not like Foreman, certainly. But he was a heavyweight boxer, his six-foot-three frame capable of concussive leverage from time to time, his right hand possessing surprising force. Foreman did a sort of pirouette, as if he were screwing himself into the canvas for some reason. "Oh, Lawdy!" Bundini screamed at ringside. "He on queer street!" Down Foreman went—no, this is the image—as if circling a drain. Wait, one more image, this from Mailer: "His mind was held with magnets high as his championship and his body was seeking the ground. He went over like a six-foot 60-year-old butler who has just heard tragic news, yes, fell over all of a long, collapsing two seconds." Ali stood above him and had his right cocked if it was necessary—"a wholly intimate escort to the floor," thought Mailer—but he realized immediately he'd thrown the last punch of the night. This was over.

Had it been an act of improvisational genius? Or just a spontaneous reaction, a visible manifestation of the survival instinct? It didn't matter. Ali was champion again, about ten years after he'd beaten Liston the first time, about four since he'd returned from his exile. Maybe it had been the most exaggerated form of patience ever witnessed, a calculated redemption, all the more satisfying for the preposterous conditions in which it was gained. Maybe this was all part of some cosmic plan, to return Ali's title in the most theatrical way possible. Poor Foreman was just a stage presence, a big fool, an overly dramatic obstacle that made Ali's reward all the more deserved. It was, in any case, a big surprise.

Foreman, who was led from the arena in a blue towel, had definitely not been prepared for the result. He was hurt, of course, but above all perplexed. Back in his dressing room he wondered where his dog was. His handlers got him back on the rubbing table, where he quietly reposed. He began counting backward from one hundred and then, as if to further demonstrate his rapid response from the concussion, rattled off the twenty-one members of his entourage.

That seemed to trigger something in him, something he had been meaning to redress.

"I have a statement to make," he announced, the press who had gained entry to the steam bath of his dressing room now readying their pens. "I found true friendship tonight. I found a true friend in Bill Caplan." Bill Caplan? The scorned press agent? The man who beat him every afternoon at table tennis? The writers looked at each other, silently registering the effects of brain injury, or fatigue, or just the catastrophic blow of an unexpected defeat. Caplan nearly fainted.

Foreman continued, but was hardly more lucid. "He won," he said, "but I cannot admit that he beat me. It's never been said that I have been knocked out." Perhaps he wasn't neurologically damaged, just trying to find a way out of his humiliation. "When the competition is tough, there is never a loser. No fighter should be a winner. Both should be applauded." The press grew uncomfortable as if they were guilty of journalistic rubbernecking. It didn't seem right to linger, as if taking professional advantage of a man's personal disintegration. They backed out.

Ali and his group motored back to the compound in N'Sele, the skies having just opened up. A monsoonal rain had arrived, so torrential that it surely would have ruined the broadcast had it happened an hour earlier. All systems shut down, the satellite connection knocked out, the dressing rooms under water within minutes. It was a deluge, with winds driving the water horizontally. But even in this downpour, even at this predawn hour, his route was lined with people, children in their arms, cheering his modest cortege. Everybody remarked on it, how the rain, after all this time, just poured down.

1975

CHAPTER 17

COKE-BOTTLE GLASSES, A FLORIDA DOG TRACK, AND A MUMMY

HOW had it come to this? He had long since been crowned, his title a mere symbol of the world's welcome back. It had taken time (eight years), and it had taken effort (eighteen fights). But his championship was restored, and so was every iota of his former popularity. A national pariah? Maybe in 1967. Two months after the Foreman fight, President Ford had invited him to the White House, to help "heal the wounds of racial division, Vietnam, and Watergate." Ali, who'd once divided the nation, was now an instrument of its reconciliation.

And, also, thanks to his travels, he'd become as beloved around the world as at home. There was nobody who could claim the level of recognition he enjoyed. Of course, he could shut down Los Angeles by scheduling a public workout (the fire department canceled it when the crowd blocked fire-access routes). But now he was an international disrupter as well. When he traveled to Kuala Lumpur to make a defense against Joe Bugner in June, twenty thousand Malaysians met him at the airport. Girls swooned, it was reported. It took a police wedge thirty minutes to get his car to the highway.

So how had it come to this? Sitting on a stool in the Philippines, every bit of his humanity pooling at his feet. So drained, so exhausted. So hurt. Ali could barely lift his head. His eyes seemed to loll in their sockets. But he finally forced himself to look across the ring at Frazier, a man grown nearly blind after ten rounds, his face a welter of lumps, his humanity departing him, too. Squat Joe Frazier. The "gorilla in Manila." Frazier glared back with his good but narrowing eye, his fury in need of no refreshment, his pride untethered by physical condition. What was with him? There was no stopping him. Maybe he had no humanity in the first place. Ali turned to Pacheco. "This is what dying's like, closest thing I know," he said. He'd done enough; there was nothing more he could do. Whom would he satisfy by stepping over that brink, into a nothingness? No return then.

His manager, sensing imminent retirement, tried to storm up to the corner, struggling through the usual crowd. "You a nigger like him," Herbert Muhammad hollered in his direction. "You gonna quit? Get your ass out there! You hear me?" Bundini was weeping, but no less insistent, no less panicked. Everybody was hysterical. Pacheco was trying to tell him this wasn't dying, nothing like it. But what did he know? He'd always been on the other end of the stethoscope. "Go down to the well once more," Bundini begged.

They pushed him out for the eleventh round, onto that precipice. Ali walked slowly toward the middle of the ring, and stepped off.

This whole thing had started as a lark, which was the most frustrating part of it. Yeah, now anybody could see it had turned into a disaster, but going in? A lark. Another big payday (boy, these dictators were just giving it away, weren't they?), another easy fight, the guys having a good old time at Deer Lake, and everybody assembling in Manila, to have pictures taken with that guy and his wife, the one with all the shoes. A lark. Best part of it, his wife, Belinda, would stay home, and he could import Veronica without fear of reprisal. Well, he hadn't feared that much reprisal, let's be honest. But it was a hassle, always introducing her as a cousin or babysitter. This was going to be fun.

Ali truly was astride the world after the Foreman fight. It wasn't just that he'd won his title back, but it was how and against whom. Shrugging off the hardest puncher, maybe in heavyweight history, and then clubbing him to the canvas like that—well, that was persuasive. He had already proved he was a man of all seasons, bridging both political and athletic eras. Now he proved he was a man of all styles, as capable of scattering every one of your neurons as he had been of dazzling you to death. *Sports Illustrated* named him Sportsman of the Year. "Return of the Big Bopper" was its headline.

He had finally erased his competition, destroyed the very idea of contention. They hadn't known, way back in 1971, that a three-man tournament was about to develop, but it had, and now it was over, conclusively so. Ali may have had problems with Frazier, going just 1–1 with him, but Smoking Joe also had to be judged by that horrible loss to Foreman. And then with Ali beating Foreman so easily, well, the laws of transfer just might have transferred Frazier right out of boxing.

As for Foreman, he could yap all he wanted about an Ali re-match, but it was looking more and more like he was broken, damaged beyond all fixing. He'd come up with a list of excuses for his performance in Zaire, most having to do with his corner. He was telling people that Sadler might have poisoned him; his prefight drink of water tasted "mediciny." He also blamed Sadler for not motioning him up in time for the ten-count. There was the issue of the cut, of course, and how for the first ten days of its healing, he couldn't even sweat, much less spar. "That was the best thing that happened to Ali when we were in Africa," he said, "the fact that I had to get ready for the fight without being able to box."

On and on he went. The lizards, the mysterious weakness, the eggs in his orange juice that made him even weaker. He also suspected that Dundee, Ali's coconspirator, had loosened the ropes the day before the fight, allowing him his rope-a-dope strategy. In fact, not only had Dundee been tightening the ropes, but both Sadler and Moore had been at the ring while he did so. They had declined to help; it was too hot.

Singer Marvin Gaye, concerned for Foreman's confidence, suggested a way back. Fight an exhibition, five men for three rounds each, in one night. Ali had already done something like that right after their own fight, facing off against a series of boxers, some of them former sparring partners, in Kansas City. But it had been conceived entirely as a goof, all in the spirit of professional wrestling. For Foreman, though, this mattered. He took it as seriously as possible, although he did agree to lift a six-hundred-pound steer at his Texas ranch for a publicity photo that ran in *People*. He trained hard for it.

But the promotion went awry. King had managed to sell the affair to ABC, and that meant Howard Cosell at ringside, proclaiming it a "farce" and a "discredit," even as his network scrapped for its ratings. Worse, Ali had been brought, apparently just to heckle from ringside. Together, Foreman thought, "they made a mockery of the whole thing." Foreman knocked three of the five men out, and at least knocked the other two down. But it was not a terribly convincing enterprise, either for Foreman or for the public. "It is safe to say," *Ring* said, "that it will be some time before Foreman recovers from the mental and physical setback he suffered in Zaire." Its headline? "Foreman's Confidence Gone, Former Champion's Circus Turns into Burlesque."

But Frazier wasn't making any real news, either. Since losing to Ali in their second fight, he'd fought just twice, beating Jerry Quarry and Jimmy Ellis. It was not the schedule of somebody trying to make a case for a rematch, either with Ali or with Foreman. He'd gone just fourteen rounds in twenty months. He had his reasons, though. He was by now legally blind in his left eye, so clouded by a cataract, he probably could have made better use of Daggo than Foreman. He could undergo surgery or resort to "Coke-bottle glasses," either condition dampening demand for further Frazier action. Anyway, he just wanted the one fight. Ali. Without those prospects, he appeared somewhat unmoored. "Joe appears to have fallen by the wayside," *Ring* reported. Noting that possible fights at the Garden had fizzled, it added, "Joe is having a difficult time fitting into the post-Zaire picture."

And what was the post-Zaire picture? It was no longer very interesting. Ali had completed his agenda, in showstopping fashion, and was now without his rivals, all discredited or just quiet. The tournament seemed to be over, his dynasty safe as long he wanted to continue and box.

Despite a five-month layoff, long for Ali during his comeback, he very much wanted to continue. He wanted the dough. "The papers made a big thing out of the $5 million guarantee at Zaire," he told some boxing writers. "Do you know that I took home with me only $1,250,000 out of the five million? The expenses are unbelievable." He said, "I have to fight often not only to collect, but also to keep sharp."

He would probably have to fight a legitimate contender, someone of the caliber of Quarry, Norton, or Ron Lyle, to really collect. Madison Square Garden thought the real moneymaker was Lyle, a hard puncher who'd lost just one of his thirty-two fights and was ranked third in the division. The Garden got so far as drawing up contracts. But here came King, no longer operating under the promotional umbrella of Video Techniques, but wheeling and dealing on his own. King's appeal to Herbert Muhammad and Ali was attractive and went far beyond his blarney about helping another black man out. He proposed much less dangerous competition than Lyle, for more money than the Garden's.

The mystery among the boxing aficionados was how this could ever be possible. But King had seen the magic of acquiring outside investors, an African dictator, for example. They asked few questions and attached fewer liens. As it happened, no dictators were interested in a fight between Ali and the Bayonne Bleeder, as Chuck Wepner was called. King had traveled to London and Jamaica, and nobody there was buying, either. But in Cleveland, his hometown, where he still maintained some dubious connections, the seed money of $1.3 million was magically made available.

The investor of record was a Cleveland millionaire, and King pal, named Carl Lombardo. Lombardo had quite a portfolio: construction, a Florida dog track, auto raceways, and thoroughbred track near New Orleans. As legitimate as he sounded, the rumors in Cleveland were that King, desperate to gain entry to heavyweight promotion, had actually gotten most of the money—altogether it cost about $2.5 million to put on—from his underground connections. Whatever the case, Ali was guaranteed $1.5 million, the third-largest advance in boxing history, to meet a fighter whose best punches, by his own estimation, were "the rabbit punch, the choke hold, and a head butt."

It was not worth a tenth of that, either economically or artistically. The fight, held in March, was a box-office bust and, despite a "knockdown" that might have inspired a certain cinematic franchise (it was not a knockdown; Wepner stepped on Ali's foot and pushed him over), the result did not add luster to either man's career. But anecdotally, as boxing writers turned the Wepner tale over and over, it was a tremendous success. They were reminded, first of all, that Wepner was the opponent of record for Sonny Liston's final fight, a bout that gave Wepner his nickname. Before it was finally stopped in the tenth round, Liston had produced a lasting masterpiece of arterial spray. Wepner needed seventy-two stitches to close all the wounds and provided Liston an occasion for his last memorable quote. Asked if Wepner was the bravest man he'd ever faced, Liston said, "No, but his manager sure is."

The upshot was that Ali and the Black Muslims had gotten their money, wherever it might have come from, and now King was truly in the business of boxing. King had hired Video Techniques to handle the technical requirements. Hank Schwartz, his old employer, had once predicted that it wouldn't be too long before he was the one riding in the back of the bus. King, not so long out of Marion Correctional, was just now negotiating a lease of office space, two floors above the Rainbow Room in New York City's RCA Building, for $60,000 a year.

That King had come a long way was obvious, but it was not equally clear whether he was a fight promoter or a flimflam man. He was putting fights on, all right, but it seemed that only King and his fighters escaped with the money. Cleveland had been a fiasco, the arena there just two-thirds full and papered at that. Even Zaire, where he'd worked so hard to bring "dignity and recognition and solidarity," was left patting its back pocket. Where is my wallet, anyway? Fourteen million dollars for that? "They got most of that back," King said proudly.

And now he and the Ali gang were off to Las Vegas, where Ron Lyle would get his chance. Lyle was one of those fearless yet overlooked fighters who were circulating beneath the bigger names during those years. Quarry and Norton, the two others, had already had their chances with Ali. For $1 million, Ali didn't mind giving Lyle his and, forced to go through his entire repertoire (he rope-a-doped, he floated like a butterfly and stung like a bee), eventually disposed of him in the eleventh round of their May fight. Ali had not had as easy a time of it as he pretended, and his magnanimous offer, waving the referee in to stop the beating ("I can't kill a guy," he'd said), was not much appreciated by Lyle. Still, it was a win. He'd collected.

Collection was still on everyone's minds by June 30, when Ali met his next challenger, Joe Bugner. There was no other justification for the bout, Ali having already beaten him two years earlier. But King found moral and athletic cause for the event in the support of international relations. King said the groundwork had been laid a year earlier when Ali visited Jakarta for a fight with Rudi Lubbers. According to King, Ali was walking "through the streets when a millionaire put $50,000 in his hand and told him to come back there to fight some day."

Putting aside the idea of putting that much cash in another man's hand—"Must've been big bills," scoffed a fight manager—there was no question Ali would come back. King had met a king, a king whose name he couldn't quite recollect—"I don't have to know his name," he said, "a king is a king"—and gotten a sizable guarantee for a June 30 fight in Kuala Lumpur. A Malaysian politician, the equivalent of a governor there, stitched together a consortium of bankers and came up with $3 million for the two fighters—$2.5 million going to Ali—plus training and transportation expenses for Ali's fifty-person entourage, "in order," said Dato Harun Idris, "to project Malaysia to the world."

There was hardly anybody but Malaysia and their bankers excited to see the fight. Bugner, a Hungarian blond who was now campaigning as an Englishman, had already lost six times, and to much lesser foes than Ali and Frazier. He was not an especially exciting or aggressive fighter, either. As writer Hugh McIlvanney said, "When the bell rings, it's not a bugle call for him."

The bout went as expected. Bugner stood there, according to King, "like a 1,000-year-old mummy," and Ali scored an easy and unanimous decision in his third title defense of the year. Also, Malaysia may have lost a little money. "What can you do?" asked King.

It turned out Malaysia was not so much a fight venue as it was an agreeable and well-paying location for a press conference. Immediately afterward, sufficiently dabbed of his sweat, Ali confirmed King's earlier announcement that he was going to fight Frazier again, completing a trilogy and, no doubt, ransacking yet one more country. This time, Ali told the world, he was taking everybody to the Philippines.

The next day Ali was joined in Kuala Lumpur by Frazier himself, so they could get this promotion off the ground. Bugner had not yet been packed away, but there was no sense wasting time. Ali seemed to have grown bored with boxing, possibly even himself, the past year, the opposition so faint it couldn't inspire the slightest couplet. It was collect, collect, collect. Nobody was complaining. The Black Muslims were profiting greatly, Ali was doing fine, King doing best of all. But he'd been without his great foils, without the comedy of his outrageous and mostly invented antagonism.

Here's what he'd been missing. Before the Foreman fight the two had appeared for a press conference that became known as the Battle of the Waldorf-Astoria, a strange affair during which Foreman ripped Ali's jacket right off him and Ali peppered him back with dinner rolls. When a fan of his appeared at the dais, offering him a candlestick from her table, Ali was genuinely surprised to be so misunderstood. "Oh, thank you, ma'am," he'd said, "but I'm just playing." And he then threw a glass of water that sailed twenty feet above Foreman's head.

So wasn't it good to have Frazier back? To play again? Somebody worthy, somebody who could get the juices flowing again, somebody who could take it?

At that press conference, back in his element and his mood heightened by this opportunity to make a fight that mattered, Ali began setting the publicity parameters. "It will be a killer," he said, everybody excited by the possibility of a rhyme, after all this time, "and a chiller, and a thrilla, when I get the gorilla, in Manila."

Oh, jeez! Did he just say "gorilla"?

CHAPTER 18

ECONOMIC TECHNICIANS, THE OTHER WIFE, AND THE WILDLIFE FUND

Unless King had acted quicker and chosen Saigon itself—the money might have been there before its fall in April—the point couldn't have been much clearer. Ali was now roaming the world with a remarkable bravado, impunity even. Eight years earlier he'd risked a prison sentence rather than go anywhere near Vietnam. But now he was being paid millions to more or less endorse a country that was right next door, just across the South China Sea. Once, he divided a country. And now, he unites the world.

Of course, his role was less military or political than it was theatrical. Despite the raft of Ali books coming out just now (one by Mailer, of course, but also by Wilfred Sheed and one by Ali himself), finding significance in his fights as well as his stands, he had not acquired cosmic meaning. He was an ambassador of anarchy, a missionary of mischief. But that was exactly what these times called for. That spring South Vietnam fell, the president flying to Taipei with three and a half tons of gold (there were your fight guarantees), leaving one of the messiest and most dispiriting cleanups in world history for the occupying United States. It was a horrible but entirely appropriate end, a fiasco even to the finish.

A C-5A transport, the world's biggest plane, left Saigon with 243 orphans, part of a plan to find homes for 2,000 children dispossessed by the failed war. Like all of the United States' intentions—good, but poorly executed—this went up in flames, probably 140 of those children dead when the plane crashed into a rice paddy and exploded in fire. The United States couldn't even extricate itself with honor. An airlift meant for women and children was rushed by soldiers, pushing the weaker aside. A trailing plane radioed there was something hanging from the tail, probably a body. The panic of escape overrode all dignity, all good sense. Chopper after chopper ferried the refugees to waiting carriers, so many that US Navy crews had to push the empty Chinooks right off the deck, just splashing them into the sea, to make room for the next incoming.

It was the kind of spectacle, metaphors of waste brought vividly to the nightly news, that did more than any number to confirm the US failure abroad. But there were numbers. In sixteen years there were fifty-eight thousand US dead, three hundred thousand wounded, $150 billion down the drain. This did not even address the consequences on the home front, where a nation became nearly paralyzed in its polarization. Faith in supposedly omniscient institutions was shot. A previously unquestioned authority was suspect. Self-hatred a new mode of expression. An unhappy place.

Yet it did have the unintended effect of creating a counterculture, grudgingly accommodating alternative movements, giving necessary voice to rabble-rousers. The dangers of headlong conformity, which used to mean patriotism, were not entirely replaced by original thought, but at least there was now a safer place for it. Individualism, sometimes grown so extreme it verged on narcissism, was now possible. Just in the eight years since Ali had gone from the country's most famous draft dodger to its greatest export, the United States had been transformed from the gloom of civil war to a hothouse of self-indulgence.

It was, even a curmudgeon would admit, a less unhappy place.

Ali, who was as much the poster boy for self-importance as he'd been a countercultural icon, may not have been the principal change agent, but he was an accessible symbol for the revolution. He'd stood his ground, said his piece, endured the backlash, and saw his point made in the end. That he did it with such grace and even good humor encouraged a nation that might otherwise find refuge in bitterness. His was a way out, the best way.

So, even as the cloud of Vietnam was finally passing over the American landscape, regrets still at the fore, he would cheer us up again. Rowdy Americanism, with its confidence in the powers of personality, was in full flower in Manila, as Ali once more exercised his considerable charms.

And why Manila, anyway? The usual reason, of course. It was not the serendipity of location; its proximity to Vietnam was just a coincidence of narrative. It was money. President Ferdinand Marcos, like rulers before, had seized upon the public relations punch of a heavyweight championship fight, especially one featuring Ali. And like rulers before him, he somehow had the cash at his disposal to make it happen. Rulers are often lucky that way. He certainly had more than the folks at Madison Square Garden who had hoped to complete the trilogy where it had begun. Marcos provided guarantees beyond $6.5 million—$4.5 million for Ali, $2 million for Frazier, and $500,000 for King's promotional fees and expenses, and Garden officials suspected, some on the side, just to make the deal go down.

As King's role in these promotions increased, so did the size of his rhetoric, which had gone from jailhouse patter, accented with literary asides, to soaring oratory. "This ain't just a sportin' event," he said. "This here is a dramatic contribution to the world's economy. Waiters will be waitin', bartenders will be tendin' and the brothers and sisters gonna be buyin' new clothes. Why, I got enough people on my payroll alone for this here happenin' to buy a jet plane, and go back and forth to New Orleans up until the year 2000."

As usual, King was careful not to create too much expectation for the host country. Once signed up, these rulers were left to their own devices, guided by the crazy, wishful thinking that, if they'd only asked for references, would never have checked out.

Marcos admitted that it might not seem like a national fund-raiser. "Frankly," he said in an interview before the fight, "the economic technicians don't look with favor on flamboyant events like this. But I have always maintained that they have their place in the scheme of things in our development plans."

One thing that Marcos hoped to achieve was a softening of opinion of the type of country that operates under martial law, a condition that was meant to bridge its colonial occupation with a more democratic future. "We have this publicity," Marcos said, "but it is not the common crowd-getting type of publicity. It is the word of truth about the Philippines. Undoubtedly martial law connotes something oppressive, and therefore always meets with antagonism from people who don't understand that under our system, martial law has been utilized not as a weapon of the status quo, but a weapon of reform, which of course is anathema, an outrage to the classical constitutionalist. Martial law here was proclaimed at the insistence of the people. I sought their advice."

This fight had too much publicity value to be dribbled away as a simple championship bout. With Ali's ability to capture a world's attention, and divert it wherever he chose, his events represented watershed moments in a nation's political future. "We have bene-fited already," Marcos said. "The fight publicizes our country. Many people do not know where the Philippines are and don't know what the situation is here. They think that the military runs the government, are on the streets. Have you seen any tanks? They think people are arrested on any pretext. That there is oppression, tyr-anny and the civil government is nonexistent or inoperative. That there are no judges. But whatever you fellows say, you must see that the fight can be held here in peace and order."

And Ali, with his odd backstory, was key to the restoration of image. "No matter what one says," he continued, "Ali symbolizes success in that part of the world which sees white men as colonial and the like. The old voices against colonialism are all over Asia again because of the Vietnam debacle, and Ali symbolizes a continu-ing protest against this racism and dominance because of color and birth. And while this may not be fascinating to the Western world, it is to Asians a highly-charged matter."

Ali was no longer only a boxer, but a symbol of independence that might be rented out and used to create new story lines for ambitious nations. He didn't come cheap, but why should he? There wasn't another man in the world who could generate occasions for such useful propaganda.

Also, there wasn't anyone in the world who was as much fun to have around. They loved Ali in Manila. As many as five thousand spectators, paying from 30 cents to $3, were showing up at his training sessions, Ali turning them into cabarets. He loved entertaining for the masses, and was good enough to create worry of insurrection. "If he was a Filipino," Marcos said, "I'd have to kill him. So popular." He quickly added, "That's a joke now, of course."

Possibly more worrisome to Marcos was the effect Ali was having upon his wife, the glamour puss Imelda. "She is in love with Ali," he admitted. "She has a taste for the feminine in men." Imelda was indeed dazzled by his presence, telling Ferdinand, who was a Frazier man, attracted to his "danger," that "he doesn't act like a boxer or athlete. He is brilliant in his repartee. He would make a damned good politician."

Imelda Marcos might have been referring to a session, ten days before the fight, that she and her husband had with the two fighters and their pared-down entourages. Part of the duties of a personality for hire like Ali is to mingle with the royal hosts, a meet and greet that will produce an agreeable photo spread in the local press. Ali had grown accustomed to the obligation, by now thoroughly enjoying these little summit meetings.

By now Ali had also become quite brazen in the exhibition of his mistress. She was always around, in some ill-defined capacity, at home. But here? It was way out front. In fact, many in his camp thought the whole point of traveling all the way to the Philippines for a fight was so that Ali could leave Belinda home and have a comparatively worry-free escape with Veronica. This was the kind of ethical inconsistency that ought to have been noteworthy, especially as supposed moral underpinnings instructed him to "give great honor to womanhood, the black woman mainly." He was always going off on the subject, not that anyone paid much mind to his religious rants anymore. But it had been scant months since he delivered a long and rambling sermon in *Ebony*—entitled "Ali Challenges Black Men"—about the demands of marriage. "If a man doesn't respect his woman," he'd said, "then he doesn't respect himself."

But nobody paid any attention to his inconsistencies, having long since identified him as a man of impulses, some good, some bad. The traveling press was certainly fully aware of what was going on but didn't feel the need to become the agents of reprimand, and definitely not divorce. Let him do what he wants, as long as he keeps providing their newspapers with excuses for these fabulous junkets.

Less aware was Marcos. Seeing Veronica, such a tall and slinky specimen, on Ali's arm, he felt it was only polite to take notice. "You have a beautiful wife," he said. Ali not only failed to correct Marcos but compounded the error with some of the sparkle that Imelda had remarked upon. "Your wife," Ali replied, "is quite beautiful, too."

Well, now there's a problem. It was a problem because a *Newsweek* writer named Pete Bonventre had been assigned a lengthy profile in Manila and, while he was not particularly interested in Ali's domestic permutations, felt he needed to report this possible imbroglio or risk getting scooped. So, in a story headlined "The Ali Mystique," he alluded to the fighter's growing hypocrisy, or at least the inconsistent treatment of marriage: "Solemn Muslim guards have given way to streetwise hustlers. Liberals who cherished him as a symbol of pro-black antiwar attitudes have been replaced by wry connoisseurs of his pure showmanship. Even Ali's women, invariably beautiful and black, have now been brought out of the back rooms of his life and openly flaunted. As of last week, Belinda was still at home in Chicago, and the stunning Veronica Porsche, sometimes know as 'Ali's other wife,' was touring Manila with the champ."

Even with the publication of the article, Ali might have softened the scandal, or at least ignored it. Instead, unasked, he began trying to justify the nonsense at his daily press conferences. Nobody particularly wanted to expand on the issue, but here he was, wrapping up training and justifying his philandering in fairly ridiculous arguments. "I know celebrities don't have privacy," he said. "But at least they should be able to sleep with who they want to." It was clear that he didn't understand the potential for outrage. "This is going too far. They got on me for the draft. They got on me for my religion. They got on me for all sorts of things. But they shouldn't be able to get on me for having a girlfriend. I could see some controversy if she was white, but she's not. The only person I answer to is Belinda and I don't worry about her."

At about that moment, Belinda, habitually aggrieved for certain, but nevertheless the mother of four of his children and not so far a subject of international shame or ridicule, was on a plane west. Dave Wolf, of Frazier's group, was on the same flight and had heard what was happening. Watching Belinda stare straight ahead with a "Sonny Liston glare" gave him the impression Frazier's work might get done for him. He thought Veronica might go "out a window and maybe Ali after her." Belinda was a tall, strong woman.

Once at the hotel, she barged into Ali's room, where he was taping a segment for *The Today Show,* dragged him into an adjoining bedroom, and began yelling and throwing things. It didn't last long. Belinda exited the hotel shortly afterward and made the very next flight back to the United States. A student who was next to see Ali, to deliver a poem he'd written about the champ, reported that he was "not looking too happy, he's in a bad way, his eyes are red." But otherwise, he didn't seem the least bit chastened. "This is good publicity," he said, which, after all, was why he was there.

Anyway, Belinda was the least of his problems. He'd instigated a far-riskier campaign than infidelity, choosing to heighten his hate crimes against Frazier. This, too, was in the spirit of good publicity, though, like Belinda, Frazier was getting rather bristly about it. He hadn't liked it the first time around, not at all the second. By now, Ali creating even new forms of iambic denigration, he was getting ready to explode.

The campaign had begun back in Deer Lake, Ali delivering his postworkout riffs from the ropes. At least before, Ali had given Frazier the dignity of racial meaning, even if Uncle Tom was a terrible slur of the times. But now, he'd unloaded him of even that loathsome freight. Now, Frazier was not even human.

After a fairly routine call-and-response, Ali asking, "Who am I?" and Bundini crying out, "The king of all he see," Ali got down to business. Addressing his usual mountain crowd, Ali departed even his low levels of decorum and sent the promotion on a path that grew only uglier as it got longer. "Joe Frazier should give his face to the Wildlife Fund! He's so ugly, blind men go the other way." Ali held his nose. "He not only looks bad! You can smell him in another country! What will people in Manila think? We can't have a gorilla for a champ. They're gonna think, looking at him, that all black brothers are animals. Ignorant. Stupid. Ugly. If he's champ again, other nations will laugh at us."

Ali's riffs were often premeditated, the whole idea his personal amusement. He once dragooned Cosell into a sketch of his devising, a racially inflammatory encounter in the coach section of a flight they were taking. "Look here, nigger," Cosell addressed him, exactly as he was told, Ali reacting with alarm, his eyes as big as pie plates. "Did you say Trigger?" Coach section got its money's worth that day.

But with Frazier he seemed always to be going further than was absolutely necessary, either for publicity or for human decency. It was one thing, though not necessarily a good thing, when Ali was teasing Frazier about his education. Ali could barely read himself; everybody knew as much. So it was kind of a joke when, at the press conference announcing their fight in Malaysia, Ali began correcting Frazier's diction. When Frazier began, "I'm gonna . . . ," Ali jumped in: "I'm going to. Not I'm gonna. Talk intelligent." Frazier resumed, Ali picking him apart at every phrase. "How far did you go in school?" he asked.

Even the "gorilla" characterization might be forgiven of a man who was inescapably drawn to the power of rhyme. If a man doesn't want to be called a "gorilla," he should not consent to a fight in Manila. "He's a nice fella," Ali would say. "I just like to get a man mad."

Even Frazier seemed to be giving him a pass. He didn't like it much, saying, "Look at my beautiful kids. How can I be a gorilla?" But he had to admit, "He's gonna talk. Ain't no way to stop him." It was Ali. He'd been down this road before. He felt he could offer retribution enough in the ring, just as he'd redressed that Uncle Tom business in the first fight (and, still, in his mind, the second one, too). "There'll come that moment when he's gonna hear that knock on the door, gonna hear it's time to go to the ring, and then he's gonna remember what it's like to be in with me, how hard and long that night's gonna be."

There had been a witness for Frazier at Ali's camp, when he'd gone off the rails and pinched his nose at the thought of Frazier. The witness, Gypsy Joe Harris, who'd been in and out of Frazier's own camp, had been there primarily to report on Ali's decay as a heavyweight. "He ready to be a corpse," Gyp told Frazier. "The right hand slow if you ask me."

"He never looks good in training," said Frazier. "What else?"

Gyp was hesitant. "Well, Smoke," he began. "It was a big crowd. Couldn't move in the place. He hopped 'round like an ape. Said you not fit to be champ. And you smell so bad they can smell you in another country."

Just as you might conduct a dalliance, everyone giving you a pass right up until you introduce your woman to the world—the world!—as your wife, so can you finally go too far in the attraction of publicity, removing your opponent to the animal kingdom. Frazier considered the report with rising bile. He turned to his trainer, Eddie Futch, and said, "Whatever you do, whatever happens, don't stop the fight. We got nowhere to go after this. I'm gonna eat this half-breed's heart right out of his chest. I mean it, this the end of him or me."

If Ali knew what kind of intensity he was stirring in Frazier, he did not show it. He just didn't care. He thought Frazier was washed up and was not only provoking him accordingly but training for an easy night. No fighter would try to juggle two women if he thought his heart could possibly be torn from his chest. Frazier was considered a shot fighter, never having recovered from the Foreman knockout and, having had just four fights since, never having tried. So Ali continued to rile his opponent at every opportunity. When Frazier's son Marvis, who turned fifteen in Manila, showed up at an Ali session to sing a song called "First-Round Knockout," all in good fun, Ali couldn't resist a dig at the father. "He's better looking than his father," Ali said, "and he makes more sense."

Then there was the matter of the pistol. Ali loved pranks. Once he rigged up Dundee's hotel curtains so that he could pull them back and forth from his own room, creating a kind of haunted house for his trainer. For Ali, any sort of reaction was worth the effort. If props were needed, no problem: butterfly nets, carrots, and, lately, for Frazier, a man dressed in a gorilla suit who went down rather easily in sparring. Whether the gun was from a security officer, as some claimed, or was a toy pistol, as Ali said, it was probably beyond the pale of a practical joke to fire anything upon your opponent at three thirty in the morning.

Ali had learned the ploy when Liston once pulled his heater on him, causing Ali to leap onto a Las Vegas craps table in fright. So there he was, in those homicidal hours of the morning, hollering for Frazier outside his hotel window. When Frazier appeared on the balcony, Ali "fired" off all chambers. It would have been hard for Frazier to believe Ali meant to kill him before collecting on a $4.5 million payday, but Ali had long since blown past personal parameters for erratic behavior as far as he was concerned. Anyway, when an "armed" man is yelling, "Go back in your hole, gorilla. You gonna scare the people. Come out again and I'm gonna kill you before time," you have to pay him some attention.

Frazier threw a pillow and some publicity photos down at him, but the story quickly circulated that Ali was becoming a bit unhinged. Between the marital discord, the mistress on hand, and now this strange gesture, it was possible to think that Ali was simply too distracted to conduct a proper training camp. What fighter could accommodate so much turmoil on the eve of an important bout?

Possibly just the one, Ali. Hadn't he demonstrated his capacity for chaos, fighting for a championship even while a prison sentence hung over him? This, Belinda barging in and then promptly leaving him to his mistress, was going to interrupt his concentration? What concentration? Five days before the fight, Frazier left the hotel where his camp had been staying and decamped to the outer city, to a place overlooking the bay. In the afternoons he'd sit outside and stare, running fight scenarios through his mind.

Ali? He was looking for toy guns.

CHAPTER 19

SUBDURAL BLOSSOMS, COOLERS OF SAN MIGUEL, AND GIN

Neither Ali nor Frazier had ever killed a man in the ring. Foreman, for all his supernatural punching power, had not killed a man in the ring. Sonny Liston had not killed a man in the ring. In fact, few heavyweights ever had. Strangely, the deadliest of this crop of fighters was the relatively light-hitting Joe Bugner. He did kill a man in the ring, or at least contribute to his death. Ulric Regis died from a brain injury three days after their fight in 1969.

It was a mystery. The dangers of boxing were real, but very unpredictable. In 1975 there were twelve ring deaths throughout the world. Quite a lot. Yet none of them was among heavyweights, whose size and strength ought to account for most, if not all, of the sport's mortality. That's just physics. These are 200-pound men, and when they hit things, as Norman Mailer observed, they leave dents. They have TNT in their mitts. Nuclearology as well.

Yet they rarely kill. Doctors believe it's the very force of these single blows—no hunting and pecking for heavyweights—that actually protects the fighter. The smaller fighters, who can muster just fractions of the heavyweights' blunt force, achieve neural destruction with repeated jackhammer blows to the head, the subdural blossoms of blood developing slowly but certainly into hemorrhagic necroses and then, worst case, a fatal brain edema. So Emile Griffith pounds a helpless Benny Paret to death, two dozen unanswered punches, Paret tangled in the ropes, long past self-defense. Or Sugar Ray Robinson outclasses Jimmy Doyle, a journeyman, and punches him to death. Did he know Doyle was in trouble, a writer asked Robinson, as if the pounding had been needless? "Getting people in trouble is my business." It hadn't been needless at all. Tragic. But hardly needless.

With heavyweights, who tend to deliver a single sledgehammer blow, boxing may actually be safer. Of course, there can be frightful barrages. But more likely, that single haymaker, the crowd tolerating the tedium of all those rounds, just waiting for the bomb to drop. That's what heavyweights do. That's why they get paid. The lights-out punch, the one that made Foreman twirl so ridiculously, not only is a crowd pleaser, but might also be a safety precaution. As horrific as a knockout might look, it may actually inoculate the fighter against further damage. All circuits are down, however briefly, but the fighter is, in this case anyway, protected by his obvious helplessness. Ali wouldn't, his hand cocked or not, deliver a second strike on top of that. It would be manslaughter. Bad sportsmanship, certainly.

Foreman recuperates more or less immediately, the circuits restored, and while he might not make sense at first, he is at least spared continued concussion and a brain edema of his own. The embarrassment of the knockout—there is hardly any way to look sillier than to have an electrical power outage in public—is a small price to pay for its collateral protection. And now, given enough time, the cellular damage can be repaired and Foreman is raring to go, hardly remembering the "lost time," as boxers sometimes describe their brief vacancy in the ring.

Liston once put it another way: "If you take a bad hit, your brain flops out of its cups—plop! And then you're knocked out. Then your brain goes back into the cups, and you come around." It's as good an explanation as any and, thankfully, or else the game would have been outlawed long ago, accounts for almost all the action. Almost all. The only danger to the boxer, according to Liston, was "if the punch is hard enough, then your brain never goes right back into the cups. And then you need other people to help you through life."

That was the kind of punch Joe Frazier intended to throw, October 30, 1975, in an outdoor ring in the Manila outskirts, the whole world watching. He would throw a punch to cripple or maim, even to kill, if he could. "To do damage," he thought. Nobody, no fight, had ever made him believe he was doing something besides a sport. It was about winning, not hurting. It was never personal. When Foreman had bounced him off the deck to dislodge his championship, his brain flopping out of its cups, he had not been insulted. Foreman offered some consolation afterward, but Frazier would have none of it, simply thanking him for the fight. This was a job. This was their work. Better some days than others, that's all.

But Ali, in a campaign that had gone on well over fifty-three months, had done more than just get under his skin. Frazier could handle the promotional friction, the jibes that were natural to a sustained and demanding competition. Affronts at press conferences, slights at weigh-ins, constant deprecations in the press—this was all to be expected in a rivalry that had gone on so long and without a satisfying conclusion. Especially when an inventive motor mouth like Ali was involved. It could be hurtful, especially as Ali would always have the upper hand in that kind of contest, but it could be endured. This was the business, the give-and-take outside the ring just as important as inside it.

Frazier got Ali as well as anybody, how spontaneous he was, how desperate for attention, how quickly he could turn on you for the slightest advantage. For something as cheap as a quick laugh. He'd throw you right under the promotional bus. Their early friendship probably couldn't have survived the twenty-seven rounds of close-in warfare they'd already waged. That would have been a lot to ask of two men as driven as them. But it didn't have to devolve into a grudge match, either. The importance of a third and deciding fight between them, the interims having been complicated by Foreman on both counts, made it intense, but not necessarily intolerable.

Ali had gone just too far and for too long, though. Maybe it wasn't so much the tenor of this new assault, though it had gotten increasingly personal and increasingly ugly. Why did Frazier have to smell? Did that really sell tickets? Maybe it was just the accumulation, four years of it, enough to finally erode any man's civility. On the eve of the fight, here he was again, this time returning to the drumbeat of Frazier's ignorance. "Go talk to Joe Frazier," he said, and "try to carry on a conversation. He's illiterate. I spoke at Harvard. They wanted me to be a professor of poetry at Oxford." These were stinging asides, coming from a man who, in the very same interview, confessed, "I can't read too good. I read one page and turn it and get tired. I just look at the pictures."

It was simply a character assassination. "Who does this son of a bitch think he is?" Frazier said one day in Manila, talking to Marvis. "I ain't no goddamn gorilla. Enough is enough. I'm gonna warm his ass good, make him suffer."

"Do it, daddy," Marvis said. "Smoke him."

Ali had no idea what he'd done. He never did. He oozed through life with equal charm and insolence, completely unmindful of consequence, always removed from the results of his affairs. If something happened, he would react. Drafted? He declined. Bulled against the ropes in the biggest fight of his life? He'd suddenly and perversely accept. It always seemed to work out, not to plan, of course—he never made plans, just lived moment to moment—but according to his dazzling improvisation, his uncanny ability to adapt. Did he mean to drive Frazier to a deadly kind of distraction? No. Why would he? Did he care? Absolutely not. Would it matter one way or another? How? How could it matter?

He was completely careless of what he wrought, here in the ring or anywhere. Did it matter that he introduced a mistress as his wife to the leader of a foreign country? Not particularly. His wife had stormed across the ocean, blistered him a bit, then stormed back. And there he was, still, with his mistress, just the way he wanted in the first place. Did it matter that he pushed Frazier so close to the edge that the man was now looking into mirrors, at his children's pictures, inspecting them for signs of deformity and defect of appearance? That Frazier was now a coiled spring of fury, a lethal instrument of resentment? How? How could it matter?

In the ring, growing hot even at this midmorning hour, Ali cavorted like a small and unruly child. A large trophy, "provided by his excellency," according to the ring announcer, had been placed in the middle (as if the championship belt were not enough), and Ali impishly rushed over to retrieve it for his corner. As if he had nothing else on his mind. A crowd of about twenty-eight thousand, settling in with their coolers of San Miguel, gasped and laughed at the antics. He couldn't have appeared more offhand or dismissive if he'd shown up in a clown suit, or maybe one of Bundini's robes.

He just didn't seem to be respecting the occasion, and certainly not the opponent. His problem, it more and more seemed, was boredom. He'd done everything and been everywhere, and he was simply exhausting all opportunities for excitement. "My personality has attracted the world," he said before the fight. "My personality has gone so far until America can't afford me anymore. The American promoters can't have me no more because they can't bid against so many countries. My personality and the power that Allah has given me has gone so far out that America is crying." He added, "No nation can contain me anymore." And having already ranged so far around the globe, the implication was that, very soon, the world couldn't contain him, either. He was above and beyond the day-to-day concerns that occupied mortals. The downside of his obvious greatness was that he no longer could engage in meaningful or satisfying ways. He was bored.

Just before being called to the center of the ring for the introductions, he leaned over the post at his corner and spotted his manager, Herbert Muhammad, already tipping a bottle of water. "Watcha got there, Herbert?" Ali asked. "Gin? You don't need any of that. I'm gonna put a whuppin' on this nigger's head." The tone was too unconcerned to register contempt. "Just another day's work," he said.

In the middle of the ring, called for instructions, Ali continued to jabber flippantly. Frazier shifted from foot to foot. "I'm gonna kill you, Clay," he said. "You're dead."

Was this how the adventure was going to end, all these twists and turns, all this fun, all this hoopla, so much amazement, so much surprise? Was this enterprise, begun in glory and uncertainty, going to end so far from home, on a dull note of redundancy? Were these holy wars, with so much at stake, going to end with this profane little exercise?

Questions, so many of them. You would have wondered, also, watching them in the center of the ring that hot, hot morning in Manila: Had Ali, whose physical and moral courage had been a beacon through a dark and gloomy time, now become nothing more than a hired hand, a troubadour of whatever politics paid the most, Don King and the Muslims happily scraping their half for what was effectively an advertisement of martial law? And had Frazier, that blue torch of pure desire, become this flickering, sputtering wick of hatred? Was this all there was?

Someone rang a bell.

CHAPTER 20

NURSERY RHYMES, PRETTY SHOES, AND A HORRIBLE SOUFFLÉ

The people tipped their San Miguels in the morning heat, slightly expectant, mildly hopeful. It was finally happening, this little amusement. So much talk, so much foolishness. Around the world, viewers settled in for the broadcast, waiting for this to be settled, once and for all. It was a little more than an amusement for them. It had been fun, the buildup, but now this rubber match had to be fought. Their twenty-seven rounds had been too close to declare a winner and, the opportunity for comparison provided by Foreman aside, required something conclusive, something very final. Ali, though older by two years, seemed the fighter in ascendancy, Frazier even at only thirty-one in decline. But you never knew. These were the two most powerful men of their era, and the most important totem of the sports world was at stake. This just had to be done. The fighters, their little rituals of intimidation concluded, moved toward each other in the middle of the ring, the air inside the arena suffocating.

It was important to remember, after so much blather and posturing, that these were action men, among the last of their kind. That, despite their fantastic colorations, they were the most transparent men of a generation, their true purpose, their character, revealed only in their work. They had fooled us, had maybe fooled themselves, into thinking half efforts would be sufficient, that they could glide to lasting achievement on patter and, maybe, just history. Neither cared to revisit their first crippling fight. Their rematch, even as violent as that was, had been an example of mutually assured destruction, the fighters agreeing to keep their missiles in the silos, lest they both be vaporized. Perhaps something in between would get the job done. Or perhaps—and few considered this—they just couldn't help themselves.

Surely, nobody expected, either in the arena or in those millions of closed-circuit seats, that they were about to wring something both wonderful and terrible from the occasion. Not even the fighters would have predicted they would range so far beyond their comfort zones, would push themselves to such terrifying limits. Nobody in his right mind would enter a fight, thinking something like *this* would ever be necessary. Nobody could prepare for that. Nobody would.

Ali, expected to dance as usual, made a presentation of arrogance instead, meeting Frazier in the middle and staying there. Whatever plans he made, whatever scenario his corner might have had in mind, became dispensable at the bell. It is a wonderful thing, to have that much self-confidence in your options. Ali had decided he would knock Frazier out. It's true, he'd been somewhat emboldened by his fight with Foreman. Also, he'd seemed to have gotten over hand troubles that had hobbled his punching power before. He claimed to be using the heavy bag, one that was easier on his fists, more than ever. Still. This was Frazier.

The first three rounds were Ali's, his jabs landing easily. Frazier, neither as squat as he usually made himself in the ring nor as close as he usually fought, was also catching Ali's right hands. Several times, Ali staggered him. At the end of round two, Ali cracked him with a right hand, and Frazier, his brain sloshing dangerously in its cups, dropped several inches before instantly righting himself. "He won't call you Clay no more," screamed Bundini.

Maybe he would knock him out. Ali, who had pretended to cry at the introductions when the crowd cheered a bit mightier for Frazier, the underdog, was now blowing kisses to the presumed converts. This would be easier than even he thought.

It was more of the same in the third, Ali snapping Frazier's head back with right-hand leads. Frazier was just eating the leather. Ali began singing nursery rhymes. Referee Carlos Padilla, like the three judges picked for the fight a Filipino, could scarcely believe what he was hearing: "Jack be nimble, Jack be quick." Then, pow! But toward the end, coming out of a clinch and still at close range, Frazier caught Ali with a left to the chin. Ali tried to laugh it off, but . . .

In the fourth round, but especially in the fifth, Frazier took control. He was built for a much longer run than any three rounds and, as Ali's arms began to drop, was able to bore in much closer. He popped Ali a couple of right hands—a weapon he rarely if ever deployed—with his head in Ali's chest. To that point, Ali hadn't ever considered Frazier to have two hands. Frazier was also forcing Ali into the ropes. This was far different from when Ali allowed Foreman to back him into the ropes. "Get off the ropes," Dundee yelled. Frazier was pounding away at the body. "Get back to the center of ring," the trainer said. "That's where you gotta live."

Ali was annoyed that Frazier hadn't had the good grace to fall down. "What you got in that niggah head?" he asked after the fourth. "Rock?" And now he was worse than annoyed. He was in doubt. Nobody should be able to trap him in his own corner. That was just ridiculous.

Frazier had somehow entered that gated community where Ali had always lived in smug security, his superior speed having always protected him from infighting. But now Frazier was inside the perimeter, free to ransack freely, vandalizing his defenses. If help was on the way, it might not arrive in time. Frazier whaled at Ali's sides, his hips, his arms.

By the sixth round, it was obvious that Ali's rope-a-dope would not offer him a lifeboat. Not only had Frazier tagged Ali—two sharp hooks to the head early in the round, the champion recoiling in trouble—but he was doing amateur surgery inside. A year earlier Foreman had swung wildly with Ali on the ropes, as if there would be a cumulative effect, Ali just crumbling from so much percussion. Ali absorbed them painlessly, laughing them off. But Frazier's punches were shorter, more accurate, sharp daggers to vital organs. Ali was not absorbing punches on his arms this time. Frazier was digging at his liver. And Ali was flinching.

In the corner, where Bundini was in tears meeting his man, Dundee was trying to communicate the danger zone he'd just entered. "We blew those rounds," he told him. "You don't rest on the ropes against Joe Frazier. You take a licking." Several rows behind him, Ali's number-one fan, Imelda Marcos, was having trouble dealing with the sounds of flesh being tenderized, and she stared down at her pretty shoes.

The seventh opened with Ali on his toes, less inclined to suffer Frazier's ravaging against the ropes. "Old Joe Frazier, why I thought you was washed up," Ali told him in the ring. "Somebody told you wrong, pretty boy," said Frazier.

Ali could not keep even that little bit of boxing, or even bravado, up and was soon pinned back in the corner in the eighth, Frazier a giant drill face, scouring the champion with his characteristic and unstoppable abrasions. If he kept this up—and what could possibly stop him?—he would simply grind Ali out of existence. Earlier Ali had bounced off the ropes for round-stealing flurries. It looked like he could no longer muster the effort. He was just sagging, eroded to nothingness.

Frazier was so crude in comparison, without the slightest elegance. Ali would shoot out a right hand, double the speed Frazier could ever shoot one out. But it wasn't mattering. Frazier continued in, anesthetized by rage, eating every punch just so he could keep pounding on his sides. It was painful for Ali, of course. Fatiguing, obviously. But more than that, it was disheartening. If Frazier could ignore the hurt he was delivering, and it was massive, just to dig at his kidneys in a childlike fury, there might not be a possibility for relief.

He was not dealing with another human being here, and it wasn't fair. After ten rounds Ali, winning the fight or not (he was ahead on just one of the cards, the other two even), was understandably in crisis.

Ali would never quit, but if there was a time to consider it, this would be it. His corner sensed his dread, and they, even from their safe places, felt the hurt. Yes, if there was a time to quit . . . "Force yourself, champ," Bundini yelled, tears down his cheeks. "The world needs you, champ."

He plodded to the center of the ring, Frazier having already hurried there, to meet his doom. Five rounds remained, all that was left of a war begun five years earlier, just minutes until the costs of so much pride could have a final summation. Ali tried to get up on his toes, but he really couldn't. And Frazier bore in.

Now there were four rounds left. Perhaps Ali's earlier sharp-shooting would save the day. Perhaps he was winning the fight on the scorecards. On the other hand, he might not even live out the morning, Frazier so murderous, his fury so calculated. There was nothing to be done with him, just go out and—what? What was Ali doing now? Suddenly, beginning in the twelfth, he was raking Frazier's head with machine-gun blows, four-punch flurries. Frazier's head had become a speed bag. Where was this coming from? How was this possible? Just like that, the fight had turned again, for no obvious reason except that Ali must have wanted it to. Ali pursued him through the next two rounds, pushing Frazier beyond his comfort zone, popping him in the middle of the ring.

By the thirteenth round, Frazier's face was rising like a horrible soufflé, huge welts forcing themselves to the surface. Worse, his eyes were closing. He had only one good eye anyway, but now he was slowly going blind in that one too. And it was Ali's turn to become a remorseless executioner, holding Frazier at a distance, too far away to see the coming right hands. Poof! Here came one right now, Frazier's mouthpiece flying out of the ring. Perhaps to rest in Imelda's lap.

Frazier's corner, meaning Eddie Futch, considered the prospects at this point. Well, they were poor. Frazier could no longer see a thing—"I can't pick up his right," he told Futch—but there was a possibility that Ali had punched himself out. If Frazier could nestle himself inside Ali's wingspan and belt away, his blindness might be irrelevant.

The fourteenth round—and it would be the last one, the final three minutes in their shared agony—was a kind of science experiment, an investigation into the extremes of human behavior. Just exactly what was a person capable of, how far could he go, how deep could he reach? Nobody had ever seen it conducted at this level, precautionary measures usually in place that would abort any further research, saving the subjects, somewhere just short of death. So, to that extent, nobody really knew what desire and pride could accomplish, or, rather, destroy. Now they did.

Ali, plumbing his final reserves, hit Frazier with every punch he had. Jabs, right-hand leads—he threw them all and connected with every one. Frazier, unable to see or simply unable to penetrate that protective cocoon of Ali's, caught them all flush. All. It was odd, Frazier having gone down so often and comically in his fight with Foreman. And now he remained so dangerously resolute, his head on deadly shocks, bouncing back every time. Ali hit him, stopped him in his tracks, and Frazier took an instant to regroup and slogged forward again, an apparition, the kind of haunt Ali might see in the wee hours. And was hit and . . . on, and on, it went.

This was too much. It shouldn't come to this. Their arrival on the world stage, their coming together, had been a marvelous happenstance. Two spirits of this size occupying this platform—well, there wouldn't ultimately be room for two, and certainly not for a third, that hulking menace, Foreman—made for a lively time. The world, America, hadn't enjoyed so much sheer potency at all, and definitely not all at once. The three men, having been pared to two by now, had made for a once-in-a-generation show. Or maybe it had been rarer even than that.

That this was at an end, this terrible tournament over, was now obvious. The three men had fought each other in every combination, a total of fifty-one rounds across four countries, and produced a survivor, although barely at that. Even as Ali was telling his corner to cut his gloves off after the fourteenth, Futch, who'd seen eight men die in the ring, was shutting Frazier down across the canvas—"Joe, it's over," he said. Camp spies waved frantically from each corner, hoping one surrender might trump the other's, but even if Ali had managed to quit first (not likely, not with that corner), his advantage had been clear. He was the survivor, after all this. However barely.

They were each now ruined, as Foreman had been ruined before them. This was the price of spectacle, the cost of glory. Ali went to a reception later that night but soon retired when he realized what a ghastly vision he must be. Indeed, wrote Dave Anderson in the New York Times, "The champion's face resembled a mask that had been stretched to fit."

The next day, not looking much better, he told Sports Illustrated's Mark Kram that he had been pushed into a strange and frightful place. "It makes you go a little insane," he said. "I was thinking at the end, why am I doing this? What am I doing in here against this beast of a man? It's so painful. I must be crazy. I always bring out the best in the men I fight, but Joe Frazier, I'll tell the world right now, brings out the best in me. I'm gonna tell you, that's one helluva man, and God bless him."

Frazier had been unable to appear at that same reception, resting in a dark room instead. When Kram reached him, he found a similar appreciation. "Man, I hit him with punches that'd bring down the walls of a city," he said. "Lawdy, Lawdy, he's a great champion." Later that night, though, he was able to make a party of his camp's making and, though still unable to recognize most people, did manage to sing with his band.

The mutual gallantry might be short-lived. Ali's apology to Frazier's son Marvis, in the dressing room, would not prove sufficient. And Frazier's initial respect for the victor might not last beyond the night. But, then, if a storybook ending could be fashioned from such an exaggerated competition as this, could it have really been authentic in the first place? They had very nearly fought to the death. Friendship does not bloom there.

In fact, hardly anything survives it. The heat of their rivalry turned into a kind of self-immolation, each man consumed in his own desperate effort to destroy the other. There wasn't anything left of them. They fought on, of course—Foreman, too—but never to any similar effect, never again approaching greatness or any form of brilliance. It was over, even if they didn't know it yet. They had, for the benefit of a country that just then needed the warm glow of glory, made a bonfire of themselves. Their embers, after all this time, still smolder away.

1996

CHAPTER 21

A STEAMBOAT, LEPROSY, AND A CAESARS PALACE PARKING LOT

The opening ceremonies of any Olympics are a kind of international one-upmanship, the host country desperate to produce something at least one level more outlandish than its predecessor. That the spectacle is completely disassociated from the athletic events that follow it is a given. Nobody stresses over relevancy; this is pure theater, where organizers test the world's patience for surrealism. It's just tradition.

The Atlanta Games were no different, setting the stage with a psychedelic preamble of its own. Some kind of mechanized bird, with a huge silver beak, swept across the stadium floor, mowing down a field of butterflies. Green gnomes, white pixies, and yellow whirligigs produced a colorful formation of uncertain significance. Also, cloggers (twenty-four), cheerleaders (five hundred), and Chevy pickup trucks (thirty). They played Martin Luther King Jr.'s "I Have a Dream," but also Gladys Knight's "Georgia on My Mind." And just when you started thinking it might all make sense, giant catfish pulled a nineteen-foot-high steamboat onto the field.

This, then, represented the American experience, circa 1996. The country had been shaken anew just days earlier when TWA

Flight 800 had exploded minutes after takeoff, killing all 230 aboard. Coming as it did on the eve of the Olympics, a quadrennial exercise in domestic security to begin with—eight-foot fencing encircled the Olympic Stadium—there was this additional overhang of tension, one more impediment to amazement. But not even a threat of terrorism could stand up against such an Olympian onslaught of the outrageous. By the time a formation of dancers had spelled out HOW Y'ALL DOIN? on the stadium carpet, everybody just had to agree: pretty damn good.

Still, nobody was prepared for what came next. The official opening of the Olympics—and this is tradition, too—calls for some athlete or otherwise meaningful personage to transfer the flame from its around-the-world journey to a cauldron that will burn for the duration of the Games. This happens after the field has been scrubbed clean of all its hallucinatory production value and been replaced by actual athletes. It is a hushed and dramatic moment in its own right, but it is given even more power by the choice of the final torch bearer, presumably a symbol for the times. As usual, the identity was kept secret. Evander Holyfield, maybe? Janet Evans? Nobody knew.

No, not them, because here came Holyfield, Atlanta's favorite son, chugging down the track, handing it off to Evans, America's favorite daughter, who took the torch up a long ramp, stopping on a platform way beneath the cauldron, where a man in a white track-suit was emerging, as if from behind a curtain. He was holding an unlit torch in one hand. The other was shaking uncontrollably. It was Muhammad Ali.

Until that instant, Evans touching her torch to his, Ali's legacy had not been fully considered. He'd been one of America's most famous citizens, one of the country's greatest athletes, the most colorful performer of all time. He'd been a source of controversy and division in his youth, a religious and political poltergeist scaring the bejeezus out of responsible citizens. But he'd also been a heroic performer, gracefully steadfast in his views, responsible for some of the greatest and most satisfying spectacles of his time. Here he was, at the age of fifty-four, long past his prime, and he, now that we thought about it, still hadn't been defined.

Until that instant, Ali stooping to light a wick that would travel high above him, where the cauldron would burst into flame and provide that warm international glow for the next two weeks. Until that instant, his stooped and trembling husk a visible reminder of his sacrifice. Until that instant—we hadn't really made sense of him.

But no sooner had that cauldron caught fire than America, probably the world, realized what he'd come to mean to us. In a feel-good moment that caught everybody by surprise—"grown men and women weeping without shame," according to one account—we suddenly understood that the turbulence he'd imposed upon us, and the punishment he'd accepted on our behalf, had been altogether necessary, good for us, actually. Seeing him in his physical decrepitude—his Parkinson's had not only destroyed his animal grace but made his once-lively face a mute mask—was shocking, of course. The frailty was not just tragic but ironic. The quickest man in the world was slowed to a tremulous standstill; the loudest man in the world was stilled by a paralytic disease. But it was not humiliating. In his physical humility, he seemed prouder than ever. Certainly, everyone in the stands that night was. A chant of "Ali, Ali, Ali," once a call to battle, now grew and grew. The hairs on your arms stood on end.

He had traveled a longer and more difficult road here than any Olympic torch had. If, according to the epiphany in Atlanta that hot night, Ali had become beloved and was now a national treasure, well, that took both some doing and a lot of time. Not even the humility that was enforced by a terrible disease could account for his newfound acceptance. He had done more than grow sick to earn this.

Probably he could have coasted to this iconic status, just on the basis of that last fight with Frazier. Frazier had not only allowed him the title that stifling morning, but given him the opportunity to demonstrate an otherworldly courage, something that now had to be counted against the flippancy of his youth. He had grown less and less ridiculous, bout by bout, until he'd finally proved his seriousness beyond all question in Manila, willing to fight to the death if he had to. Not many have the chance to make such a statement. But all who do enjoy a kind of respect ever after. The Thrilla in Manila, it gets you a lifetime pass.

But he didn't coast. He certainly didn't retire. He'd taken some easy fights, including a laugher with Jean-Pierre Coopman. That fight was enough of a mismatch that even Ali felt bad for his public, or at least the network that was broadcasting it. Leaning over the ropes after the first round, he shouted to some TV types, "You guys are in trouble. Ain't no way you're gonna get all your commercials in." Coopman, who'd been swilling champagne between rounds, hit the deck for good in the fifth.

Ali might have been forgiven if he'd continued like this, working his way through the Coopmans of the world, easing into a well-deserved retirement. What was left to prove? Who was left to fight? He'd emerged from the sport's single most important and deadly tournament the undisputed winner. He'd gotten all the acclaim that might ever be available. And, while he was just thirty-two, he'd suffered enough punishment, most of it from Frazier, to qualify for an early pension in anybody's opinion. Rocky Marciano had retired undefeated at that same age and was held in high esteem as much for his sensible withdrawal as for his record.

But Ali was not getting the same advice the Rock did, and, besides, why not take this show a little further down the road, collect some more paydays for the gang? What's the harm? And so he disposed of Jimmy Young and Richard Dunn in the boxer's equivalent of a victory lap. The fights verged on the grotesque, Ali out of shape and uninterested. He brought some of his promotional gifts into play, promising a bounty of $1,000 for Howard Cosell's toupee before the Young fight, but the public seemed to be losing interest even as he was.

An exhibition with a Japanese professional wrestler in Tokyo further tested his public's patience. That was supposed to be a highly scripted affair, Antonio Inoki even agreeing to cut himself with a razor during the bout, but instead degenerated into an insufferably boring free-for-all when Ali would not agree to the fix, Inoki crab-walking, kicking Ali in the legs from time to time.

Ali recognized he was exhausting all the goodwill he'd created in Manila, the respect for that achievement slowly petering out with each subsequent debacle. Also, the promoters' willingness to pay him his accustomed rates—this was not irrelevant anymore; his infidelity, given worldwide exposure in Manila, had just cost him his marriage to Belinda (he'd make if official with Veronica the next year), and a costly settlement loomed.

So three months after he wrestled Inoki, and a year after he fought Frazier, he agreed to meet Ken Norton, his old nemesis, again. There was no colossus on the horizon, no Foreman or Frazier to dream of Ali's title and get the world all agitated again, but at least there was this one fighter who'd once given Ali trouble. It might be worth as much as $6 million to Ali to see if Norton could give him some more.

Fighting in Yankee Stadium in September 1976, Norton gave him some more trouble. He was built to give Ali trouble, always coming forward when Ali was more suited to advancing. Ali had taken this fight seriously, at least, but, even beyond the problems Norton was always going to present, it had never been more obvious that he was not the fighter he once was. Still, he prevailed, mostly because Norton, told he was winning easily, gave away the last round. Ali, with Dundee exhorting him to "close the show," fought with the greater urgency.

But, victory or not, this was a real wake-up call. Mark Kram wrote in *Sports Illustrated,* "There's no question now that Ali is through as a fighter. The hard work, the life and death of Manila, the endless parade of women provided by the fools close to him, have cut him down."

Just days later, appearing in Istanbul with Wallace Muhammad (the head of the Muslims in America after Elijah's death), Ali seemed to agree and announced his retirement. "Mark my words," he said, "and play what I say right now fully. At the urging of my leader Wallace, I declare I am quitting fighting as of now and from now on I will join in the struggle for the Islamic cause."

There was some reason to believe him. Even he must have recognized he was slipping. This way he would retire with his title and, according to him, "$6 million tax-free, saved up, drawing seven per cent interest. What I gotta keep on fighting for? Wise for me to get out now. There's nothing else to prove. This thing is dangerous."

On the other hand, there was very little reason to believe him. He'd announced his final fight so many times already—one more, he'd said in Malaysia; one more, he'd said in Manila—that it was clear he never really saw himself outside of boxing. As many cynics suspected, his retirement didn't last long. Less than eight months after the Norton fight, Ali was back in the ring again.

It was a boring bout, against a virtual nobody named Alfredo Evangelista. The Spaniard had been fighting less than two years and would have been better matched with Coopman than Ali. Yet Ali was unable to put him away or, for that matter, mount any kind of crowd-pleasing attack. Everybody could see it. The end was near. "The fact that the bout went 15 rounds," Cosell said, "told you Ali was shot."

Except for Marciano, who probably retired because of a bad back, heavyweight champions do not tend to leave the game on their own terms. They have the most drawing power, after all, and continue to collect large purses even in their decline. It is just too tempting to fight one more time. And maybe one more time after that. The list of champions who frittered away their legacy is long. Even Joe Louis, coming back for a payday that would satisfy creditors, submitted himself to a horrible beating. Was that where Ali was headed?

In September 1977, he fought again. Earnie Shavers was a step up from Evangelista, for sure, and with Foreman's own retirement earlier that year was considered boxing's most powerful puncher. He lost a lot of fights for a contender—he was 54–5–1—but the ones he won were generally without the aid of a scorecard. Only two had gone the distance. This was not a safe opponent by any means.

And Shavers did get him in trouble, rocking him with an over-hand right in the second round that Ali admitted was, "next to Joe Frazier, the hardest I ever got hit." But, once again, drawing on those mysterious reserves, Ali outlasted Shavers for the decision, rallying heroically in the final round.

The wake-up calls were coming fast, one after the other, and everybody was hearing them but Ali. Alarmed at the transformation of his fighter—the man who couldn't be tagged was now becoming famous for his chin—Ferdie Pacheco washed his hands of the whole affair, warning Ali and his manager that Ali's health was now at risk. Even Madison Square Garden announced it wasn't going to be making Ali any more offers to fight there. "Why take chances?" asked Teddy Brenner, the matchmaker.

And still the Ali caravan rolled on. From now on, though, just easy fights. The Coopmans, the Evangelistas. People like that. Leon Spinks.

These things happen to every fighter, no matter how great he is. It would have happened to Marciano, too, if he'd offered the same exposure as Ali. It is inevitable. Once the decision is made to continue, hoping that degraded skills can be offset by decreased competition, an upset becomes unavoidable. Nobody can manage that particular calculus. Nobody ever has, anyway. So for Ali, who had battled Frazier and Foreman, and who had withstood the steady assaults of those fighters from a historically wicked second tier, it was going to be Leon Spinks. It was going to be somebody, some-day. It was Leon Spinks, February 15, 1978, in Las Vegas.

Spinks had been part of a remarkable Olympic boxing team in 1976, a team that included his brother Michael, Leo Randolph, Howard Davis, and Sugar Ray Leonard, all gold medal winners. But it had been only two years since those Montreal Games, and none had a chance to acquire much experience. Spinks had only seven fights under his belt. In addition, he was barely a heavyweight. Like that young Cassius Clay in 1960, Spinks had won his gold at light-heavy. Unlike that young Cassius Clay, he was slow growing into the division. By the time of the fight—they don't pencil out any easier than this—Spinks was not yet 200 pounds. Ali, on the other hand, was reducing frantically, losing 18 pounds in ten days on a diet of juices and cereal. It's what you do for a $3.5 million payday.

So this, finally, was the one. He'd clowned in the early rounds, reprising his old hits like this was an oldies concert. He danced, shuffled, refused to punch, languished on the ropes. Spinks, however, was not running out of gas, as Ali had hoped. And why would he? He was twenty-four! Spinks kept pounding on his body, his arms, his shoulder, then moved the attack vertically, battering him about the ears.

Ali was trailing on the scorecards going into the final round, but so what? Isn't this where he always steeled himself, gathered his resolve, did something unbelievable? He was thirty-six! Spinks kept pounding and nearly floored him at the final bell. Ali never made a peep when the majority decision was announced. "Nobody got robbed," he had to holler later, his hard-charging followers trying to put a good face on the evening. "I lost the fight."

With the upset, additional retirements became problematic. He could have busied himself in various missions. In fact, the day after the fight he was off to Bangladesh, to dedicate a sports stadium to be named in his honor. There was no shortage of opportunities to both satisfy his call to Allah and his need for attention. They could often be combined on a single trip. But if he couldn't leave boxing after a victory over Frazier, he sure wasn't going to leave it after a loss to Spinks, a kid who didn't even have front teeth and rarely bothered to disguise the deficit with a dental bridge. That would just be too much.

A rematch was arranged seven months later in September, a bout that had the unintended consequence of delivering the heavyweight championship, the World Boxing Council's (WBC) version, anyway—after all those hard and contested and, maybe, improperly judged rounds—to Ken Norton. Spinks would rather fight for Ali money than face Norton, the mandatory challenger. If that was karma, though, it was short-lived; Norton turned the title over to none other than Larry Holmes, Ali's old sparring partner, even before Ali and Spinks could meet again.

Ali increasingly identified himself as ambassador to the world, available at almost any global capital you might name. Between the Spinks fights, he found time to jet off to Moscow and central Asia, even returning to Moscow to meet Communist Party leader Leonid Brezhnev and perform a couple of boxing exhibitions there. And he'd even come up with a plan, with its own acronym, by which means he would combat everything from famine to leprosy. His organization would be called WORLD, for World Organization for Rights, Liberty, and Dignity, and would be financed by his global constituency, his fans paying $25 each for a membership.

Oh, he had plans, all right. "I'm going to put on a three-piece suit, carry a briefcase and fly around the world, working for human rights and dignity. I'm going to form my own United Nations with a headquarters in Washington and the flags of the world flying from the top. I'm going to have a big warehouse in Cleveland filled with food and clothes, and when there is a disaster anywhere in the world, I'm going to fly there in my Lear jet and help the people."

But whereas he might have drifted into that line of work full-time as a retired heavyweight champion, he could not yet commit to it as somebody disgraced by a boxing tyro like Spinks. Once back home, he delayed his WORLD scheme and trained harder than ever, sparring more rounds than before. He told *Sports Illustrated,* "I've never suffered like I'm forcing myself to suffer now. I've worked this hard for fights before, but never for this long." He told the magazine he could only bear the sacrifice knowing it was for a final fight. "I know this is my last fight, and it's the last time I'll ever have to do it." He said, "I've been doing if for 25 years and you can only do so much wear to the body. It changes a man. It has changed me. I can see it. I can feel it."

Spinks was not training quite so hard. His manager, Butch Lewis (who got his start in Frazier's camp), was having difficulty keeping tabs on the fighter, who was determined to enjoy his championship spoils. There was cocaine, moonshine whiskey—not even a fledgling bodyguard named Mr. T could keep Spinks from his rightful diversions. Not even when Spinks finally arrived in New

Orleans for the fight could his management relax. Lewis watched in horror as the Spinks motorcade arrived at the hotel and the fighter got out of an arriving limousine and simply stepped into a departing limo. Where to, nobody knew for sure. "He was drunk every night he was here," promoter Bob Arum said. "Leon went to places our people didn't dare go."

The fight was a huge draw. It was a TV fight, none other than Cosell back at the microphone, but the Superdome still filled with more than sixty-three thousand fans, producing a record gate of nearly $5 million. ABC, meanwhile, was poised for the second-largest audience ever, only the *Roots* finale surpassing it. There was a lot of drama at play, not the least of it Ali trying to become champion for a third time, four months shy of his thirty-seventh birthday. Critics had been watching him slowly disappear in the ring for some time now, but it was impossible not to root for him, to hope Ali could somehow muster the magic to leave that ring as a winner.

He did, although there wasn't a lot of magic to it. Ali could only give glimpses of that youthful grace by now, but he sure could demonstrate a veteran's guile. Keeping Spinks in the middle of the ring, he jabbed, clinched, jabbed, and danced away. Spinks had acquired a cacophonous entourage of his own since winning the championship, and he was now served by a corner of no fewer than eleven bucket carriers, each with conflicting instructions. "Well," Dundee said, in genuine admiration from across the ring, "their crazies can match our crazies, anyway."

But Spinks, to the relief of anybody who valued a symmetry of narrative, could not match even this old and reduced version of Ali. Ali endured, winning a unanimous decision in a fight that was far more moving than it was exciting. This was the coda he'd earned, the postscript he deserved. The relief at ringside was palpable. He'd survived, after all. Cosell even delivered a few rhymes of his own, though these had been crafted by that other sixties radical Bob Dylan: "May your song always be sung. / May you stay forever young."

And so Ali rode off into his version of a sunset, retiring with Veronica and their two new children to a mansion in Hancock Park, an old but distinguished part of Los Angeles. International Management Group, the large and respected agency, came on board to line up endorsements, movie and TV deals, and even a ten-city farewell tour in Europe that earned him $1 million. Campus speeches, too, $15,000 a pop. He had crafted, out of a career of utmost difficulty, a virtual gravy train. Who would have ever thought? All he had to do was sit still and enjoy the ride.

But Ali could not sit still and, listening to just about every promoter and schemer who could get his attention, soon derailed that train. He was no friend of money, anyway; his largesse was legendary. And he was not terribly sophisticated when it came to signing deals, which he often did without professional advice. Not even his record purses, which were more than the combined earnings of all previous champions, could withstand the erosion of his good intentions.

Many of the cons came from within his own camp. One such intrigue involved a man named Harold Smith—or was it Ross Fields?—who had persuaded Ali to lend his name to a couple of outfits, one that promoted track and one that promoted boxing. This was a reverse con in a way, in that Smith was paying Ali. But he was ransacking his name. It finally came to light, after nearly four years, that Smith (his alias) had been running these rather lavish operations from funds he embezzled from Wells Fargo bank—like, $21,305,000 worth! Ali was not ruined by the association in the end, and even managed to take some pride in the victimization. "A guy used my name to embezzle $21 million," he said. "Ain't many names that can steal that much."

But he was hurt, even as he was enriched, by one final con. Bored outside of the ring, and not particularly triumphant in a couple of international diplomatic missions, Ali became vulnerable to a pitch by none other than Don King. King had been cut out after the Manila promotion, having run afoul of Herbert Muhammad, but had gone on to gain considerable control of the heavyweight division, including the WBC champion Larry Holmes. Ali had ballooned to 270 pounds, had been noticeably slurring his speech, and was, in any case, thirty-eight years old. But King presented him with an offer of $8 million to meet Holmes in Las Vegas, in the fall of 1980. It was an offer he wouldn't refuse. (Oh, the other offer made to Holmes, including a leather pillowcase filled with $1 million in cash up front? Made by Harold Smith—the money from "oil men from the Middle East.")

Visitors to Deer Lake were not encouraged by what they saw, and their reports on Ali's condition were doubtful enough that the Nevada State Athletic Commission asked for a workup from the Mayo Clinic. The neurological report suggested that, this one time, it was Ali performing the con. Noting that there had been reports of slurring and staggering, the report addressed it as follows: "He stated that he was tired on the day of the examination here and that he had gotten little sleep. He denied any problems in coordination as far as jogging, sparring, or skipping rope. He also says that his memory is excellent and that he can deliver five 45-minute lectures without notes." Further: "Other than occasional tingling of the hands in the morning when he awakens which clears promptly with movement of the hands, he denied any other neurologic symptoms. . . . The remainder of his examination is normal except that he does not quite hop with the agility that one might anticipate and on finger to nose testing there is a slight degree of missing the target. Both of these tests could be significantly influenced by fatigue."

This report was not released, except to say that Ali had passed the physical exams. He was probably tired was all. So neither Nevada nor the sporting press could press any objections to the fight. Holmes voiced some: "As a friend, I have this advice for Ali. You don't need all those house and cars. If you're broke, sell the house and the cars. You can do other things. Don't swallow your pride just to make some money. Don't get into the ring."

But nobody, least of all Ali, was listening to Holmes, the one-time sparring partner who'd become a reliable, if not quite charismatic, champion. Instead, as with all Ali fights, an alternate reality began to take hold, until it came to seem like a really good idea. Ali was thirty-eight, hadn't been in the ring for two years; Holmes was just thirty, coming off seven title defenses. Yet here was *Sports Illustrated,* coming back from Deer Lake where Ali had slimmed down (with the help of a thyroid medication, as it turned out), reporting, "Better Not Sell the Old Man Short." The magazine went on: "It is as if he has turned the clock back to 1971, when he was 29."

Common sense dictated that this was a travesty in the making, if not a looming tragedy. But Ali, whatever he had lost over the years, maintained his gift for turning something as ordinary as real life into falsehood. "A Miracle in Las Vegas," suggested the *New York Times,* partly buying into the Ali legend. Reports of extraordinary amounts of calisthenics, roadwork, and rounds sparring were coming back down the mountain. "It's not gonna be no match," Ali assured readers.

Las Vegas, which was becoming the fight capital in favor of the global outposts boxing had been employing, was filling up with fans and high rollers, all eager to see that old Ali magic. Even Sinatra was there, although this time he was singing at Caesars Palace, not taking pictures in the vast parking lot that had been transformed into an arena. Holmes had been a 3–1 betting favorite, but the odds were drifting toward Ali until it was almost pick 'em. Ali always did have a way of setting the terms of engagement.

But what were they thinking? It had been five years since Ali had fought Frazier in Manila, the time since a demonstration of all that he'd left there. What were they thinking? Ali was a total shell in the ring, not even a ghost of what he'd been. No jab, no loaded right, no defense. Holmes was surprised in the fourth round when a right hook to the kidney—a shuddering blow—did little but elicit a moan. It was then he realized what he was up against. Ali couldn't fight, but he was absolutely prepared to take a beating. For $8 million (actually $7 million, after King reneged on the contract), you got valor, nothing more, but nothing less, either.

Holmes was in a quandary. "What am I supposed to do with this guy?" he asked his corner. Short of murdering him, which was looking more and more a possibility, there was little recourse. Finally, Dundee, acting on a signal from Muhammad, stopped the fight after the tenth round. "It's over," he told Ali. The fighter said, "Thank you."

Yet it still wasn't over. Ali, cheered by test results that showed the thyroid medicine might be responsible for his fatigue that night, could not quite let it go. There were no extravaganzas left in him, just a little send-off, something he could use to finish out his career in a more triumphant way. Embarrassment and humiliation had been the parting shot, a picture of Ali slumped on a stool the lasting image. Maybe fighting Trevor Berbick, a little more than a year later in 1981, would give him the exit he needed.

It wouldn't. In as sketchy a promotion as was ever held—the fight, held in the Bahamas, was delayed two hours while promoters looked for the key to the gate to the outdoor arena—the little-known Berbick won a unanimous decision. Ali was days from turning forty, so he hardly had to state the obvious: "Father Time caught up with me. I'm finished. I've got to face the facts." The single most exciting, exhausting, maddening, glorious, infuriating, spectacular career had finally come to an end.

In the years that followed, his marriage to the beautiful Veronica, the poster girl in Zaire, crumbled. His health deteriorated. Eventually, there was a divorce, and, eventually, there was a diagnosis. Parkinson's disease, a condition that gradually robbed him of voice and movement, exactly the things he was best in the world at using. Whether boxing contributed to that is a medical guess. Probably it didn't help. Whatever the case, Ali was now at the point suggested by none other than Sonny Liston, that point when "you need other people to help you through life."

In 1986 he married his fourth wife, Lonnie, a neighborhood kid from Louisville. And she helped him through life. His finances were stabilized, his health addressed. He was finally allowed a version of peace and tranquillity, although nobody ever believed those were states of mind he preferred. And he was allowed privacy. Although that, too, was never something he sought. But whether by design or disease, he gradually receded from the public eye, the most famous man in the world diminishing year by year. He'd pop up here and there, working his rigid mask of a face into something resembling a smirk, a reassuring impishness. But mostly he retreated into history, not forgotten, of course, but remembered less and less. He just percolated in a nation's consciousness, more of an idea than a man after all this time.

And then that hot night in Atlanta, stepping out of the shadows to accept a traveled flame. What a night that was! An opportunity for a shared relief, all of us grateful that we'd gotten it right after all, that we'd been there, seen this. "Ali, Ali, Ali." The chant went 'round and 'round.

2011

CHAPTER 22

A SECOND BANANA, BETSY ROSS, AND A DODGE DRAFTER

There was a defiance to his obituaries, as if the sport's curators were doubly determined in his death to finally set the record straight. This was their last chance, after all, to restore Frazier's reputation, every bit as battered and ruined as he'd been in Manila. Over the years the legend of his reckless desperation had dimmed, until he'd been reduced to the role of accomplice, Ali's foil, not quite a survivor. He'd lost two of those three fights was the problem. He'd grown poor and bitter, as Ali, even in his silence (maybe because of it), became rich and revered. That was a problem, too. Not even his supporters, of whom legions remained, could reverse the cruel logic of history, or even ignore facts. He was a broken man, living in a room above a boxing gym, haunted by defeat, the echoes of those wonderful yet horrifying bouts growing weaker each year.

Toward the end he existed simply as an example of collateral damage, the result of an athletic urgency taken too far, of an exaggerated competition that just got out of hand. His health was going south even as his fortune evaporated, his legacy likewise fading. All that remained was an ugly bitterness. He had pushed Ali to the brink of extinction, in a brutally choreographed and lightly regulated self-destruction, and had instead stepped over the edge himself. He was never the same. Frazier—that's what happens when pride and ambition become so inflamed that survival is no longer a part of the game plan. Take a look, if you can.

He had been useful, popular opinion had it, as an accessory to Ali's greatness, forcing him to explore the boundaries of human determination and set its outer limits. He'd been useful, Ali fans agreed, his plodding stoicism better illuminating Ali's free-form genius, his one-dimensional style a perfect backdrop for Ali's performance art. He had been useful, his mainstream politics, to the extent he had any at all, a relief for Ali's progressive inevitability. He was Ali's man Friday, his Watson, his Robin, his Jimmy Olsen. He was necessary to the act and was a high-performing functionary, but was surely a secondary character.

But when Frazier died, November 7, 2011, at the age of sixty-seven, the obits began rolling out, almost all of them in rebuttal of that cruel sentence of history. "No One's Second Banana" was one of them. Frazier, they all were at pains to remind, had died of liver cancer, not disgrace. The facts, as they were dutifully trotted out, supported his claim to the championship elite, where fighters of very special abilities and temperaments reside. Smokin' Joe had burned briefly, but brighter than most. There had never been as relentless and remorseless an extension of simple purpose before or since. And that left hook—good Lord! Once, before a fight, an opponent's family had reserved a hospital room in advance. To fight Joe Frazier was to approach the far threshold of dread. That had to be recognized.

When he died it was a shock to realize just how poorly he'd been rewarded for his career and his decency. He had almost nothing to show for it. The huge purses he'd gotten for the Ali fights were all but gone. His position in the '70s, as one of those three most electric performers on a world stage, was strictly emeritus. He didn't matter; he was a historical artifact. When they first put up a statue of a boxer in his hometown of Philadelphia, it was not of him, but of the fictional Rocky Balboa, a character that Sylvester Stallone had chiseled from Frazier himself. The make-believe Rocky, who'd trained on hanging sides of beef, endured longer than Frazier, who really did train on hanging sides of beef.

The obit writers were almost furious at how underappreciated Frazier was. "The Death of the Disrespected" read one headline. "Smokin' Joe deserved so much better," it ended. Another: "He deserves in death the stability of reputation he so often was deprived of in life." Not a few of them were expressions of guilt. The admiration of so much honest resolution, such uncomplicated effort, was too late in coming. "Joe Frazier never got enough from us," one such appreciation went. "Never enough affection, never enough respect. Joe Frazier never got the love we poured down so freely on Muhammad Ali." The writer, who had been too young to contribute to either man's reputation, one way or another, shouldered a shared shame. Yet he concluded, "For this I blame myself."

And it's a good question. Why wasn't he celebrated better in his time? Except for failing to beat Ali two out of three, thereby becoming trapped in the trilogy, Frazier did it better than almost any other fighter. He did not trouble us, as Ali did, with a long twilight. He wrapped his career up rather quickly once he'd fought in Manila. Ali continued to dent his own reputation, fight by fight, until he'd been beaten by a wild kid everybody called Neon Leon. There had been no possible upside to Ali's continued career. In fact, except for the heart-warming moment Spinks allowed him in the rematch, it was all downside, both immediate and deferred. Frazier, on the other hand, wasn't going to linger needlessly.

There was, of course, the matter of Foreman, a rematch that probably couldn't be avoided. There was an economic imperative to that. People wanted to see that, whether Foreman could deck him six times again or whether Frazier could take advantage of Foreman's new rupture of confidence. Either way, both were Ali victims, but even so they were still on that championship tier, another level above the available contenders. Frazier–Foreman II was the next best thing to whatever Ali happened to be doing at the moment.

But this was a fight that only Foreman needed. He was still recovering from the psychic wallop of Zaire, helped along by a decision over Ron Lyle more than a year after losing his belt. If he ever wanted his title back, he'd have to regain some credibility against a marquee fighter just like Frazier.

Frazier, however, didn't need anything. Eddie Futch, who probably saved him from death by keeping him on his stool in Manila, would have preferred he kept on his metaphorical stool. His family had understood, at least hoped, Ali was the last bout. He'd assured them right there in Manila he was through. Really, what was there to gain by pressing on? His contract with Cloverlay had expired in 1974, and he'd been able to enjoy two bouts without financial partnership, making him ever more rich. By his own accounting, he had a house in Philadelphia, that plantation in South Carolina, a pension fund of $500,000, and additional trust funds. And this didn't take into consideration his remarkable fleet—six cars, everything from a custom Corvette to an Austin taxi.

In a way, he even had his health. The damage to a boxer accrues slowly, irreversibly, and sometimes invisibly. So there might be no telling, year by year, what the toll actually will be. But the one thing he could fix, he did, getting cataract surgery in 1975. He could see better than ever, although he now required contact lenses.

But, as he explained to doubters, the impetus to continue is not always financial or even pride. "The most thing is," he told the *New York Times,* just as they were about to announce a contract for a June 15 bout with Foreman, "I love to fight." Anybody who had seen that third Ali fight would have been within their rights to ban Frazier from fighting again. But you cannot easily quench desire, and certainly not the public's appetite for intriguing rematches. Also, promoter Jerry Perenchio, the man who dreamed up the Fight of the Century all those years ago, was offering Frazier, only thirty-two years old after all, $850,000 to step back into the ring.

Frazier, in other words, did not have a problem coming out of retirement. "I can sense that I should still be fighting," he said. "In the morning, nobody has to touch me with an electric pole to get me up to do roadwork. I even been out late at night dancing and when I get home, my body's still wide awake and I go get my running clothes and do my roadwork. And then nobody has to make me go to the gym. Boxing is willpower and knowing that you have to sacrifice. I believe that's still there inside me."

He was even willing to appear in drag as Betsy Ross to help market the fight, coming as it did during the country's bicentennial celebration in 1976. He also appeared in spots as Sitting Bull and Ben Franklin. Foreman dressed up as Paul Revere, issuing the following promise: "Listen my children and you shall hear / Joe Frazier knocked on his ear." In fact, Perenchio seemed to be insisting on a very high level of costuming for the fight, as if that had been boxing's missing angle all along. For the poster Perenchio had the fighters dress up in gladiator attire borrowed from the 1959 movie *Ben-Hur.* It was the "Battle of the Gladiators," after all.

It wasn't so much. Frazier entered the ring with a shaved dome and a new fight plan. The one worked about as well as the other when it came to convincing Foreman to quit. Frazier believed his best chance to do just that was to wear him out and then drop him in a later round. He'd been at ringside for Foreman's return and watched Lyle floor the big man twice, a surprise. "When he got hit," Frazier observed, "he went down. I didn't know that about him before."

And who knows? It might have worked. If only Frazier had gotten past the fifth round. Critics who saw him get into the ring for the first suddenly understood the need for a bald head. It drew attention from his waistline. Frazier, despite running the wee hours away after a night of clubbing, came in at 224 pounds, same as Foreman and 9 more than he'd ever weighed for a fight. Even though he was just thirty-two, he was the picture of an old fighter. "It was as if Jersey Joe Walcott, who had been introduced to the crowd from the ring," *Sports Illustrated* reported, "had stayed to substitute."

Foreman was surprised at Frazier's new defensive tactics. Joe was no longer smokin', but mostly retreatin'. "I was under the impression Frazier could fight only one way, moving right at you," Foreman said. After just one round of such bafflement, Foreman decided to press on, lest this develop into a long night, and to end it as quickly as possible.

By the fifth round, with Frazier borrowing Ali's rope-a-dope, a failed strategy in this case, Foreman was scoring heavily and Frazier was puffing up, as he did increasingly in fights. Finally, Foreman, not so perplexed anymore, splashed a left hook against his head, Frazier sinking to the canvas in a kind of delayed reaction. He was up at the count of four but was immediately pinned against a ring post, where Foreman hit him with a thudding right. And, as they say: down goes Frazier!

Though he made it back up in time, which was an improvement over his performance in Jamaica, nobody was willing to watch anymore. Futch once again raced to his man's rescue, stopping the fight, probably seconds before the ref would have. Not even Frazier offered an argument this time.

He was good-natured afterward, accepting the defeat along with the idea, finally, that he should retire for good. "It's time for me to put it on the wall," he said, meaning his gloves, "and go boogie, boogie, boogie. The whole doggone game was a highlight, a lot of fun. And if I had the chance to do it again, it still would be a lot of fun."

Maybe he should have retired sooner, but it's hard to see how he could have retired better. He realized he was used up as a fighter, and, while nobody likes to go out a loser, he was satisfied he'd given it all he could. As it happened, he didn't stay completely retired. He almost mounted a comeback in 1978, two years later, when promoters tried to exploit his name for a bout with Kallie Knoetze. A bout of hepatitis kayoed that. And then, three years after that, in 1981, he allowed himself to get sucked into one more good-bye, this time a fight with Floyd Cummings that ended in a draw. Frazier had been doing so much time in the gym, training fighters, that he thought, why not? The fight was more or less coincidental with Ali's last bout, his fight with Trevor Berbick in the Bahamas, and the two shared a rueful telephone conversation before their fights: "We're old men and we gotta show the world we can do it," Ali told him. They were old men, and neither could do it. But nobody took the fight or the result seriously, least of all Frazier.

In fact, he mostly boogied. He'd been fooling around with his band for years but now decided to devote all his energy to the re-tooled "Smokin' Joe Revue," an eleven-piece band he'd formed. He even moved to New York City, hiring a choreographer and a voice coach. The group did not penetrate the Top 40 and, aside from a gig at the Rainbow Grill, didn't play a lot of big rooms. A 1980 stint at Frenchman's Reef Supper Club in the Virgin Islands—"the folks at the Reef say dress semi-formally"—was more like it. His singing was not as transcendent as his boxing and even, with his winking permission, became something of a joke. In a beer commercial, during that era when retired athletes were busy hawking Miller Lite, Frazier told the camera he liked the suds so much, "it makes me wanna sing!" The camera panned to a room, clearing out in panic.

But Frazier enjoyed the work, and if all it amounted to was an expensive hobby, well, it was less dangerous than boxing (though he did once break an ankle doing his signature split onstage).

He was probably more serious, and better suited, to his role of trainer. Once retired from boxing, he did not let his gym go fallow. He'd bought it out from Cloverlay, his original investor, along with their stable of fighters, and began managing fighters such as Duane Bobick and Willie (the Worm) Monroe. Frazier liked nothing more than sitting in his office above the gym, examining the action below.

One of his best prospects turned out to be his son Marvis. Marvis Frazier was a heavyweight boxer, and Joe Frazier had been a heavyweight boxer. Yet if you watched either in the ring, you would not recognize any transference of DNA. Marvis had no power whatsoever, relying on quickness entirely. Nor did he possess the maniacal sense of purpose his father had in the ring. Who did? But he was skilled and, left to the care of trainer George Benton while Joe was on tour, developed into a promising amateur, going 56–2, beating three men who would later become champions.

In 1980 he turned pro and, still under the tutelage of Benton, ran off a series of wins. He wasn't a likely candidate for this world, or even a likely son of Joe's, as he was becoming more interested in religion (eventually becoming a licensed minister) than fighting.

Plus, he'd needed surgery to repair a pinched nerve in his neck and suffered additional layoffs as well. But he was a Frazier and undefeated. And therefore a promising contender. In 1983, with Joe managing and training Marvis full-time now, they got a match with Larry Holmes. It was a $750,000 payday, the money mitigating any qualms about Marvis's inexperience. Holmes blasted him out of the ring before the first round ended.

Although Joe seemed to have gotten Marvis back on his feet, after wins over James Tillis and James Smith, he derailed his son's career for good, putting him in with an up-and-coming Mike Tyson. That fight, in 1986, made the Holmes bout look like contract bridge. He might as well have fed Marvis to a wood chipper. Tyson blew him up in less than thirty seconds, one of the more remarkable destructions in ring history. He fought three more times over the next two years, but it was clear he belonged in the pulpit more than the ring. He was soon spending more time at the Faith Temple Church of God in Christ than at Joe Frazier's Gym.

That left Frazier himself at loose ends. Neither the music business nor boxing management offered him, in the end, a sustainable career. Nor did they do much to supplement his finances, which were being slowly overwhelmed by failing businesses such as a limousine service and the gym itself. It is the same old story with high-profile athletes: the spending continues long after the earning stops. He lived in an apartment above the gym for a reason, and not necessarily to examine the action below.

As his future dimmed, he grew more and more preoccupied with the past, which, in his mind, consisted of way too much Ali. He tried vainly to reorder their history, to find a way for him to emerge triumphant. He'd argue that he won the first two fights, that he was the true survivor. In the hallway of his gym hung a blow-up picture, Frazier harpooning Ali in the jaw in their first fight, the one he won. Well, he definitely won that. But that was never enough, not as the years rolled on. It finally occurred to him, if he couldn't claim the edge in their trilogy, he could at least claim authorship of Ali's physical decline.

This was an ugly way to promote his legacy. But he'd been scalded too often by Ali's barbs, his small-time wit. He'd been an Uncle Tom, a gorilla. No apology, no explanation, could ever be satisfactory. What was it about Ali? The two men had once convened in Frazier's office above that gym, hatching plans for their fight, how they'd promote it. They'd been friends. And then Ali would leave, flip his promotional switch, and cast Frazier into the animal kingdom, smelly and stupid. How do you ever forgive that? Ali stung him with such offhand effort, his charisma giving his arguments their only persuasion, that Frazier could only gulp down his humiliation. He was, Ali once told reporters, the only black man "who didn't have rhythm." Ali couldn't even give him his Smokin' Joe Frazier Revue. He had to mock him for that, too.

By the time Ali's authorized biography came out in 1992, Ali was signaling his intention to forgive and forget. "The roughest and toughest was Joe Frazier," he said. "He brought out the best in me." He added, "I'm sorry Joe Frazier is mad at me. I'm sorry I hurt him. Joe Frazier is a good man. I couldn't have done what I did without him, and he couldn't have done what he did without me. And if God ever calls me to a holy war, I want Joe Frazier fighting beside me."

But Frazier was neither forgiving nor forgetting. He was determined to lay siege to Ali's reputation, to take advantage of his silent and mummified tormentor. "He's damaged goods," he said for the very same book. "I know it, you know it. Everybody knows it. . . . He was always making fun of me. I'm the dummy, I'm the one getting hit in the head. Tell me now, him or me: Which one talks worse?"

The satisfaction Frazier took in Ali's decline was unseemly, especially in counterpoint to Ali's apology, his grace in decline. This, the recorded message on his answering machine: "My name is Smokin' Joe Frazier, sharp as a razor. Yeah, floats like a butterfly, stings like a bee? I'm the man who done the job. He knows. Look, see."

There didn't seem to be any bottom to his well of bitterness. He concluded his own 1996 autobiography by saying, "It'd be easy for me to fall in line and act as if Clay was some fuzzy old saint to me, like he is to so many others. I know that's what people would like to hear. Forgive and forget. But I'd be shuckin' you if I told you that." Instead, he continued, "I'd like to rumble with that sucker again, beat him up piece by piece and mail him back to Jesus." And: "Now people ask me if I feel for him, now that things aren't going so well for him. Nope. I don't. Fact is, I don't give a damn. They want me to love him, but I'll open up the graveyard and bury his ass when the Lord chooses to take him. You see what the Lord did to him." He ended the chapter this way: "Now let's talk about who really won those three fights . . . "

And this was before Ali was chosen to light the Olympic cauldron at the 1996 Olympics. Frazier, who attended the Games, found the honor too much, saying, "I wish he'd fallen into [the flame]. If I had a chance, I'd have pushed him in." Later, at a press conference there, he seemed to be mystified by the Ali mystique. "The butterfly didn't do that much," he said, his speech garbled and slurred, even less in command of the English language than ever. "You look at it, he was a dodge drafter, he didn't like his white brothers, all the things he said was really against America."

Just as Ali had puzzled and disappointed him all those years ago, with his hurtful promotional rants, so had he continued to rattle him, his popularity all the more infuriating in this athletic afterglow. Frazier had to wonder: What did he have to do? What could he possibly say? Ali had finally been silenced—he'd done it himself!—yet his voice remained far more powerful than Frazier's own.

That feel-good moment, the one they certainly deserved after so many contentious seasons, eluded them. There never was a proper reconciliation, Frazier never really overcoming his bitterness. This hurt him with the public, of course, everybody expecting Frazier to accept Ali's apology and then thinking him the smaller man when he didn't. In fact, Frazier did finally come around a little bit. Months before he died, during the fortieth anniversary of the Fight of the Century, Frazier sounded a surprising note of resolution. "I forgive him for all the accusations he made over the years," he said. "I hope he's doing fine. I'd love to see him."

But the sentiment, if it was true or just a grudging appeasement of public demand, did not have time to blossom into a proper reunion. That was a lot to ask, in the first place, that the two principals in the greatest rivalry in sports should drop their hands, become a bickering but lovable odd couple. These two men, alone in the world, understood what the other was capable of, and it was simply otherworldly. It was frightening. Maybe a lifelong wariness was all anybody could expect, after all. We'd just have to let the obit writers figure it all out.

2013

CHAPTER 23

A SMELL OF SORROW, HAM HOCKS, AND THE GOURMET PRODUCTS SHOW

Almost everybody was gone now. Ali was all but gone, trotted out on occasion, sometimes the author of a statement, sometimes the recipient of an award, sometimes the silent but benevolent host of an event. All but gone, though. Everybody else, really gone. Nobody remained from his camp, all those hard-charging followers. Pacheco lived on, having parlayed his Fight Doctor notoriety into a broadcasting career and a series of memoirs. He also became a painter, creating vivid tableaus in the studio of his Miami Beach home. Gene Kilroy lived on, too. He also found an afterlife, becoming a casino host in Las Vegas. Once a fixer, always a fixer. But the rest, gone. Bundini, too hard charging for his own good, long gone. He didn't even make sixty. Angelo Dundee, who trained Sugar Leonard to a number of titles after Ali finally retired, died in 2012, just weeks after Ali's seventieth birthday bash in Las Vegas. Angie, whose ringside patter was a dialect of its own, was ninety. He was well remembered.

The Frazier camp had been cleared out, too. Frazier was the last to go, really. Eddie Futch, whom he'd never really forgiven for stopping the fight in Manila, was also ninety, just like his counterpart across the ring, when he died in 2001. He was really well remembered, as much for saving Frazier from that fifteenth round as for his Hall of Famer career as a trainer.

Not many of their ring contemporaries were in for the long run, either. That whole second tier of heavyweights, any one of whom might have starred in some other era, one without Ali, Frazier, and Foreman, was gone, too. Jerry Quarry, who'd given Frazier so much trouble and who bothered Ali in their two fights, died in 1999 at the age of fifty-three. He had fought too long and too hard; he was in full-blown dementia, living on Social Security when his end came. Ron Lyle, who fought Ali and Foreman close, died in 2011. He was seventy. And Ken Norton, who not only beat Ali but busted him up, died in 2013 after a series of strokes. He was sixty-seven and had been in very poor health, some boxing related probably, some the result of a car accident years before.

But what would you have expected? This was a violent trade, and these were the most determined men in it. And it all happened a long time ago. Time would destroy what the crippling effects of boxing hadn't.

Yet one of them had survived. More than survived. Foreman, who'd seemed the most fragile of them all, not only came out of this demolition derby intact, but emerged changed and improved. It was Foreman, enjoying one epiphany after another, taking dizzying turns in his life, who parlayed his role in this debilitating tournament into a fame that might even have eclipsed Ali's, not to mention the kind of wealth that was beyond even most professional athletes.

It was the single unlikeliest development to come out of the whole shebang. Of all of them, Foreman seemed the least equipped for the long run. He was headstrong, unsophisticated, a fast spender, and a man of such varying temperament that a single loss, that unfortunate Rumble in the Jungle, was capable of derailing his entire career, threatening his manhood. He hardly seemed equipped for adulthood, much less success.

Really, would anybody have thought that Foreman, who cobbled his personality from public service announcements and suspect role models, would have had the stuff to become an interesting and complete character? That this onetime thug would end up beloved? That this gloomy hulk would have been the one to leave this all behind, become happy, satisfied, a grinning role model for us all?

No one should have. Nothing could have predicted it. Ever since his loss to Ali, for which he'd found dozens of excuses, he'd been single-minded in his pursuit of a rematch, as if only that could restore his peace of mind. Certainly, he'd been unsettled and scattered immediately after the defeat, entirely unmoored. His personal life was a mess; by 1977 he was expecting his fourth child by a fourth woman. He was increasingly holing up in his five-acre ranch in Livermore, rewinding that Zaire fight on his projector over and over, or tending to his growing zoo, which now included five horses, five pedigreed German shepherds, a five-hundred-pound tiger and a four-hundred-pound lion. Also, a two-thousand-pound bull.

None of it, not even the wins over Lyle and Frazier, had replaced his previous self-confidence, though. Only a return with Ali could. And he possibly was on the verge of getting that, a bout that not only would satisfy his appetite for revenge but might mean a purse of $5 million. Or so said Don King.

All he had to do, King assured him, was "play it smart" in his next fight, the last one the two had with ABC. To Foreman, ranked no. 1 by now, with the WBA hinting it would force Ali to meet him or else strip his title, that meant he had to toy with Jimmy Young a bit, give the network its money's worth. His last three fights, all of them encouraging him to think he'd recovered the old mystique, had gone four or fewer rounds, which, on the other hand, discouraged broadcasters. "Don't try to knock him out too early," King told him before the fight, held March 17 in San Juan. Keep the network happy.

There is one thing Foreman was not good at, and it was toying with opponents. Ali had already demonstrated the game plan for all who would follow. Just keep out of Foreman's range for eight rounds or so and then take advantage of his lack of stamina. Could an unremarkable fighter like Young make that work for him? Yeah, he could. Foreman got Young in trouble several times but was strangely unable to finish him, even when he was satisfied he had toyed sufficiently. Instead, here he was, drifting into these late rounds, past any point he'd ever fought. Both Young and the San Juan heat were putting him in peril as the fight went on, in this uncharted and increasingly uncomfortable territory.

By the twelfth and final round, Foreman was spent. Young recognized as much and suddenly countered one of Foreman's wild rights with an overhand right of his own, sending Foreman to the canvas. Foreman was up immediately, but if it hadn't been clear who was winning the fight earlier, it was at the final bell, Foreman vomiting in his own corner. Young's unanimous decision, which had been unthinkable an hour earlier, was now quite obvious. Some big plans had just been scuttled.

Then it got weird.

Most people in the dressing room thought it was a combination of that last blow and the heat, a one-two punch that sent Foreman into a strange delirium. "Heat prostration," said Gil Clancy, a veteran trainer who was working Foreman's corner that night. But Foreman was recognizing something else, something beyond any physical condition. Anyone else might call it a hallucination or vision. But for Foreman, it was as real as could be. It was practically a visitation.

At first, as he cooled off on the rubbing table in the dressing room, he was able to reduce the defeat to a kind of speed bump. "Who cares about boxing?" he told himself. "I still got everything. I'm George Foreman. If I wanted to I could retire now, go to the country. I could retire and die."

He caught himself. What had he just thought? He could die? Suddenly, in this confused rush of emotions, he was overtaken by a sensation of nothingness. His entourage rushed around him, consoling him, toweling him off, but Foreman descended into the terrifying pit of his mortality. He was going to die. He suddenly knew it. He felt he was "in a deep dark nothing, nothing but nothing." He was experiencing this gloom fully, with all his senses, too. "A smell of sorrow. You multiply every sad thought you've ever had in your life and you would come close to this." He thought of everything he'd worked for, the very things that had initially consoled him, the money in his safe-deposit boxes, his children——"And it just crumbled. It was as if someone took a match to it and, you know how paper burns and then you touch it and it crumbles? It crumbled like I'd fallen for a big joke."

It occurred to him: "Wait, I don't think this is death. I still believe in God." And with that, he was back to this world and sprang upright on that dressing table, telling his horrified handlers that "Jesus Christ was coming alive in me." They scurried around him, trying to reassure him——"Champ, you'll win a fight again." But Foreman was now raving uncontrollably. He was reciting scripture, telling them he was born again. People were panicking. Look, he told them, look where he was bleeding from the thorns. The dressing room was in chaos. They tried to hold him down, but it was no use. "Look," he said, "where they crucified me." They finally got him to a hospital. He'd be all right, they thought. He might have had a concussion. Maybe it was the heat. He'd be all right.

He wasn't all right, at least not in the way a boxer needs to be. He might not have been all right in the way anybody needs to be. He'd been reborn, transformed——whatever. But if he was better prepared for an afterlife, he was having difficulty in the here and now. Back in Houston, he joined a charismatic church and was speaking in tongues with the rest of the congregation, foaming at the mouth, writhing on the floor. One of the most valuable properties in sports was now on the sidewalk, reading apocalyptic scripture into a microphone. Not even the chance to reclaim his title, once Spinks beat Ali in 1978, tempted him to come back to the ring. He wandered the streets in rags, drove a Ford Fiesta, stopped passersby to issue warnings of doom.

Foreman was gone, out of boxing at least. King tried to coax him back, saying he'd seen a vision himself, Foreman striding across a ring. But he'd have none of it. Eventually, time and champions passing, Foreman dropped out of the conversation altogether. He'd announced his retirement, and he seemed beyond temptation. An ordained minister, he soon had his own church, a small outpost outside of Houston called the Church of the Lord Jesus Christ. He settled rather easily into this new and strange life. He'd visit his parishioners, sit at their table, and devour plates of fried chicken and biscuits and gravy. "You want another of these ham hocks?" they'd ask their preacher. He did. His weight crept to 300 pounds, and he wore bulky bib overalls to better hide the fat.

That might have been it. Over the years reporters trooped down to Texas and visited him at his ranch in Marshall, four hours outside of Houston, or at his church in the Houston outskirts. It was an odd but always uplifting story, this onetime menace now booming gospel from a pulpit. It could have gone on this way forever; Foreman still had a generous income from a fund set up during his boxing days and wasn't living on much besides fast food anyway. That ranch in Livermore had been sold years before, the animals sent back to the wild kingdom, most of his rolling stock—the Rolls, the mobile home, the Excalibur—sold, too. On and on he preached.

And then he came back to boxing.

Not even Foreman had a good explanation for it. Not even a vision. He was thirty-seven, now well over 300 pounds and a full decade removed from the ring. Ali was retired by this time. What possibly could entice him back to the sport he'd grown to hate, or at least distrust? Foreman trotted out a grocery list of reasons at the time, including fitness, the financial demands of a growing family (he'd remarried), the chance to expand his Marshall ranch. But the most persuasive reason might have been his desire to fund a youth center. He'd been humiliated when he tried to raise money at speaking engagements, where the church folks were too poor to make anything greater than a token contribution. However, he recalled, he used to make money quite easily, and in large amounts. Just for knocking another man senseless.

But this was a new and quite enormous George Foreman. No longer an intimidating force but a grinning, self-effacing, down-to-earth blob. Yeah, it was a joke—fat, foolish, and going on forty—but he was in on it. He took his comeback from town to town, places like Sacramento and Springfield, fighting no-names for small purses, just $2,500 his first time out. Every place he went he participated in the self-abuse that went with it. And he did it with a laugh.

Still, it didn't seem to amount to much, boxing-wise. He was far removed from that five-year flurry when three boxers circled each other with such entertaining resolve. If he wasn't foolish, he was every bit of forty by 1989, and still kind of fat. Critics who wanted to hold on to their own vision of a fierce and indomitable boxer were having trouble with this new version. "A fraudulent second career," sniffed Ferdie Pacheco. "A traveling road show," said another boxing veteran. Not even promoter Bob Arum could stomach Foreman's litany of "hand-picked bums," almost dropping him when Foreman refused to fight somebody named Anders Eklund. "Hits too hard," Foreman told him.

Yet, fight by fight, the idea began to take hold that Foreman, who retained his brute strength after all, might eventually become the one man to stop Mike Tyson, a pocket-size terrorist who was just then scorching the heavyweight landscape. Well, said Angelo Dundee, after Foreman had dispatched twenty straight opponents, "I give him a shot. I'm open minded. I can be showed."

In 1990, down to 253 pounds but up to forty-one years old, Foreman met the first opponent of any name recognition, Gerry Cooney. In fact, Cooney had been a boxing nonentity since losing in a title bid with Larry Holmes in 1992, but he did have the recall of a murderous left hook. No longer an Anders Eklund, perhaps, but still a onetime contender. Foreman destroyed him in two rounds and just like that, according to *Sports Illustrated,* "had vaulted—well, sort of—into the position of Most Viable Candidate for Tyson."

It seemed real enough that King had prepared a contract, offering Foreman $5 million to fight Tyson sometime that year. Foreman refused, saying, "I was more afraid of Don King and the dotted line than I am of Tyson." But it was clear that Foreman had somehow, in this ridiculous comeback, become marketable, if not altogether credible.

Alas, the whole raison d'être vanished barely a month later, when Tyson got himself upset by Buster Douglas in Tokyo. But

Foreman was not about to fold up his tent show on that account. He'd invested a lot of roadwork, if nothing else. In April 1991 he fought the wonderfully sculpted Evander Holyfield (who had beaten Douglas rather quickly and rather easily) for the WBA, WBC, and International Boxing Federation titles. Foreman, it was observed at the time, was not so sculpted but was the reigning AARP champion. Still, he was guaranteed the incredible purse of $12.5 million, somewhat justifying this four-year journey. Critics pointed out that that was a bargain, all the same, only $50,000 a pound.

What was more incredible than the purse, somewhat justified by a viewing audience even bigger than the Holyfield-Douglas fight, was the action in the ring. It had actually been a marvelously competitive fight. Holyfield, the better boxer, had his hands full in winning the unanimous decision. Foreman had stung him with those thudding punches of his. Moreover, Foreman did not run out of gas for once. At the age of forty-two, still fat, he no longer seemed so foolish. He was actually becoming something of a folk hero.

Then, five fights later, and almost exactly twenty years since he lost to Ali (and wearing the same red trunks from that disastrous bout), Foreman won the heavyweight championship. Michael Moore had beaten Holyfield out of the title in the spring of 1994 and, for his first defense, agreed to meet Foreman for a championship fight that November. Foreman was now forty-five (but still hovering around that 250-pound mark) and still more a novelty than a true contender. His likability forced the match—and accounted for his $3 million payday—as much as anything; oddsmakers still pegged him as a 3–1 underdog. Yet it turned out to be quite a simple feat, Foreman retrieving that old sledge of a right hand, and driving it right through Moore's mitts, early in the tenth round. This was almost nostalgic. Just like victims of yore, Moore sank straight down, lifted his head briefly, and then, as he'd been sufficiently relaxed, lowered it again, as if ready for sleep.

It was reasonable to wonder how different the world might have been had Foreman been able to do just that in Zaire. Of course, Moore was no Ali. Yet it could hardly have been more interesting than doing it two decades later. This was one of those improbable events that readjusted everybody's expectations of middle age. A heavyweight champion at forty-five? It also readjusted everybody's understanding of Foreman. His competitive zeal had been cloaked in fat and buffoonery. Turns out he had taken this much more seriously than anybody else.

Foreman proved to be an indifferent champion, allowing the WBA to void his title for failure to defend and ultimately losing his final fight in 1997. At the age of forty-eight! But he'd made his point, made his money, and, if he never got to enjoy redemption against Ali, did win his crown back. But by then—and his story just gets more improbable—he was already on to bigger things.

And not just his broadcasting career. HBO, the preeminent fight presenter, had hired him in 1992, alert to his growing popularity. Foreman was a cheerful-enough analyst, though not one given to homework. Before one fight he asked blow-by-blow man Jim Lampley how to pronounce a fighter's name. Nor did he especially believe in teamwork. He rarely consorted with his cohosts before fights and always took the red-eye (until he bought his own jet) immediately afterward to be home in time for his Sunday sermons. But HBO was happy to have his quirky spontaneity ringside, and, often, he turned out to be the most entertaining boxer at the event.

His endearing jack-o-lantern smile earned him other opportunities as well. Capitalizing on his well-earned reputation for gluttony, he was hired to endorse products from companies such as KFC and Doritos. But his really big break came in 1995 when a man whose best-selling appliance had been a radio that was built to float in a swimming pool invited the fighter to the Gourmet Products Show in Las Vegas. That man, Leon Dreimann, was trying to market a countertop grill, its hook being its ability to magically sluice away the fat. He'd been told that Foreman, who had become as famous for eating cheeseburgers as dispatching opponents, might be just right for the product.

Dreimann was astonished at the pandemonium Foreman created at the products show. He decided on the spot to make Foreman a partner, not simply a pitchman, agreeing to a 45 percent split for the fighter—cheeseburger eater. It seemed a preposterous deal, except that the machine had already been around a while and had never made a dent in the market. Forty-five percent of nothing was still nothing.

But once the company realized that infomercials of Foreman cooking away with the grill, the fat just dripping from the machine, instead of footage from his fighting days, were what was resonating with homemakers, sales took off. It turned out that it was his good humor, not his pugilistic pedigree, that was moving the grill. Once, during a segment on QVC, while the host was rambling on about it, Foreman absentmindedly picked up a cheeseburger and began chomping away. Suddenly, red lights began blinking in the studio, calling all available salespeople to their phone stations. Looking at the video the next day, they realized that Foreman's random appetite had triggered the sales tsunami.

The George Foreman Lean Mean Grilling Machine became one of those marketing sensations, its appeal entirely tied up with its celebrity endorser. Outside of the Franklin stove, there is not another appliance that is so singly identified by its creator, or presenter. The machine had been a dud. Then suddenly, with this grinning corpulence waving his spatula in round-the-clock commercials, it was one of the most iconic appliances in American culture.

Foreman had vaguely dreamed of making $1 million out of the deal. And at first, the monthly checks just dribbled in. But they were growing every month—$5,000, then $10,000. In 1997, when he was preparing to fight Shannon Briggs, his attorney came to his Atlantic City hotel room with a monthly check for $1 million. It took some of the sting from the loss, a controversial one. No wonder it was his final fight.

So this is how you handle celebrity! Once he thought the correct response to attention was a forbidding curtness. Maybe a shot to the snoot. That's how Sonny Liston handled fame. But perhaps this was better, smiling away, signing every autograph request, returning every public consideration with good humor. By 1999, his boxing career over simply because he had forgotten about it, the monthly checks were approaching $4 million.

It was that year, when fears that sales might be flattening (by then, who in America hadn't already bought a version of it?), that Foreman agreed to conclude his deal, taking a lump sum of $137.5 million. Nobody had ever made more from endorsements in a single year. Not Tiger Woods, not Michael Jordan. Only George Foreman, the guy who looked so stupid over in Zaire, just flailing away.

Foreman had led a life of serial self-improvement, as alert to opportunity as revelation. There were zigs and zags along the way, as he tried on different personalities, undertook different occupations. From surly enforcer to cheerful endorser, a heavyweight champion and minister in there somewhere. He'd grown up in a country, in a time, when ambition was rewarded in direct proportion to its recklessness. Reinvention was not the miracle it seems today. You could be anybody—a champion at forty-five as easily as at twenty-four!—and you could do anything. You could sell kitchen gadgetry or preach a gospel.

Foreman alone among his blood brothers got out alive. Frazier died poor and bitter. Ali withdrew into his disease. But Foreman was left to enjoy the spoils. He tootles around Houston, between his ranch in Marshall with its herd of Icelandic stallions and his home in Humble, with its German shepherds and his warehouse of exotic cars. Mechanics loiter about, looped ties in their pockets in case the boss shows up. Or maybe he drifts over to the church, or his youth center. He'd be driving his V-12 BMW either way. Or writes a check for $1,000,007 to the M. D. Anderson Cancer Center. "Anybody can donate $1 million," he says, explaining the figure, if not the impulse.

It really was strange that it would be Foreman, out of all of them, who would end up so comfortable, at such peace. Hadn't they all deserved this, after such self-sacrifice? Didn't they have that coming? Their five fights—American spectacles of ambition, excess, and unadulterated desire—cost them dearly. Nobody before or since has ever agreed to such a debilitating tournament, or paid such a price. Yet a country that basked in their reflected glory could not, in the long term, accommodate all three. It was just Foreman, healthy and wealthy after all these years, who would truly profit from their violent extravaganzas.

Well, not just Foreman. It had all been for our great amusement, after all, during a time when the country teetered on its moral ledge. So we thought. But it turned out to be something more important than just entertainment. Their unabated resolve had been reassuring, necessary, just then, as if to remind America that the right thing, certainly the hard thing, was still worth doing. They did it, didn't they? So it wasn't only Big George Foreman who survived that raucous, crazy, thrilling, and ridiculously dangerous time. The country, now that we think about it, had gotten out alive, too.

* ACKNOWLEDGMENTS

The luck of having these three figures in one place at one time is undeserved, of course. Any one of them—Muhammad Ali, Joe Frazier, or George Foreman—should have been bonanza enough. But all three? Together? Just then? Well, now we have the makings of a book, or so it seemed to me.

And yet without the accompanying journalism of their frantic era, heavyweight scribes who were uniquely up for this challenge, I doubt it would have been possible. The principals are mostly gone, their fantastic entourages thinned by time, so all that remains are the generation's archives. Here again, luck. Was there ever such a collection of writers to stand witness to this story, sportswriters who were so able to render the fun of these shenanigans, all the while understanding their importance? Not that I know of.

So I mostly want to thank them, themselves a traveling circus (and themselves thinned considerably), who not only had the wit to recognize a growing narrative but the style to give it a lasting voice. I don't know if theirs was the Golden Age of Sportswriting but I will say it was not a bad time to be reading boxing. Think of the people still pounding their keyboards at ringside in the 1970s: Red Smith, Dave Anderson, Robert Lipsyte, Jim Murray, Larry Merchant, Mark Kram, Hugh McIlvanney, Dave Kindred, Jerry Izenberg. They deserve more than a citation in the endnotes. And how about Norman Mailer, George Plimpton, or Budd Schulberg? Like I say, luck. A lot of heavyweights in one place at one time, never mind that Hunter S. Thompson gave away his Rumble in the Jungle press credential. That might have been something.

Also, in a more contemporary gratitude, I'd like to thank agent Scott Waxman and the book's editor, Robert Pigeon, who both shared my enthusiasm for this project.

* NOTES

Chapter 1

7 **"Why do I want to live in a rat bin":** Associated Press, January 30, 1970.

8 **Muhlenberg scene:** Ron Czajkowski, author interview, January 9, 2013.

9 **Randolph-Macon scene:** James Cortada, author interview, January 15, 2013.

10 **"Once you get to be champion":** George Foreman, author interview, December 6, 2012.

11 **Bugner paid him:** Howard Bingham and Max Wallace, *Muhammad Ali's Greatest Fight: Cassius Clay vs. the United States of America,* 186.

13 **Clay initially classified as unfit:** Thomas Hauser, *Muhammad Ali: His Life and Times,* 143.

13 **"You go ahead":** *Muhlenberg Weekly,* February 5, 1970.

15 **"You niggers give me":** Associated Press, January 30, 1970.

Chapter 2

15 **"Screw the tournament":** Joe Frazier with Phil Berger, *Smoken' Joe,* 55.

16 **pile of cash:** *Sports Illustrated,* July 10, 1967.

16 **"They're Talking Frazier":** *Ring,* June, 1967.

16 **"Scrap Iron Johnson gave him":** *Sports Illustrated,* July 10, 1967.

17 **a fifteen-inch Philco and other biographical details:** Joe Frazier with Phil Berger, *Smokin' Joe.*

19 **"With me around":** *Sports Illustrated,* August 14, 1967.

19 **"It was a complete success":** *Sports Illustrated,* June 17, 1968.

20 **"In the gyms guys are whispering"**: Ibid.

20 **"Here I am," he said**: *Sports Illustrated*, October 10, 1969.

21 **"Sissy, you can't hit"**: Frazier with Berger, *Smokin' Joe*, 80.

21 **"This town is too small for both of us"**: *New York Times*, February 17, 1970.

Chapter 3

23 **He'd been a thief and other biographical details**: David Remnick, *King of the World*.

24 **He'd been a small-time punk**: G. Foreman, author interview.

24 **"the silver coin toll"**: *Sports Illustrated,* July 17, 1989.

24 **"Keep it up, big man"**: Bill Caplan, author interview, October 25, 2012.

25 **the Louisville Sponsoring Group**: Hauser, *Muhammad Ali,* 30.

25 **He thought Frazier**: G. Foreman, author interview.

26 **Sadler got Foreman**: Ibid.

27 **Once, the whole gang in Sadler's car**: Ibid.

28 **"little mean guy"**: Ibid.

30 **Liston's bloated body**: Remnick, *King of the World,* 293.

Chapter 4

33–34 **Madison Square Garden scene**: Michael Arkush, *The Fight of the Century: Ali vs. Frazier, March 8, 1971; Ebony,* May 1971.

37 **Ali hunkered down**: Dr. Ferdie Pacheco, author interview, October 11, 2012.

37 **The Garden had provided**: Arkush, *Fight of the Century.*

37 **"Tonight is the night of truth"**: *Ali the Fighter.*

38 **Frazier's camp was suffering**: Dave Wolf, *True,* July 1971.

38 **Archie Moore, a former champion**: *Ali the Fighter.*

39 **"Oh, the satisfaction"**: Ibid.

39 **Pacheco wondered**: Arkush, *Fight of the Century.*

40 **"What Frazier doing right now"**: *Ali Frazier I: One Nation Divisible.*

40 **"You guys just come in start shooting"**: *Ali the Fighter.*

41 **"I'm in the belly"**: Larry Merchant, author interview, March 4, 2013.

Chapter 5

43 **"What you got there?"**: Caplan, author interview.

44 **Later, when he visited**: John Capouya, *Gorgeous George: The Outrageous Bad Boy Wrestler Who Created American Pop Culture,* 241.

45 **"Who were those little sissies?":** Robert Lipsyte, *An Accidental Sportswriter: A Memoir,* 64.

46 **"If Baptists":** Hauser, *Muhammad Ali,* 217.

47 **Ali-Frazier conversation:** Muhammad Ali with Richard Durham, *The Greatest: My Own Story,* 223–249.

48 **Martin Luther King Award:** Michael Ezra, *Muhammad Ali: The Making of an Icon,* 150.

48 **"athlete of the decade":** Gerald Early, *The Muhammad Ali Reader.*

49 **"I really don't know":** *Sports Illustrated,* January 25, 1971.

50 **"It's potentially":** Ibid.

52 **"The Battle of the Undefeated":** *Life,* March 5, 1971.

53 **"That Joe Frazier":** Bingham and Wallace, *Muhammad Ali's Greatest Fight,* 234.

53 **As Schulberg:** Budd Schulberg, *Loser and Still Champion: Muhammad Ali.*

53 **"Nobody wants to talk":** Ibid., 134.

53 **"would be especially":** *Ebony,* March 1971.

54 **"to free 30 million":** *Time,* March 8, 1971.

54 **"I don't want to be":** Ibid.

54 **"The All-Time Fascination":** *New York Times,* March 6, 1971.

54 **seats were selling out:** Arkush, *Fight of the Century.*

Chapter 6

57 **two backup generators:** *New Yorker,* March 20, 1971.

57 **"I'm gonna kill you":** Frazier with Berger, *Smokin' Joe.*

58 **"That," said Burt Lancaster:** Closed-circuit telecast, 1971.

58 **"It's amazing":** Ibid.

59 **"What's holding him up?":** Frazier with Berger, *Smokin' Joe.*

59 **"All through the first":** *True,* June 1971.

59 **"Joe was as easy":** Schulberg, *Loser and Still Champion,* 142.

59 **"It was obvious":** Norman Mailer, *Life,* March 19, 1971.

59 **"exploiting the anticipated":** Hugh McIlvanney, *McIlvanney on Boxing: An Anthology,* 45.

60 **"He snake-licked":** Mailer, *Life,* March 19, 1971.

60 **"He's out":** Arkush, *Fight of the Century.*

63 **"When Ali tasted":** Donald Reeves, *New York Times,* May 17, 1971.

64 **The fight fans:** *Ebony,* May 1971.

64 **Celebrating with far less:** Arkush, *Fight of the Century.*

64 **"He held his camera":** *Life,* March 19, 1971.

64 **"I want him over here":** Mark Kram, *Ghosts of Manila,* 148.

65 **"Did he fall?":** Ibid., 148.

65 **"That is the question":** George Plimpton, *Shadow Box: An Amateur in the Ring*, 191.

65 **His "guns" were loaded:** *Sports Illustrated*, April 5, 1971.

65 **"Must have been a helluva":** Ibid.

66 **"When you get as big":** McIlvanney, *McIlvanney on Boxing*, 47.

66 **"struck down with the flu":** *New York Times*, March 14, 1971.

Chapter 7

72 **"zip-punch-power-bang":** G. Foreman, author interview.

72 **Foreman trained his fists:** Ibid.

72 **"I've seen you":** Ibid.

73 **revealed "the techniques":** *Ring*, August 1971.

73 **in *Ring*'s opinion:** Ibid.

74 **One other thing:** *New York Times*, July 30, 1972.

74 **"We've got to get him":** Arkush, *Fight of the Century*, 204.

75 **But Chamberlain:** Hauser, *Muhammad Ali*, 237.

75 **"It's like a man's been":** Bingham and Wallace, *Muhammad Ali's Greatest Fight*, 248.

76 **"Clay Stock Drops":** *Ring*, July 1972.

76 **Part of the problem:** Frazier with Berger, *Smokin' Joe*, 128.

77 **"cool boxing experience":** G. Foreman, author interview.

78 **He fired Sadler:** Ibid.

78 **"Let me try once more":** Plimpton, *Shadow Box*, 17.

79 **"Louis was light-fingered":** Thomas Hauser, *Straight Writes and Jabs: An Inside Look at Another Year in Boxing*, 93.

80 **Moore was far more direct:** G. Foreman, author interview.

81 **"She's daddy's baby girl":** Ibid.

Chapter 8

83 **He'd bounced poor:** Jack Newfield, *Only in America: The Life and Crimes of Don King*, 4.

83 **"Donald, don't kick him":** Ibid., 5.

84 **He bet $5,000:** Ibid., 12.

85 **The first to be ensnared:** Don Elbaum, author interview.

85 **"You don't want a black":** Ibid.

86 **The gate was:** Newfield, *Only in America*, 30.

87 **He had managed to buy it:** Ibid., 21.

88 **He'd formed a group:** Elbaum, author interview.

89 **"Frazier was made to order":** Ibid.

Chapter 9

94 **accounts of the Dempsey fight in Montana:** Jason Kelly, *Shelby's Folly: Jack Dempsey, Doc Kearns, and the Shakedown of a Montana Boomtown.*

95 **"It is an island":** *Los Angeles Times,* January 21, 1973.

95 **National Sports, Ltd.:** *Daily Gleaner* (Kingston, Jamaica), January 21, 1973.

95 **"Come to fight":** *Hayward (CA) Daily Review,* January 22, 1973.

96 **"Take a gander":** *Sports Illustrated,* February 2, 1973.

96 **"Joe Frazier, sharp":** Roy Foreman, author interview.

97 **"They're talking about":** *New York Times,* December 13, 1972.

97 **"Don't let nothing":** *New York Times,* January 23, 1973.

98 **"He's always in front":** *New York Times,* January 21, 1973.

98 **"I'm rooting for Frazier":** *Hayward (CA) Daily Review,* January 22, 1973.

98 **"been with George":** *Sports Illustrated,* February 5, 1973.

98 **"hits like a tornado":** *New York Times,* January 22, 1973.

99 **"I'm worried none":** *Sports Illustrated,* January 15, 1973.

99 **"I like a man":** *Sports Illustrated,* February 5, 1973.

100 **"Look at him":** G. Foreman, author interview.

102 **"My man!":** Roy Foreman, author interview.

103 **"Don't feel bad":** G. Foreman, author interview.

Chapter 10

105 **"Do you know where":** *The Dick Cavett Show,* February 21, 1973.

108 **Cosell thought:** Howard Cosell, *Cosell,* 239.

108 **"revolutionizing the game":** *Sports Illustrated,* April 23, 1973.

108 **"The minute you hit":** *New York Times,* October 25, 1989.

108 **"The edges kept poking":** *New York Times,* April 2, 1973.

109 **"Right now":** *Ring,* June 1973.

111 **"Old heroes":** *New York Times,* September 6, 1973.

Chapter 11

113 **"When you picture":** *New York Times,* September 20, 1972.

115 **"The boxer, Sugar Ray":** Kenneth Shropshire, *Being Sugar Ray,* 155.

116 **"That was no way":** *New York Times,* September 29, 1987.

116 **"If you gonna tell him":** *Sports Illustrated,* February 15, 1971.

117 **"They not pine":** *Sports Illustrated,* September 3, 1973.

118 **"The tallest race":** Ibid.

119 **"could have killed"**: United Press International, July 3, 1973.

120 **"They are all talking"**: *Sports Illustrated*, September 17, 1973.

Chapter 12

125 **"we're having a scene"**: *Wide World of Sports* telecast.

125 **"There was no title"**: Les Krantz, *Ali in Action: The Man, the Moves, the Mouth*, 94.

126 **"I feel like an Oreo"**: *The Dick Cavett Show*.

128 **"You are a corrupt"**: Kram, *Ghosts of Manila*, 160.

129 **"It was just the way"**: *New York Times*, January 24, 1971.

129 **"Perhaps the fight will be"**: *Time*, January 28, 1974.

130 **"My, my, look at that boy"**: *Sports Illustrated*, January 21, 1974.

131 **"Champ ain't gonna try"**: Kram, *Ghosts of Manila*, 161.

131 **"Answer me"**: *Sports Illustrated*, February 4, 1974.

Chapter 13

133 **"This kind of malaise"**: *Time*, February 25, 1974.

134 **He was still furious:** G. Foreman, author interview.

135 **Foreman suddenly recognized:** Ibid.

136 **"I know Caracas"**: *New York Times*, January 31, 1974.

136 **"I want to hurt him"**: McIlvanney, *McIlvanney on Boxing*, 50.

136 **Somebody did manage:** Caplan, author interview.

137 **"Many times a day"**: *Sports Illustrated*, March 3, 1974.

137 **"It's really best"**: *New York Times*, March 23, 1974.

138 **"It's like magic"**: *Sports Illustrated*, April 8, 1974.

138 **Nobody's hotel room**: Ibid.

139 **The next day:** Caplan, author interview.

Chapter 14

142 **"a bank vault"**: Howard W. French, *A Continent for the Taking: The Tragedy and Hope of Africa*, 54.

143 **"This isn't just another"**: Newfield, *Only in America*, 59.

145 **"sooner or later"**: *New York Times*, October 27, 1974.

145 **"The time may have come"**: *When We Were Kings*.

146 **"George is the first"**: Angelo Dundee with Bert Randolph Sugar, *My View from the Corner: A Life in Boxing*, 173.

146 **Zaire's foreign minister:** Hauser, *Muhammad Ali*, 264.

147 **"to whip Mr. Tooth Decay"**: *When We Were Kings*.

147 **"George Foreman is a"**: *Texas Monthly*, December 2004.

148 **"All we see"**: Hauser, *Muhammad Ali*, 265.

148 **"Africa is the cradle"**: *When We Were Kings*.

Chapter 15

150 **"I'd rather be":** Caplan, author interview.

150 **"This is mine":** Ibid.

150 **"I can beat him":** Joe Ryan, *Heavyweight Boxing in the 1970s,* 277.

151 **"One of the more":** *When We Were Kings.*

151 **"He not only has TNT":** *Sports Illustrated,* October 28, 1974.

152 **"You must not publicize":** *New York Times,* November 14, 1974.

152 **"I'd give anything":** Hauser, *Muhammad Ali,* 270.

153 **"that swift":** G. Foreman, author interview.

153 **He told his PR man:** Caplan, author interview.

154 **"Let the big man":** Ibid.

154 **"Martin Borman":** Plimpton, *Shadow Box,* 226.

155 **"If he doesn't get me":** Merchant, author interview.

156 **"Adversity is ugly":** *Sports Illustrated,* September 30, 1974.

156 **"You are a genius":** Newfield, *Only in America,* 82.

157 **Singer Lloyd Price:** Hauser, *Muhammad Ali,* 262.

157 **"leave 'em all over there":** G. Foreman, author interview.

Chapter 16

159 **"That's the place":** Plimpton, *Shadow Box,* 171.

160 **"As we go to the stadium":** McIlvanney, *McIlvanney on Boxing,* 62.

160 **"What's wrong":** Plimpton, *Shadow Box,* 319.

161 **"like having a nightmare":** G. Foreman, author interview.

162 **"Chump," he told him:** Ali with Durham, *The Greatest,* 403.

163 **"Don't talk":** Dundee with Sugar, *My View from the Corner,* 184.

163 **"A bird's nest":** *Sports Illustrated,* November 11, 1974.

164 **"The magic was gone":** G. Foreman, author interview.

164 **"Ali swayed so far back":** *Sports Illustrated,* November 11, 1974.

165 **"His mind was held":** *New York Times,* August 3, 1975.

166 **"I have a statement":** Plimpton, *Shadow Box,* 327.

Chapter 17

170 **"This is what dying's":** Pacheco, author interview.

170 **"You a nigger":** Kram, *Ghosts of Manila,* 186.

171 **"That was the best thing":** G. Foreman, author interview.

173 **The investor of record:** Newfield, *Only in America,* 88.

174 **King, not so long:** *Sports Illustrated,* September 15, 1975.

175 **King said the groundwork:** *New York Times,* April 28, 1975.

175 **"in order," said Dato Harun Idris:** *New York Times,* June 26, 1975.

Chapter 18

180 **A C-5A transport:** *Time,* April 14, 1975.

181 **"This ain't just a sportin' event":** *Sports Illustrated,* September 29, 1975.

182 **"Frankly," he said in an interview:** Ibid.

183 **As many as five thousand spectators:** *New York Times,* September 24, 1975.

183 **"She is in love":** Kram, *Ghosts of Manila,* 174.

184 **But it had been scant:** *Ebony,* January 1975.

184 **"You have a beautiful wife":** Hauser, *Muhammad Ali,* 315.

184 **"Solemn Muslim guards":** *Newsweek,* September 29, 1975.

185 **"I know celebrities":** *New York Times,* September 24, 1975.

185 **At about that moment:** Hauser, *Muhammad Ali,* 318.

185 **"This is good":** *New York Times,* September 24, 1975.

186 **"Joe Frazier should give":** Kram, *Ghosts of Manila,* 169.

186 **"Look here, nigger":** Ezra, *Muhammad Ali,* 157.

186 **When Frazier began:** Hauser, *Muhammad Ali,* 313.

187 **"He's gonna talk":** *Sports Illustrated,* September 29, 1975.

187 **"He ready to be a corpse":** Kram, *Ghosts of Manila,* 170.

188 **Then there was:** *New York Times,* September 24, 1975.

188 **"Go back in your hole":** Kram, *Ghosts of Manila,* 181.

Chapter 19

192 **Liston once put it:** *Sports Illustrated,* February 4, 1991.

194 **"Go talk to Joe":** *Sports Illustrated,* September 29, 1975.

194 **"Who does this son of":** Frazier with Berger, *Smokin' Joe,* 160.

195 **"My personality":** *Sports Illustrated,* September 29, 1975.

195 **"Watcha got there":** Kram, *Ghosts of Manila,* 183.

196 **Frazier shifted:** Frazier with Berger, *Smokin' Joe,* 161.

Chapter 20

198 **"He won't call you":** *Sports Illustrated,* October 13, 1975.

199 **"What you got":** Kram, *Ghosts of Manila,* 184.

200 **"Old Joe Frazier":** *Sports Illustrated,* October 13, 1975.

201 **"Force yourself":** Ibid.

203 **"The champion's face":** *New York Times,* October 2, 1975.

203 **"It makes you":** *Sports Illustrated,* October 13, 1975.

Chapter 21

211 **"There's no question":** *Sports Illustrated,* October 11, 1976.

212 **"The fact that the bout":** Hauser, *Muhammad Ali,* 341.

213 **"next to Joe Frazier":** Ibid., 346.

213 **"Why take chances":** Ibid.

214 **"Nobody got robbed":** *Sports Illustrated,* February 27, 1978.

215 **"I'm going to put on":** *Sports Illustrated,* September 25, 1978.

215 **"I've never suffered":** *Sports Illustrated,* September 11, 1978.

216 **Lewis watched:** Hauser, *Muhammad Ali,* 358.

218 **Oh, the other offer:** Larry Holmes with Phil Berger, *Against the Odds,* 148.

218 **"He stated that he":** Hauser, *Muhammad Ali,* 405.

218 **"As a friend, I have":** *Sports Illustrated,* April 14, 1980.

219 **"It's not gonna":** *New York Times,* August 22, 1980.

219 **"What am I supposed":** Holmes with Berger, *Against the Odds,* 166.

220 **"Father Time":** *New York Times,* December 13, 1981.

Chapter 22

226 **"No One's Second Banana":** *Village Voice,* November 9, 2011.

227 **"The Death of the Disrespected":** *Nation,* November 9, 2011.

228 **By his own accounting:** Frazier with Berger, *Smokin' Joe,* 169.

228 **"The most thing is":** *New York Times,* March 18, 1976.

229 **"When he got hit":** *New York Times,* June 15, 1976.

229 **"It was as if Jersey":** *Sports Illustrated,* June 28, 1976.

230 **"It's time for me":** Ibid.

230 **"We're old men":** *Sports Illustrated,* December 14, 1981.

232 **Nor did they do much:** *New York Times,* November 20, 1981.

233 **"The roughest and toughest":** Hauser, *Muhammad Ali,* 326.

233 **"He's damaged goods":** Ibid.

233 **"My name is Smokin'":** *Thrilla in Manila.*

233 **"It'd be easy for me":** Frazier with Berger, *Smokin' Joe,* 196.

234 **"The butterfly didn't":** *New York Times,* July 31, 1996.

Chapter 23

241 **"Don't try":** G. Foreman, author interview.

242 **"Who cares about boxing?":** Ibid.

242 **"in a deep dark":** *Sports Illustrated,* July 17, 1989.

243 **He wandered the streets:** Ibid.

245 **"A fraudulent second career":** Ibid.

247 **That man, Leon Dreimann:** *Sports Illustrated,* December 1, 2003.

249 **"Anybody can donate $1 million":** Ibid.

✴ BIBLIOGRAPHY

Books

Ali, Muhammad, with Richard Durham. *The Greatest: My Own Story*. New York: Random House, 1975.

Arkush, Michael. *The Fight of the Century: Ali vs. Frazier, March 8, 1971*. New York: Wiley, 2008.

Bingham, Howard, and Max Wallace. *Muhammad Ali's Greatest Fight: Cassius Clay vs. the United States of America*. New York: Evans, 2000.

Brunt, Stephen. *Facing Ali: 15 Fighters, 15 Stories*. Guilford, CT: Lyons Press, 2002.

Capouya, John. *Gorgeous George: The Outrageous Bad Boy Wrestler Who Created American Pop Culture*. New York: HarperCollins, 2008.

Cosell, Howard. *Cosell*. New York: Simon & Schuster, 1973.

Dundee, Angelo, with Bert Randolph Sugar. *My View from the Corner: A Life in Boxing*. New York: McGraw-Hill, 2007.

Early, Gerald. *The Muhammad Ali Reader*. New York: HarperCollins, 2013.

Ezra, Michael. *Muhammad Ali: The Making of an Icon*. Philadelphia: Temple University Press, 2009.

Foreman, George. *By George*. New York: Villard Books, 1995.

Frazier, Joe, with Phil Berger. *Smokin' Joe*. New York: Macmillan, 1996.

French, Howard W. *A Continent for the Taking: The Tragedy and Hope of Africa*. New York: Vintage, 2005.

Hauser, Thomas. *Muhammad Ali: His Life and Times*. New York: Simon & Schuster, 1991.

————. *Straight Writes and Jabs: An Inside Look at Another Year in Boxing*. Fayetteville: University of Arkansas Press, 2013.

Holmes, Larry, with Phil Berger. *Against the Odds*. New York: St. Martin's Press, 1998.

Kelly, Jason. *Shelby's Folly: Jack Dempsey, Doc Kearns, and the Shakedown of a Montana Boomtown*. Lincoln: University of Nebraska Press, 2010.

Kindred, Dave. *Sound and Fury: Two Powerful Lives, One Fateful Friendship*. New York: Free Press, 2006.

Kram, Mark. *Ghosts of Manila*. New York: HarperCollins, 2001.

Krantz, Les. *Ali in Action: The Man, the Moves, the Mouth*. Guilford, CT: Lyons, 2008.

Lipsyte, Robert. *An Accidental Sportswriter: A Memoir*. New York: Ecco, 2011.

McIlvanney, Hugh. *McIlvanney on Boxing: An Anthology*. New York: Beaufort, 1982.

Newfield, Jack. *Only in America: The Life and Crimes of Don King*. New York: Morrow, 1995.

Pacheco, Ferdie. *Fight Doctor*. New York: Simon & Schuster, 1976.

Plimpton, George. *Shadow Box: An Amateur in the Ring*. New York: Putnam, 1977.

Remnick, David. *King of the World*. New York: Random House, 1998.

Ryan, Joe. *Heavyweight Boxing in the 1970s*. Jefferson, NC: McFarland, 2013.

Schulberg, Budd. *Loser and Still Champion: Muhammad Ali*. Garden City, NY: Doubleday, 1972.

Shropshire, Kenneth. *Being Sugar Ray*. New York: Basic Civitas Books, 2008.

Magazines

Ebony
Jet
Life
Nation
Newsweek
New Yorker
New York Village Voice
Ring
Sports Illustrated
Texas Monthly
Time
True

Newspapers

Chicago Sun-Times
Daily Gleaner (Kingston, Jamaica)
Hayward (CA) Daily Review
Los Angeles Times
Muhlenberg Weekly
New York Times

Videos

Ali Frazier I: One Nation Divisible. HBO Sports, 2000.
Ali the Fighter. Directed by Rick Baxter. Anchor Bay, 1971.
Joe Frazier: When the Smoke Clears. Directed by Mike Todd. SRO Entertainment, 2012.
Thrilla in Manila. Directed by John Dower. TimeLife, 2008.
When We Were Kings. Directed by Leon Gast. Universal, 2005.

Author Interviews

Bill Caplan
James Cortada
Ron Czajkowski
Don Elbaum
George Foreman
Roy Foreman
Larry Holmes
Larry Merchant
Dr. Ferdie Pacheco
John Shearer

* INDEX